# THE
# EXORCIST
# LEGACY

## 50 Years of Fear

### NAT SEGALOFF

**Citadel Press**
Kensington Publishing Corp.
www.kensingtonbooks.com

CITADEL PRESS BOOKS are published by

Kensington Publishing Corp.
119 West 40th Street
New York, NY 10018

All Kensington titles, imprints, and distributed lines are available at special quantity discounts for bulk purchases for sales promotions, premiums, fund-raising, educational, or institutional use. Special book excerpts or customized printings can also be created to fit specific needs. For details, write or phone the office of the Kensington sales manager: Kensington Publishing Corp., 119 West 40th Street, New York, NY 10018, attn: Sales Department; phone 1-800-221-2647.

ISBN: 978-0-8065-4194-5

First hardcover printing: August 2023

10  9  8  7  6  5  4  3  2  1

Printed in the United States of America

Library of Congress Control Number: 2023934458

First electronic edition: August 2023
ISBN: 978-0-8065-4196-9 (ebook)

*To the two Bills whose friendship and wisdom inspire me:*
*William Friedkin and William Peter Blatty*

*And to my friend and colleague Mark Kermode:*
*For his scholarship, for his passion,*
*and for not writing this book first*

# Contents

# *The Exorcist* and Me

*by John A. Russo*

In 1990, *The Exorcist* was inducted into the Horror Hall of Fame, and I was there as a featured guest, because *Night of the Living Dead* was being honored, too, along with *Psycho* and *Alien*. Four of the most iconic horror films of all time!

Jason Miller was there to accept the award for *The Exorcist*, and Russ Streiner and I were there to accept the award for *Night of the Living Dead* (George A. Romero couldn't be there because he was directing *The Dark Half*). The host of the show was Robert Englund, and some of the presenters were Anthony Perkins, Kane Hodder, Roger Corman, John Landis, and Roddy McDowall. It was a black-tie affair, and as they say in Hollywood, "everybody who was anybody" was there, and there were throngs of people behind the velvet ropes wishing they could get in. One of them was my friend Tobe Hooper, and I was able to get him a pass.

This was a lavish, star-studded event, definitely one of the high points of my career—and I almost didn't go. Russ Streiner and I had received our invitations while we were on location coproducing *Night of the Living Dead* (1990), but we had never heard of the Horror Hall of Fame, so I suggested that if Columbia Pictures could be talked into paying for our flights, then it might be worth going. They agreed, and we went, and I've been extremely happy with that outcome ever since.

Of course I had read William Peter Blatty's terrifying novel when it was first published, and I had also seen the movie that was splendidly directed by William Friedkin. Therefore I was glad to meet Jason Miller in person at the Beverly Hills Hotel, where all the Horror Hall of Fame honorees were lodged in classy rooms and chauffeured to and fro in long black limousines. I was impressed that Jason had been nominated for an Academy Award as Best Supporting Actor for his role as Father Karras. And both of us had grown up in small Pennsylvania towns, he in Scranton, and I in Clairton. So I felt that we had that connection, as well as being the same age and both fighting our way through the very tough and demanding entertainment business.

I have to confess that, as an agnostic, I was not as badly frightened as millions of other folks were by *The Exorcist* either as a novel or a movie, even though both versions were masterful depictions of demonic possession and its terrifying psychological manifestations. I'm not sure that the human body can be invaded by malevolent spirits. But I can suspend disbelief enough to temporarily be immersed in the horrors of what I am reading or watching. However, beyond *Night of the Living Dead* and *Return of the Living Dead*, I've written a vampire novel, *The Awakening*, from which I made my movie *Heartstopper*, and I've also written a screenplay, *Intensive Scare*, featuring a woman possessed by the soul of a serial killer. Therefore I can have fun exploring supernatural themes and using them to entertain readers and moviegoers.

Knowing that my friend and colleague Russ Streiner was profoundly affected by his first exposure to *The Exorcist*, so much so that he often says that it scared him more than any other movie, I asked him to explain why for the benefit of this foreword, and his explanation follows:

"When I first saw William Friedkin's film *The Exorcist*, I was a relatively new parent of a very young daughter. By an odd coincidence I was watching the film during a weekday afternoon, in an almost empty movie theater. That environment provided no comfort.

"As the early signs of possession began to take hold of the young girl, Regan, my own imagination began to grip my thoughts. And the horror set in. As a parent I imagined what I would do if my own daughter started showing some of the same behaviors that were showing up in the film character. How helpless would I feel? What would I do to protect my young daughter from an ailment that we couldn't see and when—at first—my daughter was helpless to describe what was taking control of her?

"To this day I cannot watch *The Exorcist* without flashing back to that very first time I sat, alone, watching that film and thinking of my own daughter—who is now fifty."

I think Russ's reactions are probably quite typical of the millions of people who have been thrilled, excited, and frightened in a soul-searching way by Blatty's novel and Friedkin's movie. Horror films like *The Exorcist* and *Night of the Living Dead*—and many others that are equally well crafted and realistic—invite all of us to confront the demons inside of us.

If the cinematic experience cuts deeply enough, we can vicariously learn some important things about ourselves. We can begin to assess how brave we might be, or how cowardly, in the face of extreme danger. We can weigh the chances for survival of ourselves and our posterity, especially if those chances depend on ourselves as individuals. We must strive to understand evil so we can stoutly confront it. That is what Russ Streiner was trying to do when he was as emotionally pent-up as Regan and her distraught mother were. The terrors they were facing on screen produced the anxiety he was disturbingly confronting in his imagination.

At bottom, that is the very real virtue of horror movies. They force us to weigh and consider our own attributes, or lack thereof, while we're having fun with the thrills and chills they provide. They present sharp insights into the meaning of life and the psychological motives and character traits of real people who we encounter outside of a theater.

For millions of years, we human beings were prey for wild animals such as cave bears, crocodiles, and saber-toothed tigers. We harbor an atavistic fear of being devoured that has dwelt inside of us for eons. Nowadays, thanks to the current plague of twisted serial killers, we're even more scared of being set upon by strangers who might want to rape or kill us. Cave bears or saber-toothed tigers could be driven away with torches or vanquished with repeated spear thrusts, if packs of humans warily surrounded them. We human beings had a bare chance against them, no matter how slim.

But what about nameless, insidious, invisible *spirits* with malevolent intentions? Do such spirits actually exist? Many people fervently believe that they do. That is why the evil demon conjured up by *The Exorcist* still haunts our worst nightmares. And this great new book by Nat Segaloff, *The Exorcist Legacy: 50 Years of Fear*, enthusiastically explores and explains the movie's everlasting legacy in ways that will greatly entertain its millions of fans.

---

*John Russo is the cowriter of the seminal zombie horror film*
Night of the Living Dead, *which celebrates its fifty-fifth anniversary in 2023, the same year as the fiftieth anniversary of the equally pivotal possession film—*The Exorcist.

# The Secret Screening

The first time I saw *The Exorcist*, I didn't know I was supposed to throw up. I also didn't dive under my seat, cover my eyes, or run screaming from the theater and head for the first church. It was because I was guarding the door of a secret screening with strict orders to let no one in who hadn't been invited.

*The Exorcist*, easily 1973's most hotly anticipated film, was scheduled to open Wednesday, December 26, at only twenty-two theaters nationally, one of which was the Cinema 57, a twin-screen structure that was a prime showplace of Boston's Sack Theatres chain, for whom I was publicity director. The Wednesday date posed a problem for the city's two weekly "alternative" newspapers, the *Boston Phoenix* and the *Real Paper*, whose publishing schedules were such that their reviews would appear a week late. As they served Boston's commercially important youth market, the lapse was crucial.

Eager to meet his deadline and especially savvy about the ways of the industry, Stuart Byron, the film editor and chief film critic for the *Real Paper*, wired the film's director, William Friedkin, asking for an advance screening the day before. Byron, a former studio publicist, had deep knowledge of the industry coupled with flamboyance as a critic. He assured Friedkin that he had no doubt that the film would be a phenomenon and stressed that it would benefit from allowing the city's weekly papers to meet their deadlines. In fact, he added, the extra day would allow even the critics for the daily papers to give more thoughtful reviews.

Friedkin—who, I later learned, could be as flamboyant as Byron—consented to the screening, which was quickly and discreetly arranged through the New England publicity agent for Warner Bros., Karl Fasick, and Sack's executive vice president, A. Alan Friedberg. As the chain's publicist, I was instructed to invite the critics, swear them to secrecy, and break it to them that they could not invite their editors, family, friends, etc.

In case you've lost track of the date, the day before December 26 is Christmas.

The screening involved unusual logistics. Having been beset with production and postproduction delays, the film's cut negative and sound mix had been delivered so late to Metrocolor that the lab was working around the clock to get prints out to the first wave of theaters, starting with those in the east and moving west. Had Santa himself carried it to the Cinema 57 on Christmas Eve, it would have been easier than waiting for the shipper to wend their way through the holiday traffic from Logan Airport.

Only *The Exorcist* could have enticed a cadre of jaded film critics to leave their families at 10 a.m. on Christmas morning—although, come to think of it, that might have been an incentive. Some twenty Boston media scribes staggered into the Cinema 57 on December 25 with their notebooks open, if not their eyes. They spread out across the six-hundred-seat house. The print had arrived so late that the projectionist had not been able to preview it to set the light or audio levels. Those of us in whose hands the fate of the picture rested were a little tense when the houselights went down and the first eerie musical notes seeped from behind the screen. The tension would not let up for the next two hours and two minutes.

One of the joys of being a critic is seeing a new film before the start of public word of mouth (this was decades before social media invented the word *spoiler*). In the best cases, a critic is able to bring attention to films that might, for any number of reasons (budget, obscurity, content), otherwise escape wider notice. The exact opposite was the case with *The Exorcist*; the public was well aware that it was coming. They had either read the bestseller or seen the short teaser trailer whose understated message was spoken by a studiously nonchalant narrator.[1]

Because people would inevitably be arriving for the scheduled 12:30 performance of the 57's then current attraction, I was posted at the auditorium door to keep strangers from wandering in. This meant that I could not be inside watching, but could poke my head in and out when I'd hear something exciting, then go back to my post. Perhaps that's why I did not immediately succumb to the film's power.

As for the critics, after the screening, they emerged, inscrutable as always, Stuart among them. I can understand their position. They knew the film was going to be a smash regardless of anything they might say about it. Would they hop on the bandwagon or would they become a voice on the curb citing the emperor's nudity just to get noticed? Moreover, would it be a factor that this was overwhelmingly Catholic Boston? They filed out in silence. (When I became a critic a few years later I learned that post-screening silence isn't indicative of having been moved, it's to keep colleagues from stealing your wisecracks.)

The next day, when the film opened, the reviews pronounced it effective. Some compared it with the book, and nearly all made note of the extreme language and the MPAA "R" rating.

Then the bedlam began. In the Sack Theatres executive offices high atop the Savoy Theatre on downtown Washington

Street, we began getting reports from Merrill Franks, Cinema 57's manager, that people were running up the aisles and into the lobby, some of them making it out to the street before vomiting, while others did it en route.[2]

Said Tom Kauycheck, the company's most experienced manager, who was hurriedly dispatched to the 57 to wrangle the throngs, "I remember them throwing up, and I couldn't imagine people being affected like that. I just stood around and watched the crowd; that was a movie in itself. Part of it was getting caught up in the excitement around the film, not the film itself."[3] He's right; ticket holders waiting in line for the next performance would see the distressed faces of those leaving and pump themselves into a frenzy even before the lights went down. Inasmuch as the 57 was a twin cinema and *The Sting* opened on the same day across the lobby, people who were there to see the Newman-Redford film must have been really confused.[4]

Soon word came in from Karl Fasick, no doubt informed by studio publicist Joe Hyams, that similar reactions were being observed in the twenty-one other cities where *The Exorcist* had opened. This was before cell phones, the internet, or Twitter. How did people know they were supposed to react this way? And how did they all know at the same time?

The phenomenon had started. Even Stuart Byron wrote in his review that the film had made him sick.

Such viewer reaction, half a century later, has yet to abate. To this day there are people who refuse to see *The Exorcist*. Despite this aversion, *somebody* must be seeing it; since 1973 there have been a sequel, an official sequel, and a prequel (each of which exists in two versions), a TV series, a trilogy of continuations, and countless cultural references, all of them harkening back to the 1973 original.

That's what this book is about.

I finally managed to see *The Exorcist* straight through the following weekend. This time I stood in the back because the house was sold out (I got in for free), as it would be for weeks to come. By then it was an intellectual experience, not an emotional one. I had prepared by reading William Peter Blatty's book and wondered how he and director William Friedkin could possibly squeeze all of it into one movie (they didn't, and I later learned that the omissions had, for a time, tarnished their friendship). I tried to understand why people of faith seemed disturbed in ways that other people were not. I also saw that the artistry and thought that went into the film were genuine.

Regardless of what many people continue to believe, Blatty and Friedkin did not set out to make a horror movie. Sure, *The Exorcist* is viscerally scary, but its power comes from its ability to touch, challenge, and, yes, exploit the spiritual beliefs of its viewers. It is both a film about the mystery of faith—their term—and an examination of their own religious quests.

That's also what this book is about.

When *The Exorcist* came out, it was just a movie. Over the next fifty years it became a legend.

That's what this is about, too.

*The Exorcist* stands, half a century after it was birthed in fire and brimstone, as a unique product of a Hollywood system that no longer exists. As William Friedkin said on many occasions, "I didn't set out to scare the hell out of people as you do with a horror film. I set out to make a film that would make them think about the concept of good and evil." That remains a worthy achievement, and it's time the world acknowledged that he and his cohorts more than succeeded.

—NAT SEGALOFF
Los Angeles, 2023

## Note:

As a study of a remarkable and influential film and its progeny, this book necessarily contains a great number of spoilers.

# THE
# EXORCIST
# LEGACY

## 50 Years of Fear

## CHAPTER 1

# The Two Bills

T*he Exorcist* may be the most misunderstood classic of all time. It heads the list of the world's scariest horror movies, yet its creators staunchly regard it as a whodunnit with spiritual overtones. It's been called the scariest film ever made, but it has only one traditional screen shock (a candle flaring up) and nobody jumping out of the shadows. Scholars have said it reflects the social and political upheavals of its era, yet it draws its power from religious attitudes so old that they survived the Enlightenment. It contains images that have been called subliminal, yet the man who directed it says he had nothing in mind beyond trying to tell a good story. There is ongoing dispute about the ending. Even its victim is misplaced; many people think it's about a twelve-year-old girl, yet the secretary who retyped William Peter Blatty's manuscript, before anybody else had read it, correctly asked the author, "They're after him aren't they?"—meaning Damien Karras, the priest.[1] Like all great art, people take from it what they bring to it, and people brought a lot to *The Exorcist*.

On its surface, it's about the demonic possession of a twelve-year-old girl. Beneath its surface, however, it's about something more personal, more familiar, more threatening, and therein resides its power. Beyond the shaking beds, crucifix mutilations, streaming pea soup, and spinning heads, what makes *The Exorcist* so affecting is that its emotional core is a mother's desire to protect her child and, on a more metaphysical level, whether we, as humans, are worthy of walking on God's earth.

"That's a very good description," agrees Ellen Burstyn, who played the mother, Chris MacNeil, adding, "I see it in terms of the confrontation with the unknown. Certainly the aspect of the mother protecting her daughter is the thread of the story. As a genre I see it as a psychological drama. I never have thought of it as a horror film. As a matter of fact—I'm sure you know this—it's the only film that's called a horror film that's been nominated for Best Picture."

But Stephen King, no slouch in the horror genre, believes that the mother-daughter story is secondary to the real subtext of *The Exorcist*, namely the generation gap. "The movie (and the novel) is nominally about the attempts of two priests to cast a demon out of young Regan MacNeil, a pretty little subteen played by Linda Blair," he writes in *Danse Macabre*.

"Substantively, however, it is a film about explosive social change, a finely honed focusing point for that entire youth explosion that took place in the late sixties and early seventies. It was a movie for all those parents who felt, in a kind of agony and terror, that they were losing their children and could not understand why or how it was happening. It's the face of the werewolf again, a Jekyll-and-Hyde tale in which sweet, lovely, and loving Regan turns into a foul-talking monster strapped into her bed and croaking (in the voice of Mercedes McCambridge) such charming homilies as 'You're going to let Jesus fuck you, fuck you, fuck you.' Religious trappings aside, every adult in America understood what the film's powerful subtext was saying; they understood that the demon in Regan MacNeil would have responded enthusiastically to the Fish Cheer in Woodstock."[2]

Horror scholar/historian David J. Skal builds on that observation. "The film became a highly publicized cultural ritual exorcising not the devil, but rather the confused parental feelings of guilt and responsibility in the Vietnam era when—at least from a certain conservative perspective—filthy-mouthed children were taking personality-transforming drugs, violently acting out, and generally making life unpleasant for their elders."[3]

King and Skal might be surprised to learn that their metaphor about youth rebellion is more accurate than they could have imagined, as the actual case is explored in the next chapter.

Critical sophistry aside, it's doubtful that audiences who bought tickets did so to take part in a cultural revolution. They may have come for the thrills, but they were held rapt by identifying with Chris MacNeil's tireless pursuit of help for her daughter. As such, *The Exorcist* provides one of the best starring roles for an actress—Ellen Burstyn—among a wealth of female-centric films of the 1970s.[4] This would turn out to be a factor in how audiences responded: by gender. Of the viewers who fled auditoriums during the film's initial run, it was mostly men. The women stayed. In hindsight, the reason seems basic: If a woman can endure the pain of childbirth and care for a sick child even if she, herself, is ill, surely she could remain in her theater seat in support of Regan MacNeil.

The motherhood theme is even more intimately intertwined with *The Exorcist* because the two men most responsible for its existence—writer William Peter Blatty and director William Friedkin—were especially close to their mothers.

As the only child of Rachel Green and Louis Friedkin—she from Kiev, he from Chicago, according to their son's August 29, 1935, birth certificate[5]—William David Friedkin always spoke of a happy home life, yet spent much of it on the streets of the Windy City. Rae, as everyone called her with love and respect, came from a family where she had twelve siblings, Louis from one where he had eleven, and yet his and Rae's union resulted in an only child. Consequently, young Billy was the apple of his mother's eye, *eye* being the appropriate word since she had lost one of hers in her younger years and had it replaced with a glass implant.[6] An operating room nurse who gave up her career to raise her son, she was the anchor of the family trio as Louis, an itinerant worker, was always in and out of employment. "[My father] never earned more than fifty dollars a week in his life," Friedkin says, a judgment that would surface as a series of unsympathetic portrayals of father figures in *The Exorcist* and his other films.[7]

When the Friedkins were reduced to welfare, Rae resumed her profession in the various hospitals near the family's 4826 N. Sheridan Avenue address. As soon as Billy was old enough to work, he hawked sodas at nearby Wrigley Field, ran errands for neighborhood residents, sold duds at a cut-rate clothing store owned by his uncle Sid Green, and bar-backed at a tavern run by another uncle, Harry Lang, who had married Rae's sister Sara. More at home on the streets than in a classroom, he barely graduated from Senn High School in January 1953, half a semester behind his peers.

It was Harry Lang who triggered Friedkin's lifelong fascination with crime. Lang had been a Chicago cop during the reign of Al Capone, and as Friedkin told it, he and his patrol partner Harry Miller were on the take from Frank Nitti, Capone's enforcer and eventual successor. Imagine their embarrassment when, one day, they were ordered by an anti-corruption police commissioner to bring Nitti in.

"They went into Nitti's office," Friedkin says, "where they used to go all the time, and this is how Nitti got caught, as opposed to all the fiction about it. Nitti had no weapon, but they did. My uncle shot Nitti eight times. And Nitti lived! My uncle then shot himself in his left hand and claimed that Nitti had drawn on him first." Nitti survived, but Uncle Harry's career did not. He retired from the force and opened a pub that catered to both cops and cons. And, of course, Billy, as bar back, became a captivated habitué.

When he was twenty but still looking young, as he always would, he encountered his third fascination (the first being crime and the second being women): media—in this case, television. Answering a newspaper ad for a mail boy at Chicago's WGN-TV, Friedkin began sorting packages in the mail room, using his daily delivery rounds to familiarize himself with all aspects of television production. It was at this time that his father began deteriorating and had to be taken to the Cook County Hospital, where he died within two weeks— probably, his son later offered, of cancer. Billy and his mother were devastated, both emotionally and financially. His intelligence and acumen led him from the mail room to become a gofer, a floor manager, and then a director at a succession of Chicago TV stations. Most of it involved routine chat shows and live studio-bound news broadcasts, and he began looking for opportunities to get out of the studio. A bright autodidact, he became a social animal, using his skill reading people's personalities to make his way in a hostile world.

"He was always looking for some way to better himself," says Ken Nordine, an announcer who devised the concept of Word Jazz and whose stentorian, Orson Wellesian voice made him a radio guru to a generation of listeners. "He was eager, driving, and opportunistic. His strength, outside of his energy, was his ability to size up situations and people that he could get the most out of and to learn to use in some way."[8] His breakthrough came while he worked at WTTW-TV and was befriended by *Chicago Tribune* columnist Fran Coughlin, whom Friedkin considers his mentor. Coughlin introduced

"Billy the Kid" to such Chicago literati as editor/publisher Lois Solomon of *The Paper*, *Time*'s Miriam Romwell Selby, broadcaster Studs Terkel, columnist/author Nelson Algren, lawyers Donald Paige Moore and Elmer Gertz, journalists John Justin Smith and Irv "Kup" Kupcinet, and occasional visitor Lenny Bruce.

He changed jobs as opportunities presented themselves. Going back to work in 1960 at WGN-TV with an open mandate to do specials, Friedkin scouted the city for a subject worthy of his interest. At one of the Solomon soirées, he heard of a man named Paul Crump who was sitting on death row in the Cook County Jail but was probably innocent. Friedkin asked his WGN bosses to let him make a documentary about it. When they declined, Friedkin approached Stirling "Red" Quinlan at competing station WBKB-TV and a deal was struck. The two men reached an understanding that, along with WBKB's $7,000 budget, the film was going to be a defense of Crump; Quinlan said he had no problem with that as long as the result was labeled as such.

At WBKB, Friedkin teamed with one of the station's studio cameramen, Wilmer Butler (who would later use the name Bill Butler to photograph, among other films, *Jaws*), and began experimenting with then new lightweight 16mm film equipment. The two young men taught themselves the techniques of production as they went along. The result was 1962's *The People vs. Paul Crump*.

Paul Crump, thirty-one, sat on Illinois's death row, convicted of murder in a 1953 robbery of the Libby, McNeill & Libby meat packing plant during which Theodore Zukowski, a security guard, was killed. Although Crump didn't pull the trigger, he was convicted of murder that same year and sentenced to die in the electric chair. His codefendants David Taylor, Eugene Taylor, Harold Riggins, and Hudson Tillman were also convicted but received various prison terms. Two years later the Illinois Supreme Court reversed Crump's conviction and he was tried again; once more he was convicted and given a death sentence.

Friedkin and Butler interviewed the people in Crump's life and finally got permission to film the incarcerated Crump himself. First, Friedkin pre-interviewed Crump to gauge what he was like. He proved the ideal subject: young, handsome, poised, and articulate. Moreover, when he told his story, he broke down in tears under Friedkin's compassionate questioning. Once on camera, however, he became formal and distant. Hearing the camera running out of film, Friedkin knew he needed emotion. "You're lying to me," he suddenly said to the dazed Crump, who saw his one chance for freedom slipping away. Seeing the man was on edge, Friedkin hauled off and slugged the unsuspecting Crump in the face. He got his tears.

"I did it as a calculated risk," Friedkin admitted later, contrasting the two sessions. "He was not being interviewed by the press at that time; he was a forgotten person and he sat down alone with me and he broke down telling the story. And I felt, How the hell am I going to get this guy into the same emotional bag? I'm going to have to make him feel as though I, who was his only friend, had betrayed him."

Now came another wrinkle. As powerful a plea for commutation as the film became, it also uncovered that Mayor Richard A. Daley's Chicago police had beaten a confession out of Crump. These were the Chicago police who later become a disgrace by rioting at the 1968 Democratic National Convention. Red Quinlan screened the film for opinion-makers and weighed the risks. In the end, he decided not to air it. Nevertheless, thirty-four hours before Crump was to be executed, he received a commutation from death to 199 years from Illinois governor Otto Kerner, Jr.

As the years drew on, Crump applied for parole several times but was always turned down by then governor James Thompson. This was unsurprising in that it was Thompson who had been the state's attorney responsible for Crump's original conviction, and parole boards serve at the pleasure of the governor. Not until Jim Edgar was elected Illinois governor in 1993 was Crump paroled, but almost immediately he was returned to prison for violating a family restraining order. He died of lung cancer in 2002 in the Chester Mental Health Center at age seventy-two.

In the meantime, Friedkin's very first film had saved a man's life without ever being aired. It also won top prize at the 1962 San Francisco Film Festival. The man whose films he beat was powerhouse producer David L. Wolper, who, seeing a good thing, hired Friedkin to come work for him in Los Angeles. For Wolper he directed three documentaries: *The Bold Men* (1965), *Pro Football: Mayhem on a Sunday Afternoon* (1965), and *The Thin Blue Line* (1966). He was then hired away for two scripted projects, the comedy pilot *The Pickle Brothers* (1966) and the last hour-long *Alfred Hitchcock Presents*, titled "Open Season" (1965).

By then a shining light in what was being called the "New Hollywood," he landed his first feature, *Good Times* (Columbia, 1967), starring Sonny and Cher, and moved swiftly into *The Night They Raided Minsky's* (United Artists, 1968), *The Birthday Party* (Palomar Pictures International, 1968), and *The Boys in the Band* (National General Pictures, 1970) before his breakthrough, *The French Connection* (Twentieth Century-Fox, 1971).

In 1967, once it was clear he wasn't going back to Chicago, he had moved his mother to Los Angeles and rented for her Mickey Rooney's old house on Walden Drive in Beverly Hills. At the time, he was living with director Howard Hawks's daughter, Kitty, but managed to see Rae often. "She was the one person that I've ever seen on whom he couldn't pull all those mind games," said Edgar Gross, Friedkin's business manager at the time. "He wouldn't dare to try that around her."[9]

Two years later, in winter 1969, while Friedkin was editing *The Boys in the Band* in New York, he got a call at 4 a.m. from Gross, who told him that his mother had died of a heart attack that afternoon while walking along Walden Drive. She was in her early sixties.

"I stayed awake crying that morning," Friedkin wrote in his memoir, "remembering all my mother meant to me and how much I loved and valued her. She had sacrificed her life for me." Her son had her buried without a service. "Whatever goodness resides in me comes from her and whenever I've strayed," he wrote confessionally, "I know that somewhere she disapproves but loves me nonetheless."[10]

The broad strokes obscure the details of how a Hollywood career actually advances. No one knows how many films are pitched and promised only to die on the strangling vines of Development Hell. While still a newbie in 1967, Friedkin was sent by his William Morris agent, Tony Fantozzi, to Paramount Pictures, where writer-director Blake Edwards was preparing to produce a theatrical version of his popular *Peter Gunn* television series. Proudly handed the script by Edwards, one of Hollywood's most successful filmmakers (*The Pink Panther*, *Days of Wine and Roses*, and *Operation Petticoat* among them), Friedkin sat down to read it.

"I hated it," he says. "I didn't really know what to say to Blake because I really wanted to do the picture, but not *that* picture. So I went back to Blake and said, 'Blake, I really hate this script. As a matter of fact, I think it's the worst piece of shit I've ever read in my life.'"

Edwards listened patiently to Friedkin and then pressed a button on his desk, saying, "I'd like you to tell that to the fellow who wrote the script. He's sitting in the outer office."

The writer dutifully entered, shook Friedkin's hand, and took a seat.

"He has read your script," Edwards told the writer and, nodding to Friedkin, said, "Tell him what you told me."

Friedkin did. "I didn't temper my comments too much," he says, "but after I said it, [the writer] broke into hysterical laughter and said, 'You know, you're absolutely right. It really is a rotten script and nobody here has had the guts to say it.'"

Needless to say, Friedkin didn't get to make the film, but he did make a friend. The writer was William Peter Blatty.

"The place was not in Blake Edwards's office, it was in the commissary," Blatty corrects, adding that "being rejected made me a Billy Friedkin admirer from that moment. I had cowritten *Gunn*, and part of my contribution was a dream sequence which Blake liked very much. Billy raised one objection to the script and it was simply that, it was the dream sequence. Now, you must set this into context: Billy had, at that time, only done one film (*Good Times*). I'm sure Billy will agree with me that it was not an auspicious beginning. And this interview was extremely important. I sat back and reached for another cigarette and thought, Well, now he is going to give way and like the dream sequence when he sees how much Blake likes the dream sequence. Billy did not back off, knowing full well he was not going to get this important job. He stuck to his guns and he didn't get the assignment. I never forgot that.

"This is why, when it came time to find a director for *The Exorcist*, I threatened Warner Bros. with a lawsuit because of their refusal to consider Billy Friedkin as director. Curiously, when I threatened it, I was rebuffed and I then called my lawyer and said, 'Can they do this? Can they actually do this?' and he said, 'Yes they can.' That's when I called Warner Bros. again and said, among other terrible dire threats, about going on *The Tonight Show* to expose them as savages and brigands and also that I had a solid lawsuit and they couldn't beat it. Their lawyers decided I was right! It was just an empty bluff and they're happy today that they did."[11]

In a sense, Blatty's loyalty made him the brother that Friedkin never had.

Unlike Friedkin, William Peter Blatty did have siblings— four, to be exact, of whom he was the last born, on January 7, 1928. His parents, Mary (née Mouakad) and Peter, arrived in New York by boat in 1921 from Lebanon, and both, particularly his mother, were devout Catholics. His father, who held minor jobs, separated himself from the family when Bill was very young, and Mary managed to support the six remaining Blattys by selling homemade quince jelly. No wallflower, Mary gained local fame for naively trying to present a jar of her sweet concoction to visiting President Franklin Delano Roosevelt, alarming his Secret Service squad but endearing her even more closely to her New York City neighbors.

Bill grew up in a continual con game. Mary would never pay bus or train fare, always managing to slip under the turnstiles or flummox the driver. The family moved every few months as the succession of landlords that Mary fooled into waiting for rent gave up and had them evicted. She consorted with Romas and came out ahead. The lessons of survival, tenacity, and *alwaqaha* (Lebanese for *chutzpah*) were not lost on the blue-eyed, soft-voiced baby of the family.

Mary had built-in radar. Whenever any of her children ran away, she could track them down, usually with "Willie"

(Bill) and their mongrel dog Ginger in tow. She spotted brother Mike tearing tickets at the Paramount Theater and sibling Eddie at Minsky's Burlesque. Bill never knew how she did it. Nor, probably, did she. Hers was a lonely life; Blatty remembers her leaning out the tenement window looking down the street as if eternally waiting for her estranged husband to return. He never did. "Mama stored up her dreams and her hopes in a chapel of her soul when she prayed alone," her son would write.[12]

Life with Mary was an adventure. She would get it into her head to stow away on trains and bring the kids along without a single ticket among them. She would watch when the conductor was coming to collect fares and would hide the children in a bathroom. Naturally, the conductor would bang on the door and say, "Tickets!" The kids were instructed to keep silent. "I know you're in there" was the expected response, at which point Mrs. Blatty would emerge to say, "The wind, it blew the ticket from my boy's hand." If, by chance, she happened to touch the arm of the conductor, within moments three other train employees would have arrived to remove the Blattys at the next stop. What makes these affairs even stranger is that Mama and the kids weren't really going anywhere; she just wanted to take a train ride. Gambits like that instilled in young William Peter a sense of the absurd as well as a knowledge of how to survive in a topsy-turvy world, even if the world happened to be of his own making.

When she wasn't shaking down railroads or landlords, Mary was hitting up the Church. St. Francis of Assisi on Thirty-First Street had a friary known for its generosity. On the days, Blatty writes, when the "quincing" sales were meager, mother would bring the family to St. Francis, where the brothers would ply them with free sandwiches. "They never asked you to fill out a form in quadruplicate [like municipal welfare bureaucrats] or prove you were penniless or check and ask endless humiliating questions and they checked and you waited and they checked and you waited and waited until finally my mother punched them dizzy in the stomach." Which was something else she did: She was known to attack social workers who came around inquiring after the children's welfare.

Mary had her own way of seeing into the future. When Bill won a scholarship to Georgetown University, his mother said only, "I know." "She had prayed that I would get it," he wrote. "What else is new?"

It was at Georgetown in 1949 that he encountered, first, a mention of exorcism by his New Testament teacher Father Eugene Gallagher, and then the newspaper article about a nearby one. Beset by other challenges at the time, he filed both away in his mind.

Mrs. Blatty reigned in her son's heart. Still barely able to navigate English, she was asked at her U.S. citizenship hearing, "If the president dies in office, who takes his place?" Without hesitation, Mrs. Blatty answered, "His son." The examining judge laughed and then asked, in all curiosity, "Why do you want to be a citizen?" She said, "For my children." The judge said, "You pass, Mrs. Blatty."

As the last of five children, Bill was prepared to take on the priesthood, a tradition in many Catholic homes. And yet, as he modestly said, "the notion of course was unattainable and ludicrous in the extreme, since with respect to the subject of my worthiness, my nearest superiors are asps; and yet a novel of demonic possession, I believed—if only I could make it sufficiently convincing—might be token fulfillment of deflected vocation."[13] To his self-deprecating credit, *The Exorcist* probably did more to bring people back to the Church than all the televangelists in perdition.

Moving to Los Angeles after graduating in 1950, Blatty made his way as a writer. His robust humor perfectly matched the marketplace of the times, and soon he was able to bring his mother out to live in comfort and sun. It was a heady life. When he'd finished *The Man from the Diners' Club* (1963) for Danny Kaye, Kaye invited him to see him perform at the Greek Theatre. When Blatty got there, he found himself sharing a box with Cary Grant and Clifford Odets. "I sat at the dinner table with the three of them unable to speak or even stammer," he recalled.

Hollywood didn't know it yet, but when Bill Blatty was writing successful comedies, the landscape was changing. The youth market, and with it the so-called "New Hollywood," was in the next reel. The old-line studios were still mired in banal product that held scant interest for the rapidly growing flower child audience. The founding moguls (MGM's Louis B. Mayer, Columbia's Harry Cohn, the independent Sam Goldwyn, Jack L. Warner, Twentieth Century-Fox's Darryl F. Zanuck, etc.) were either dead, dying, or retiring, and Wall Street wasn't happy with the empty soundstages they were leaving behind.

Fortunately, Bill Blatty had hitched his wagon to Blake Edwards's star. His 1964 screenplay for *A Shot in the Dark*, written with Edwards, was the second *Pink Panther* film starring Peter Sellers as the bumbling Inspector Jacques Clouseau. Reworked for the English-speaking stage by veteran writer Harry Kurnitz from French playwright Marcel Achard's *L'Idiote*, then adapted for Peter Sellers by Edwards and Blatty, the movie was an immense hit and set the format for subsequent *Pink Panther* films (in none of which, by the way, the pink panther jewel ever appeared).

Blatty's next project, *John Goldfarb, Please Come Home* (1965), introduced the writer to Shirley MacLaine, who would become the model for Chris MacNeil. A farce about an American pilot who lands in an Arab country and doesn't want to return to the States, it starred, in addition to MacLaine, Peter Ustinov and Richard Crenna. More intriguing, however, was the supporting cast of great character actors including Fred Clark, Wilfred Hyde-White, Jim Backus, Scott Brady, Harry Morgan, Richard Deacon, Jerome Cowan, Jerry Orbach, and Jackie Coogan. Blatty was responsible for casting these roles himself, and they saved the picture from director J. Lee Thompson. Thompson, who had been coasting on the success of 1961's *The Guns of Navarone*, proved so incompetent at comedy that, seven years later, he would become the model for Burke Dennings, *The Exorcist*'s defenestrated director.

*Promise Her Anything* (1966), with Warren Beatty and Leslie Caron, followed. A minor romantic comedy, it is best known for sparking a romance between Beatty and Caron that led to Caron introducing Beatty to French director François Truffaut, who connected him with screenwriters Robert Benton and David Newman and their script for *Bonnie and Clyde*. But that's another story.

The mild service comedy *What Did You Do in the War, Daddy?* (1966) brought Blatty back to Blake Edwards and led to *Gunn*, which brought him, as noted, to William Friedkin. Although Blatty wrote two more screenplays after *Gunn*—*The Great Bank Robbery* (Hy Averback, 1969) and the deeply troubled *Darling Lili, or Where Were You the Night You Said You Shot Down the Red Baron?* (Blake Edwards, 1970, later shortened to *Darling Lili,* 1990)—it was becoming clear that his style of glossy comedy was going the way of Doris Day, and he forsook Hollywood to start writing *The Exorcist*.

Over the two years during which Friedkin and Blatty prepared to shoot the movie, they grew close. "I felt a special kinship with Friedkin," Blatty observed. "He had been very devoted to his mother and had taken her death three years before very hard. I had seen a picture of his mother in the office, and the woman whom he'd cast to play the role of Karras' mother (Vasiliki Maliaros) looked a blend of Friedkin's mother and mine."

Understandably, the mother imagery in *The Exorcist* is the most affecting in the entire film. In the casting of sad-eyed Maliaros, both Blatty and Friedkin found counterparts to their maternal memories.

"Coming to the set of Karras's mother's apartment, Billy wasn't there yet, but the set decorator was," Blatty reported, "and I said, 'What is this? This is all wrong.' Everything was as neat as a pin, unlike my mother who, in her later years, [said] Eh! [so let it be messy]. I went to Billy about it [and he said], 'Oh, she would be neat.' What he was really saying was, '*My* mother would be neat.'"[14]

This realization lends extraordinary resonance to Karras's relationship with his mother. Karras feels suffocating guilt at not having been able to provide for her; later, the demon uses it to taunt him. Blatty, too, was unhappy that his success did not come in time to ease his mother's later years. Friedkin, whose mother shared the beginnings of his fame, well knew these emotions and infused them into Karras's anguish at betraying his mother's welfare. The line of dialogue, "Dimmy, why you did this to me?"—used first by Mrs. Karras and later repeated by the demon—is easily the most emotionally devastating exchange in the entire film.

A lot of people insist that *The Exorcist* is about the devil and the priests who cast him out, and it is. But the towering strength that holds it together is a mother.

"Billy and I have a common background in that we are deeply connected to a mother," Blatty proposed. "He's the only child and I, effectively, the only child, because I was the youngest. Both [of us were] tremendously affected by the death of our mothers. I would say in my case my grief could be described by an outside observer as neurotic [and] over-drawn, and one might describe Billy's reaction as the same as mine. And who knows what deep psychological effect it had on both of us."[15]

Somewhere Sigmund Freud is smiling.

## CHAPTER 2

# The Actual Case

There has been confusion over the years about the actual case that inspired *The Exorcist*, some of it sewn by the filmmakers themselves, perhaps out of discretion, perhaps to create enigma, or perhaps both. Most news coverage at the time of the film's 1973 release echoed the Warner Bros. press materials citing a nameless fourteen-year-old boy in Mount Rainier, Maryland, a suburb about twenty miles northeast of Washington, D.C. Later reports placed the incident in Bethesda, Maryland, about nine miles northwest of Mount Rainier. In his on-screen introduction to the twenty-fifth anniversary DVD, William Friedkin inexplicably locates it in Silver Spring, Maryland, midway between Bethesda and Mount Rainier.[1]

But it's Cottage City where author/paranormal researcher Mark Opsasnick found that it took place, and he offers persuasive details that the boy was Ronald Edwin Hunkeler of 3807 40th Avenue in that small town. (This was years before an article appeared in the *Skeptical Inquirer* magazine outing the then recently deceased Hunkeler.) Cottage City was, at the time, a white working-class neighborhood in Prince George's County, on the cusp of being low-income. Founded as the village of Yarrow by early European settlers, it played a role of hostelry more than hostility in the War of 1812 and the Civil War.[2] The post–World War II boom that created the Maryland suburbs, however, bypassed Cottage City (so named after the bungalows that originally lined its roads) and it fell into obscurity.

Until August 20, 1949.

That's the date that Bill Brinkley's two-column article in the *Washington Post* broke the news about a fourteen-year-old Mount Rainier boy "Reported Held in Devil's Grip."[3]

"In what is perhaps one of the most remarkable experiences of its kind in recent religious history," Brinkley began, "a fourteen-year-old Mount Rainier boy has been freed by a Catholic priest of possession by the Devil, Catholic sources reported yesterday." The priest and a Protestant minister are both referenced in the account without being named, and the article stresses that all medical and psychiatric causes were exhausted before summoning spiritual help. "The boy was taken to Georgetown University Hospital here," Brinkley reports, "where his affliction was exhaustively studied, and to St. Louis University. Both are Jesuit institutions."

There were no subsequent articles, leading one to remember something said by Philip L. Graham: "Journalism is the first rough draft of history." Coincidentally, Graham, at the time, was owner and publisher of the *Washington Post*. Brinkley never filed a follow-up.[4]

With barely that to go on, Opsasnick teased out the boy's identity using old-fashioned boots-on-the ground journalism. By exhaustively consulting public records of births, baptisms, high school graduations, and high school yearbooks—what boy, for example, should have graduated in 1953 but did so in 1954 after losing a year to "illness"—he narrowed the field. In those days the Gonzaga High School yearbook printed the addresses of each graduating senior, so Opsasnick set out knocking on doors in the suspect neighborhood. In this way he was able to determine Hunkeler's identity.[5] He later confirmed it by tracking down then-eighty-year-old T. Westin Scott, former Cottage City fire chief, who recalled that the Hunkelers were always calling the fire station to report family troubles, including Ronald's misbehavior and fights between his mother and aunt.

Classmates and neighbors of the boy also confirmed his identity and antisocial behavior. One of them, fellow Gonzagan Bobby Canter, told Opsasnick of an incident in class: "What happened was Ronald Hunkeler started shaking the desk and wouldn't stop. It was just a disciplinary thing. It had nothing to do with demonic possession. He was doing it to rattle the desk to upset the teacher and the teacher finally sent him home. But there was no talk of it being the devil. The desk never floated. It happened like one time." Concludes Opsasnick, "Hunkeler was just making a disturbance and everything was blown out of proportion."

Who was Ronald E. Hunkeler? By existing accounts he was a troubled boy. His father, Edwin, was a lapsed Catholic and his mother, Odell Coppage Hunkeler, was a fervent Lutheran. A German-speaking grandmother who was also a non-practicing Catholic lived with them. It was an aunt, called variously "Harriet" and "Aunt Tillie," who introduced Ronald to spiritualism and shared his fascination with the Ouija board.

Whether Hunkeler was actually possessed remains a matter of conjecture. He may have been faking it to get out of going to school, where he was roundly disliked. But there are people who, without knowing him, believe he was inhabited by a demon, if not by Satan himself.

The events began on January 15, 1949, and continued through April 18 of that year. At first the archbishop refused permission to conduct an exorcism, but later he approved with the stipulation that the officiating priests keep a diary.[6] A succession of priests was called in at various times. One of them—Father William Bowdern—kept the diary. Opsasnick tracked down the elderly cleric.

"They had to come up with something," Bowdern told him, "so they wrote down everything that was told to them by the boy's relatives. I don't believe anybody ever actually saw things like words coming up on his skin."

Opsasnick asked, "'Did the boy show prodigious strength?' [Bowdern] said, 'No. He punched me in the nose one time.' And, you know, it was like, here are priests trying to hold down a fourteen-year-old boy. What do you think he's going to do? [Then] I said, 'What about this thing about words coming up on his arm?' And [the priest] goes, 'Yeah, one time there was a word on his arm.' And he said it looked like lip-stick. And I said, 'Did he speak in tongues or any unknown languages?' And he goes, 'He mimicked us. We were doing Latin prayers and the kid's making fun of us.'"

How could Bowdern's memory be so much at odds with what he wrote in his diary decades earlier? When Opsasnick asked, the priest replied, "Well, you know, they're telling me what to do and telling me what to say."

The diary was submitted April 29, 1949, not by Bowdern but by Father Raymond S. Bishop, S.J., to Brother Cornelius, the rector of St. Louis University, with the caution from their Chancery Office that it should not be made public. In the document that eventually surfaced, Bowdern identifies the Hunkeler family by name.[7] In other accounts the boy is called "R."

The turning point came in mid-February when Father Edward Albert Hughes of St. James Catholic Church in Mount Rainier was asked to review the case (this is what gave birth to the identification with Mount Rainier). He told the family to use blessed candles, holy water, and special prayers, and is said to have seen objects moving around the room during the ritual. At times the boy made obscene and blasphemous comments using a strange, evil sounding voice. The room also grew cold. Experiencing this, Father Hughes asked Cardinal Patrick A. O'Boyle for permission to perform an exorcism.

The Hunkeler events that followed are not as theatrical as those in the book and film. There is no projectile vomiting, urination, defecation, levitation, or head-spinning. But the manifestations did baffle logical explanation at the time. They ranged from scratching and knocking sounds emanating from within the walls of the Hunkeler house to tipping chairs, shaking beds, and words appearing etched on the boy's body (that could have been self-inflicted). From the diary of March 15:

> Three large parallel bars were scratched on the boy's stomach. From then on, at the name of the Lord and His Blessed Mother and St. Michael, scratches appeared on the boy's legs, thighs, stomach, back, chest, face and throat. These scratches were sharply painful and caused red marks on the body, and the marks raised up above the surface of the skin, similar to engraving. Only one scratch pierced the outer layer of the skin, similar to a very slight laceration and caused a small amount of blood to flow. This scratch appeared on his left leg. R recoiled under evident pain as each mark was made. R stated that some of the marks felt like thorn scratches, others like brands. The brand marks were the more painful.[8]

It appears that the Lutherans, to which church the mother belonged, did not relinquish the boy entirely to the Catholics. A Lutheran minister named Schulze also had the boy at his residence and experienced bed vibrations and furniture tipping over. The boy was then moved to Georgetown University Hospital.

On February 28 the word *Louis* appeared scratched into the boy. When witnesses asked him if it meant "St. Louis," a second scratch appeared that answered "yes." Posthaste, Ronald was brought to Normandy, Missouri, which is near St. Louis, to stay with an aunt. The bed shaking followed him. This is where Father Bowdern of St. Francis Xavier Church enters the scenario. Bowdern asked to attend; he read a novena, blessed the boy, and placed a crucifix under his pillow. Once the adults evacuated the room, sounds were heard from within. They re-entered to discover that a bookcase had moved, a bench was upended, and the crucifix had been rejected from the boy's mattress. No one saw it happen.

In St. Louis, Father Raymond J. Bishop, who would later deliver the Bowdern diaries to his superiors, met Hunkeler and saw the markings on the boy's body as well as the moving mattress.

On March 16, Archbishop Joseph E. Ritter granted Father Bowdern clearance to perform the rite of exorcism at the aunt's Normandy, Missouri, home. Bowdern was chief exorcist; Rev. Walter Halloran assisted him; and Fathers Lawrence Kenny and Charles O'Hara were also present. Before long, Father Halloran left the case, and the ritual was removed to the rectory of St. Francis Xavier Church. This was but a temporary location, as increased violence forced a change to the Alexian Brothers Hospital's psychiatric ward.

There seemed to be a breakthrough on March 18, per the diary:

> Then he made as though he were trying to vomit from his stomach. His gestures moved upwards, close to his body. He seemed to try to lift the devil from his stomach to his throat. He asked that the window be opened, and then in a happy, victorious mood he

said sweetly, "He's going, he's going . . ." and finally, "There he goes." His body fell limp upon the bed in a perfectly relaxed condition. Everything seemed to indicate conquest. In a moment he was normal and seemed relieved. The whole family knelt around the bed and said prayers of thanksgiving. The mother was beside herself with joy. R was asked what his experiences were during the latter part of the fight. He said that he saw a huge, dark cloud of black vapor in front of him passing out from his vision. A figure in black robes, cowl, and white walked away in the cloud.

R got out of bed, put on his bathrobe and saw the Fathers off. He was very happy. R seemed to have made a complete recovery at 1:00 a.m. and it was about 1:30 when the clergymen departed. About 2:00 or a little after R felt strange sensations in his stomach and in a few moments he began to call out fearfully, "He's coming back! He's coming back!" Father Bowdern was called at 3:15 a.m., and the three exorcists went back for more of the formula. No evident progress was made, and about 7:30 a.m. the boy dropped off into a natural sleep.

The next day the boy had returned to a state of fear and pain:

> When the exorcist asked for a sign through the prayer "Praecipio," on three or four different occasions R urinated, seemingly without control. He complained upon awaking that the urine burned him. Previous to the urination R doubled up with pain in his stomach and he woke up crying. He complained too that his throat hurt him.

On April 1, Ronald E. Hunkeler, who had been raised mildly Lutheran, was baptized Catholic. Over the next few weeks, the boy was inexplicably moved from the hospital back to Maryland (attacking Father Bowdern en route), stayed briefly at a Jesuit retreat in St. Louis, tried to drown himself, and was finally returned to the psychiatric ward, where the exorcisms continued. Finally, on April 18, 1949—Easter Sunday—the exorcism was deemed successful.

It is difficult to assess the veracity of these accounts. None was submitted for scientific scrutiny, nor were recordings or formal measurements made at the time or after the events took place. But when they were reported in the August 20, 1949, *Washington Post*, a young Georgetown University junior named William Peter Blatty became intrigued. (At the time, none of the diary specifics or anything else had been released by the archdiocese.)

In 1958, the Hunkelers sold their house and moved away, seeking to forget the past and pursue anonymity. As for Ronald himself, he finished Gonzaga High School and grew up to have a career at NASA. When occasionally questioned about his possession over the years by those who had somehow determined that he was the victim, he declined comment. He retired to Laurel, Maryland, where he died—or, depending on one's religious beliefs, passed—on May 10, 2020, at age eighty-five.

Meanwhile, the seed was sewn in the deeply religious Blatty's heart, soul, and imagination. "Here, at last," he would later write, "was tangible evidence of transcendence. If there were demons, there were angels and probably a God and a life everlasting."

And he intended to write it.

# CHAPTER 3

# The Book

Although William Peter Blatty never met Ronald Edwin Hunkeler, they had been joined forever at the spiritual hip. Yet even after eighteen years in gestation, *The Exorcist* did not spring fully formed from Blatty's soul. Reading it now, even in its supposedly imperfect first draft (q.v.), it's a striking example of a story brilliantly set forth in the exact form in which it needs to be told.

Its style is deceptively simple. Unlike his comic novels, there is no clever turn of phrase, no literary pretensions that get in the way of straightforward, effective exposition. Its matter-of-factness gives it an authenticity that becomes that legendary cold wind that chills the reader's entire body.

Simplicity is complicated. Studio mogul Sam Goldwyn once irritated writer Lillian Hellman by saying, "Writing is just putting one word after the other." Hellman replied to Goldwyn, whose idea of writing was hiring someone else to do it, "No, Sam, it's putting one *right* word after another right word, and not too many of them."

As a man known for comedy, Bill Blatty faced a massive task. The impulse to be funny is instinctive in those so gifted. Switching to a serious tack runs into unknown territory. Blatty knew that *The Exorcist* could not be funny or, worse, cynical. If he himself didn't believe it was actually taking place, neither would the reader. Persuading publishers was also daunting; a filmography that included the comedies *A Shot in the Dark*; *John Goldfarb, Please Come Home*; *Promise Her*

*Anything*; *What Did You Do in the War, Daddy?*; and *Darling Lili* was hardly a résumé for the author of a supernatural novel. Plus he needed an advance; unlike today's top screenwriters who can easily pull in six figures for a script, Blatty in the 1960s was barely making ends met. Thus when he won $10,000 posing as an Arab sheik on the Groucho Marx quiz show *You Bet Your Life* on February 9, 1961,[1] and Groucho asked him what he was going to do with his money, Blatty answered, "write a novel." It took him seven years to get around to it, and *The Exorcist* was the result.

His thirteen-year marriage to Mary Margaret Rigard from 1950 to 1963 produced three children: Christine, Michael, and Mary Jo. He had three subsequent marriages and was married to Julie Witbrogt at the time of his death in 2017.

*The Exorcist* was a struggle. Unwilling to write on spec, Blatty could never interest his movie agents, one of whom was Noel Marshall,[2] in landing him a book deal and its accompanying advance. "Stick to comedy, you're good at it," everyone insisted. Then, at a 1967 New Year's Eve party at the home of novelist Burton Wohl, he met Marc Jaffe, the editorial director of Bantam Books. As editors do, and as writers are always prepared for, the two men discussed what Blatty was working on. When Blatty went on about his supernatural tale and Jaffe didn't change the subject, he continued pitching and, in due time, was asked to submit an outline of his proposed book.

Instead of a formal outline, however, Blatty wrote Jaffe a long letter "detailing what I knew of the incidents of 1949, including some rather bizarre phenomena that had been talked about on the Georgetown campus at the time. For example, a report that the exorcist and his assistants were forced to wear rubber windjammer suits for the boy, in his fits, displayed a prodigious ability to urinate endlessly, accurately, and over great distances, with the exorcists as his target." The report, Blatty later discovered, was false, but only as to a minor detail: Instead of peeing with unerring accuracy, the boy could spit. Small difference to those on the receiving end, of course.

"Is there a man alive," Blatty's epistle to Jaffe said, "who at one time or another in his life has not thought, 'Look, God! I'd *like* to believe in you; and I'd really like to do the right thing. But twenty thousand sects and countless prophets have different ideas about what the right thing is. So if you *are* out there, why not end all the mystery and hocus-pocus and make an appearance on top of the Empire State building. *Show me your face.*'"

To him, this theme was more important than the story, yet one needed to support the other: If God really exists, why not stop all the mystery and have Him just show His face? "But I happen to believe," Blatty added sadly, "that if God were to appear in thunder and lightning atop the Empire State Building, it would not affect (for long, at least) the religious beliefs of anyone who witnessed the phenomenon. The trick to faith," he concluded, "lies not in magic but in the *will of the individual*."[3]

Before committing to Bantam, which was strictly a paperback house, Jaffe shopped Blatty's non-proposal proposal to various hardcover publishers in search of a partner to share the advance. None of them could imagine how a comedy writer would be able to produce a book about demons and priests. Eventually, Jaffe got Bantam to shoulder the entire fee (until Harper & Row kicked in later on), and Blatty began work.

On June 28, 1967, *Gunn* was released to theaters. Having been unable to sign Friedkin, Blake Edwards directed it himself. It garnered little critical or box office interest and broke

Edwards's winning streak. For Blatty it was a not-so-subtle hint to change genres, if not careers. He bought a green IBM Selectric typewriter, stocked up on coffee and Marlboros, and sat down to face a blank page.

Over the years he had made notes, such as character sketches for a menschy police detective, Lieutenant William Kinderman (long before Peter Falk's Colombo, as Blatty was constantly at pains to point out). Once, in the margins of a book called *Satan* by Frank Sheed, he had handwritten, "Detective—Mental Clearance Sale." This gelled years later into Kinderman. "I think it was in 1963," he would write, "the notion of possession as the basic subject matter of a novel crystallized and firmed."[4]

Naturally he tried tracking down the reporter who wrote the 1949 article that had caught his curiosity, but Bill Brinkley had long since left the *Washington Post* and Blatty did not know he had become a fellow novelist. Inquiries at Georgetown University turned up nothing. Blatty's research into religious writings revealed, as he would note, that "over 90 percent [of possessions] were conceivably attributable to fraud, delusion, a combination of both, or misinterpretation of symptoms of psychosis, particularly paranoid schizophrenia, or certain neuroses, especially hysteria and neurasthenia." While disappointing, this discovery may have led Blatty to include psychiatry as a major red herring in his novel.

Among the few credible examples was a 1928 incident in Earling, Iowa, that was, at the time, the last exorcism approved by the Catholic Church. An account was written in a pamphlet titled "Begone Satan" by Rev. Carl Vogl and carried photographs of the primary participants. One riveting description stuck in Blatty's mind: "It was stated that the victim, a forty-year-old woman, would repeatedly and forcefully fly up from her bed as if hurled like a dart, head first, at a point above the bedroom door, where she would hang suspended by her forehead, as if tightly glued to the spot. An extraordinary image! I instinctively felt that it could not have been invented."[5]

Still seeking information about the 1949 case, Blatty resorted to what could only be called "Jesuit geography." He asked a Jesuit-trained friend living in Los Angeles for the exorcist's name, and was surprised when he got it. Blatty wrote the exorcising priest himself and received an answer that the man considered the case to be true demonic possession but that those involved had imposed strict secrecy on all its events, a mandate kept in place over the years by orders of the cardinal himself. This freed Blatty from being a reporter and allowed him to become a novelist.

He wrote *The Exorcist* in three locations, starting July 1969.[6] First he rented a cabin in Lake Tahoe and wasted six weeks deciding whether the scratching in the MacNeil house began on April 1 or 13. Needing money, he accepted an interim screenwriting job adapting Calder Willingham's *Providence Island* for Paul Newman, a film that was never made. Going back to his novel, he found a beach house in Los Angeles where he couldn't concentrate because of the seagulls and surf noises. Finally he rented Angela Lansbury's guesthouse in Encino, just above Ventura Boulevard, for $70 a month, and spent the next nine months drinking coffee, smoking four packs of Marlboros a day, and letting his mind wander creatively. The guesthouse was not far from Blatty's own home, where the rest of his family was living, and he cherished its creative privacy.

Writing his book, he used no plot outline; it seemed to flow, especially when he wrote overnight, tapping into the dream state of the silence and darkness.

Mary Blatty, Bill's colorful, resourceful mother, had died in 1967 from a heart attack. Bill had moved her from New York to the San Fernando Valley, not far from his family's house and the guesthouse where he was now writing. He remained inconsolable over her loss but found relief by giving her warmth to the character of Mrs. Karras. Likewise, Blatty patterned Karras after himself to the extent that, like Karras, his mother's death had caused in him a crisis of faith.

The book changed along the way. Blatty originally planned the possessed child to be a boy named Jamie. The priest called in to exorcise him was first named Father Thomas and was a Black man who had escaped poverty by joining the church. Thomas (as in "doubting Thomas") would connect the paranormal manifestations with his Haitian heritage, until Blatty realized that he was in danger of, as he put it, writing Sidney Poitier.

Sans outline, Blatty was surprised when ideas miraculously popped into his head just when they were needed. "I remember, for example," he wrote, "being so surprised at the moment it occurred to me that Burke Dennings, and not an offstage character as originally planned, would be the demon's murder victim, that from my desk I cried out aloud, 'My God, Burke Dennings is going to be murdered!'"[7] Perhaps most significantly, in Blatty's original concept, neither of the exorcising priests dies, and the troubled younger one is never sure what actually happened. "What restores—no, reaffirms—his faith is simple human love, which is surely the face of God made visible."[8]

The face, or, rather, the manifestations, of Satan were also made visible. Blatty merged a litany of effects into Regan MacNeil's possession from several exorcisms he researched: the bed shaking, the scratchings on her body, the icy room, the distended tongue, the cracked ceiling, etc. But all of those paled when compared to the rotation of Regan's head by 360 degrees. (This will be discussed in the chapter on the making of the film.)

By June 1970, he was almost finished when bizarre occurrences began happening at his home. His daughter Mary Jo reported seeing ghost images. Her screams woke her brother Michael. One of the images was a book that had belonged to Mary Blatty that Bill did not know Mary Jo had kept. Similar small incidents began to haunt Blatty as he finished his book. He was never able to explain them.

He had sent the manuscript to Bantam by the end of summer 1970. He made several photocopies but kept no carbons ("I have a death wish," he joked), and he dropped one off with his neighbor Shirley MacLaine, on whom he had based the character of Chris MacNeil, telling the actress, in his nervousness, that playing the part in the movie would "save her career." Fortunately, MacLaine, one of the brightest and most well-centered people in Hollywood, understood what he meant, and sent him back to his car with a pocket full of rocky road candy. Almost immediately he contacted producer Lew Grade and began talks to make the film of his novel with himself as screenwriter and producer. Grade's offer was minimal, but Blatty almost accepted it to pay off his creditors, until he learned that Grade wanted Robert Fryer to produce. Fryer's most recent film was the notorious bomb *Myra Breckenridge*. Blatty rejected Grade's offer, and when he did, MacLaine lost interest and accepted the lead in another paranormal film, *The Possession of Joel Delaney* (1972).

He also sent a copy of the manuscript to William Friedkin, the man who had earned his respect when he refused to direct his script for *Gunn*. In late 1971, Friedkin was on a national publicity and lecture tour touting his new film, a *policier* called *The French Connection*. Blatty's manuscript reached him along the way, and he ignored it until late one afternoon in a San Francisco hotel when he had a few hours to kill before a dinner engagement. Before long he was so engrossed in Blatty's novel that he called off his dinner plans and read it straight through, then phoned Blatty.

"Bill, my God, this is wonderful!" he said, "What the hell is this?"

"Billy," Blatty said, "I've sold the book to Warner Bros. and I'm going to produce it and write the screenplay, and I'd like to know if you'd be interested in directing it."[9]

Meanwhile, Bantam was closing in on a hardcover publisher. Harper & Row was the most alert and said that it would take the book if Blatty made two changes. First, drop the Iraqi prologue (which he rejected). Second, clarify the ending so the reader knows that Karras throws himself out the window *when he is not possessed* to prevent the demon repossessing him and making him kill Regan. The scene happens "off screen" in the novel and is kept purposely vague.

"There was a feeling that the final confrontation, while it works in the novel, needed expansion in the film," Jason Miller recalled for Mark Kermode in 1992. "And the final decision was to improvise it and see what happens."[10] Miller then explained that Karras would say, "Come into me," and the film would cut to Kinderman's coincidental arrival downstairs to question Regan, and Karras would go out the window. Upon further thinking, the filmmakers realized that it was more dramatic to see Karras possessed yet breaking away to save the girl with his sacrifice. This would become the most controversial moment in the resulting film.

Blatty was still revising the manuscript as his publication deadline neared. One day he got a call from William Tennant, who represented writer-producer Paul Monash. Monash, who had been responsible for bringing *Peyton Place* to television and had just produced the hit *Butch Cassidy and the Sundance Kid*, had his eyes on *The Exorcist*. Monash gave Blatty $400,000 for a six-month option to set the project up at a studio under the proviso that Blatty would write the script and produce and Monash would executive produce. This is what brought Blatty to make the deal with Warners that he had disclosed to Friedkin. What he didn't tell Friedkin was that Monash's stated intentions of how he would change the book for the screen had given him serious reservations.

"I saw it as being extremely visual if we could find out how to get a young girl to do it," Monash said. "I also [felt] that the book was going to be enormously successful. It was such outrageously evident film material. I thought it would have the substance of a very successful horror movie. I thought there was substance in it which had kind of gotten buried and could be uncovered in the screenplay."[11]

Monash's interest apparently put him in the minority. According to Blatty, "the manuscript had already made the rounds of every studio, mini-major, major-major, fly-by-night independent from here to Panama and nobody wanted it. I never got anything more than a mimeograph form rejection slip."

Monash's reaction was different, although it was not in Blatty's favor; it developed that Monash was working on another property at Warner Bros., brought them *The Exorcist*, switched projects, and got an immediate deal. Then he started making changes in Blatty's work without telling Blatty. Blatty discovered this and exploded.

Recalled Monash, "He uncovered a memo I had written to someone—I don't know how he got it—in which I criticized certain [things], told him certain changes we would have to make." Among them were combining Fathers Merrin and Karras into one priest, moving the location away from

Georgetown, putting Chris MacNeil into some profession other than acting, and making Lieutenant Kinderman less colorful. Or, as Monash put it, less *"Bridget and Bernie.* This over-Jewish guy just seemed terribly artificial."[12]

The killer insult was when Blatty learned that Monash had turned around and sold his option to the studio for an immediate bailout of $641,000 on his $400,000 investment and would receive 5 percent of the profits for doing nothing.[13]

Blatty referred to the memo he found as "screwing the author," and admitted to copying the document from Monash's Warner Bros. office and using it to separate Monash from any control in the film (although Monash would keep a percentage). Blatty's agent, Noel Marshall, took Monash's place as executive producer.

Blatty then went to bat for Friedkin to direct. This was not received well at Warners, which was already negotiating with Mark Rydell (*The Fox*, and later *On Golden Pond* and *The Rose*), undoubtedly for his skill in handling a cast of young actors for the studio's currently filming *The Cowboys* (1972). Although it cannot be confirmed, and Blatty never named Rydell or the film,[14] it seems clear that it was *The Cowboys* that the studio screened for Blatty, who concluded that "entire novenas could be said during the pauses in its dialogue." When Blatty dug in for Friedkin, they again ignored him and offered it to Arthur Penn, who wanted to avoid another violent film after *Bonnie and Clyde* and *Little Big Man*. Stanley Kubrick, who generated and produced his own material (until, apparently, *The Shining*) also passed, as did Mike Nichols, who didn't want to attempt a film that would hinge on a child's performance.

Meanwhile, *The Exorcist* was published in January 1971 to unexpected indifference. The publisher was about to write it off when Blatty was summoned as an emergency fill-in guest on the Dick Cavett TV show where Cavett, unprepared, let him talk for the full hour. The next day the book took off.

Like the other directors, Friedkin saw the obstacles; unlike the others, however, he knew how to surmount them. But Warners cared not and still refused to consider him.

That changed on October 7, 1971, the day *The French Connection* opened.

Faster than you can say, "The power of Christ compels you," Warner Bros. scrambled to be in the Billy Friedkin business.

SIDEBAR

# Synopsis of the Book *The Exorcist*

*In order to discuss the significant differences between the original novel and the films derived from it, it is necessary to provide a close synopsis.*

## Prologue:

A man in khaki (Father Lankester Merrin, an elderly Jesuit priest) leads an archaeological dig in Northern Iraq. Finishing an inventory of artifacts, he sees an amulet of the demon Pazuzu that warns him that he is about to face an old enemy.[1]

## Part I: In The Beginning

*One:* Georgetown, Washington, D.C. In this tony section of the nation's capital, movie star Chris MacNeil, thirty-two, is awakened by strange rapping, scratching, and knocking noises coming from the attic of her large rented[2] house on the corner of 36th and

Prospect Streets, Northwest Washington, D.C., over-looking a steep staircase. It's April 1,[3] and Chris is in D.C. with one week left shooting a musical remake of *Mr. Smith Goes to Washington* with campus unrest added to make it more contemporary. Its director is the eccentric Burke Dennings. Chris rented the house for herself, her almost-twelve-year-old daughter, Regan ("Rags"), her assistant Sharon Spencer, and two married housekeepers, Willie and Karl Engstrom. Chris is surprised when Regan's room is icy cold one night despite the radiator being on. Someone has also moved the room furniture around enough for Chris to stub her toe on the dresser in the dark.

As she prepares to leave for location early in the morning, Chris tells Karl to check the attic for rats. Karl says he has done so and that there is no evidence of them.

Walking home from location, Chris sees a young, unshaven priest conferring with another priest and wonders if Jesuits have to go to confession. When she gets home, she checks in with Sharon and finds Regan in the basement sculpting a clay model bird. She notices a Ouija board, but when she tries to use it with Regan the planchette flies from her hand. Regan blames someone named Captain Howdy for interfering. Burke Dennings visits, drunk and obnoxious as usual, but also charming. Sounds continue to come from the attic. Chris wakes in the morning to find Regan in bed with her, complaining that her own bed was shaking.

*Two:*  The unshaven priest whom Chris saw, Father Damien Karras, goes to New York for a psychiatric conference.

He gives a subway vagrant his last dollar and continues to his mother's apartment in a rundown section of Manhattan. Karras binds his mother's wounded leg and feels ashamed that he cannot provide for her. He has applied for a transfer from Georgetown to New York so he can look after her, but it has not yet come through. He celebrates Mass.

*Three:*   It's April 11, and Chris asks her doctor in L.A. for a shrink referral for Regan. Ever since her father, Howard, missed her twelfth birthday, Regan has been moody and restless. She has an imaginary playmate, the Captain Howdy from the Ouija board, and is suddenly doing poorly in school. Chris is worried. And Regan's bed is shaking. Her LA doctor refers her to a Dr. Klein in D.C. who, on examining her, says she has a hyperkinetic behavior disorder. She has also started swearing and smells "something burny" in her bedroom.

*Four:*   Chris throws a party at her house. One of the guests is a Father Joe Dyer. Other priests are present. Chris learns that someone has obscenely desecrated a statue in Dahlgren Chapel. Dyer jokes with an astronaut[4] that he would like to be the first missionary on the moon. Burke Dennings insults Karl, who is Swiss, calling him a Nazi. Suddenly Regan enters the room, tells the astronaut, "You're gonna die up there," and urinates on the rug. After the party, Chris bathes Regan and tucks her in. After she leaves the girl's bedroom, she hears screams and rushes back in. The bed is shaking violently and tossing Regan around.

## Part II: The Edge

One: Father Karras buries his mother in New York with her brothers present.[5] When he returns to his Georgetown dormitory, he is met by Father Dyer and a bottle of Chivas Regal. They drink, and Dyer tucks Karras into bed once he passes out. Karras dreams of his mother. Awakened, he recalls how his uncle summoned him to the charity ward of Bellevue where his mother was placed. In the morning, a young priest confers with Karras about another church desecration. It turns out that the young priest was a decoy sent to check on Karras's emotional state.[6] Karras is removed from his counseling duties and is assigned to lecture in psychiatry at the Georgetown University Medical School.

Two: Regan is examined by Dr. Klein. Klein theorizes that Regan might have moved the heavy furniture around the room by herself without remembering. Prescriptions, tests, and speculation follow. Finally a neighbor, Mary Jo Perrin, gives Chris a book about the occult. The next day the book vanishes.

Three: Sharon summons doctors to the house. Regan is contorting violently, talking in tongues ("nowonmai ... nowonmai"), and screaming, "It burns" and "Make him stop." She backhands Chris and, in a dreadful voice, claims, "The sow is mine." The doctors manage to sedate her and outline more tests they want to give the girl. In a hospital, Dr. Klein does a spinal tap that comes out normal. Only then does he suggest that Chris consult a psychiatrist.[7]

A night or two later Chris gets back to the house to find Regan alone. When Sharon returns, she explains that she went out to fill a prescription, but it was okay because Burke was there. Except Burke isn't there. Chris gets a call from an assistant director telling her that Burke Dennings is dead, having fallen down the huge flight of steps outside the Mac-Neil house.[8] The next morning Chris and Sharon witness Regan crawling backwards down the stairs like a spider and flicking her tongue. Regan follows Sharon around the house licking her ankle.[9]

*Four:*   April 29.[10] Dr. Klein and a psychotherapist trained in hypnotism put Regan into a trance. They ask who is inside her. Suddenly she emits horrible smells. Another personality emerges and she grabs and crushes the shrink's genitals. Eventually she is sedated, the second personality seems to withdraw, and the doctors again confer with Chris about additional treatments.

Detective William F. Kinderman visits the Mac-Neil house. Chris already suspects that Kinderman, whose business card places him with the homicide division, is there to inquire about Dennings's death. He acts bumbling and charming, but he is no fool, which Chris senses right away. Kinderman is a movie fan. He wonders if Dennings was visiting the house on the night he died. Chris says that Regan has been sick. Kinderman then inquires about Karl and Willie, who were off work the night that Dennings died. Later a pathologist's report shows that Dennings's head was completely turned around.

Kinderman looks further into Karl and Willie, who said they were at a movie when Dennings died—or was murdered. Checking on Karl, Kinderman finds mention of a narcotics theft several years earlier when he was working for a doctor in Beverly Hills, but the doctor nevertheless wrote him a recommendation for the MacNeil job.

Five: Lieutenant Kinderman interviews Father Karras. He tries to make his questions sound innocent, but he actually wants to know if a satanic murder has taken Burke Dennings. Later he matches a paint chip at the bottom of the stairs where Dennings died with the paint on Regan MacNeil's bird statue. He also shadows Karl Engstrom to a tenement in a poor area of Washington and later sees him emerging in tears.

Six: By May 11, Regan has become a prisoner in her own room, a victim of the doctors' insistence that her malady is physical. Chris finds a book on demonic possession in Regan's room. She asks Karl if he put it there. He denies it. When Kinderman visits the house, he is solicitous, but Chris and Sharon quickly suspect he is pursuing Burke Dennings's death. Did Sharon have a boyfriend who visited the house that night? As Kinderman leaves, he accuses Karl of killing Dennings because the director had abused him at Chris's party. Once Kinderman has gone, terrifying sounds come from Regan's bedroom. Chris races in to see Regan masturbating with a crucifix while speaking in Dennings's voice.[11]

## Part III : The Abyss

*One:*   Chris meets Karras furtively and asks him to perform an exorcism on Regan. A skeptical Karras visits Regan to investigate, and she tells him she's the devil. When "it" mimics the man who had asked Karras for help in the subway, Karras is stunned. He tape records their conversation. Regan spews a stream of vomit at him. Helping him clean up in the basement, Chris asks Karras what he'd do if he heard a killer's confession, for by now she suspects that her daughter killed Burke Dennings and she is afraid that Lieutenant Kinderman thinks so, too.

Karras still is not convinced of possession and studies literature on the subject. He remains skeptical, as does his friend Father Dyer. Karras reads about the work of Father Lankester Merrin, who, years ago in Africa, spent months exorcising a possessed boy.[12]

Karras visits Regan again, and the two have a civil conversation until she taunts him about his dead mother's activities in hell. Exiting the MacNeil house, Karras speaks with Karl, who is also leaving. Karl proceeds to a slum where he meets his drug-addicted daughter who is hiding in an apartment. When Karl exits his daughter's flat, he is confronted by Kinderman.

*Two:*   Karras learns that Regan's supposed "unknown speech" is really English spoken backwards: "I Am No One." Karras counsels Chris, who confesses that Regan told her she killed Burke Dennings. Karras speaks with Dr. Klein, looking for evidence he can give the bishop to permit an exorcism. Visiting Regan again, he witnesses her conversing in German with Karl about

Karl's daughter. Soon after, Regan also speaks in Latin and French, neither of which she has ever studied.[13]

Sharon summons Karras and shows him the words "Help me" raised in the girl's handwriting on Regan's midriff.

Karras asks the bishop to summon Lankester Merrin.

## Part IV: "And let my cry come unto thee . . ."

*One:* Lieutenant Kinderman ascertains that Karl Engstrom is innocent of Dennings's death; at the time he was not at the movies but had been visiting his daughter, Elvira, to give her money to buy drugs to feed her addiction. Elvira clears her father but jeopardizes herself as an addict.[14]

A cab arrives at the MacNeil house and an old man emerges. This is Father Lankester Merrin. The demon rages upstairs. Merrin asks Karras to assist him in the Roman Ritual of exorcism. Karras offers to describe the case to him; Merrin says, "Why?" Karras and Merrin enter Regan's bedroom to begin. Regan/demon has been expecting him, saying, "This time you are going to lose."

The ritual proceeds, complete with cursing, shaking, levitating, and intensely personal insults. Chris administers sedatives to Regan to the edge of killing her.[15]

During a break, Karras asks why the demon possesses people. Merrin opines that it must be to make us ask how God could possibly love us, given our flaws. Merrin confesses that he long ago gave up on man, until he realized that God would never ask him to do anything of which he was incapable. Karras, still in a crisis of faith, is shaken when the demon impersonates his mother and asks him why he forsook her in her final illness ("Why you do this to me, Dimmy?").

As the exorcism proceeds, Kinderman shows up at the MacNeil home talking about satanism to the point where Chris and, especially, Karras become nervous and impatient. They finally get rid of him. Karras returns to Regan's bedroom, where he finds Father Merrin dead and Regan/demon gloating. Chris and Sharon wait downstairs and hear a commotion upstairs. Karras has thrown himself out the bedroom window to his death at the foot of the steps. Chris races into Regan's bedroom to find her daughter free of possession. At first Chris is hesitant to embrace her. Father Dyer, finding Karras dying at the foot of the steps, gives him last rites.

## Epilogue:

It's late June and the MacNeils are returning to California.[16] The investigation of Dennings's death was closed by Kinderman, although he suspected that Karras might have done it, having become consumed with belief in possession. Father Dyer visits Chris. "Well, like you say," she tells him, "as far as God goes, I am a nonbeliever. Still am. But when it comes to a devil—well, that's something else. I could buy that . . . the devil does a lot of commercials." As Dyer sees Chris and Regan off, Regan stares at his priest's collar. Does she remember Karras? There is a glimmer of hope that Chris will be open to accepting the existence of God. The MacNeils drive away just as Kinderman shows up and is as friendly to Dyer as he had been to Karras.[17] They walk off together talking about movies.

## CHAPTER 4

# Making *The Exorcist*

Like many artists, William Peter Blatty wasn't necessarily the best interpreter of his own work. He never thought of *The Exorcist* as a horror story, despite millions of other people regarding it as such, but his description of it as "a supernatural murder mystery" fell short of the actual effect. Sure, there are deaths and suspects and red herrings. Yes, Regan was with Burke Dennings when he died and paint chips from her sculpture were at the bottom of the stairs where he landed. Sharon is into spiritualism and meditation, and perhaps the Ouija board was hers. Father Karras, who has lost his faith, blacks out from drinking and might have defaced the chapel. Karl, the butler, who has a criminal past, goes off to an unknown rendezvous. And then there is the demon who says he's the devil himself, yet is known to lie.

Although *The Exorcist* wants to be a murder mystery, thanks to word-of-mouth, every reader already knew who the killer was before opening the book. Why should the filmmakers pretend otherwise? That's the first thing William Friedkin recognized in June 1971, before the novel was published, when Blatty proudly handed him his 225-page first draft script (most feature screenplays at the time ran 97–120 pages). Finally able to work with the director he admired, Blatty was shocked when Friedkin gave him back his own screenplay with the complaint that it wasn't faithful to the novel.

Blatty was floored. Of particular concern to the director was Blatty's use of cinematic tricks in telling the story:

flashbacks, quick visual intercuts, changes in narrative tone, etc. Too many gimmicks, Friedkin explained, when a story this unbelievable needed to be told in a linear fashion. Discussions between the men produced an adaptation that presaged how the film would play to a theater audience. A number of subplots were removed, much to Blatty's disappointment, but all in service of Friedkin's reasoning that audiences knew the little girl was possessed, and any delays in getting there would just frustrate them. As Blatty had to admit, "Let's get on with it."[1] The final shooting script was 136 pages (though Blatty makes reference to a 133-page script) that underwent typical changes during the course of production.[2]

One concern was plotting the development of the demon's character. They held its personality textures to a minimum until he (it?) was in full control of Regan and began doing battle with Karras and Merrin. That is where the pageant of vulgarity began as well as the quest for a believable villain.

They began by totally rejecting Hamlet's notion that "the devil hath power to assume a pleasing shape." Blatty had written definitively otherwise. But he had also—and this is something Friedkin and special makeup artist Dick Smith instantly realized—always described the demon's appearance in terms of Regan's appearance. *Her* throat swelled. *She* had scratches on *her* face. *Her* skin broke out in pustules. *Her* lips were cracked. The demon had to be within Regan, almost bursting through, using the instrument of her body.

Smith, who was confident in his skills, sometimes clashed with Friedkin, who was equally confident in his, yet each man respected the other. "He was tough," said Smith, "but it was very stimulating. He drove me to do some of the best work that I'd done up to that time. A makeup artist gets a great thrill changing someone's face because, in a sense, he is creating a new, living creature. I was faced with the problem of making this twelve-year-old little girl, a pretty little girl with apple cheeks and butterball nose, into a demon. It was an incredible challenge."[3]

The first task Smith faced was his own limitations. "My training in television had been quality for a low price," he said, "one of the lessons I learned on *The Exorcist*. I dismissed out of hand our doing something [of which] I said, 'Oh, it would be much too costly to do it.' And Billy Friedkin admonished me, 'That's not your problem. I'll decide if it's too expensive to do it.' And his option was to do it. I realized, of course, I'm thinking like television. . . . I had to get used to the reality of film. My job then became to promote even the most costly thing if I thought it would be better, and not worry about the cost."[4]

Needing to manufacture an endless supply of the foam latex appliances in the visionary process that he had invented, Smith enlisted the help of a young man who wanted to follow in his footsteps: Rick Baker. "With the makeup like this, a foam rubber appliance makeup," Baker explains, "it's pretty much a new set of rubber appliance pieces every day that you work. Dick was pretty much a one-man show. He worked in his basement. If Linda [Blair] worked fifty days, he would have to pretty much make fifty sets of appliances. He had prepared all this and was ready to start filming, and the first day Linda worked, one of the grips said, 'Oh, she's got her mask on today.' [Friedkin] heard that and said, 'It's too masky, do another one.' And Dick said, 'What do you mean, "do another one"? This took me months to prepare.' 'Well, we can't shoot this. It looks like a mask.'" At the time, Baker says, he was offended that anybody would question Dick Smith, although in hindsight it was the right thing to do. "But it was fortunate for me," Baker continues, "because they were in production . . . so he called and said,

'Rick, would you mind coming out, living in my house, and working in my lab in the basement and helping me with *The Exorcist*?' So I got to live in the master's house, work in the basement, and learn from him."[5]

Max von Sydow posed a different problem, but one that Smith had long since perfected in such films as *Little Big Man*: old-age makeup. "The only good makeup is the makeup that you don't see as makeup," he said. "Max von Sydow was forty-two and I made him look approximately eighty. Most people, because Max was not a familiar face, didn't realize that he was made up. They accepted him as an old actor. That was a great one."[6] While Smith was whitening the actor's hair and applying old-age facial appliances, Baker painted liver spots on his hands.

The mechanical effects had to be equally novel, if not downright visionary. Friedkin's declaration that the possession would only look real if it was really happening (albeit for earthly reasons) led him to Marcel Vercoutere, a mechanical genius whose dedication to his craft rivaled Friedkin's. Born in Detroit in 1925 to a French father and Belgian mother, after serving in World War II, Vercoutere moved to Hollywood with his wife and found work in the movie studios that were wallowing in the postwar box office boom. He developed an interest in special mechanical stunts such as those used in car chases, gunfights, and exploding structures. By the 1970s at Warner Bros., he had contributed to *Deliverance* and *McCabe and Mrs. Miller* before diving into *The Exorcist*.

"He was a strange soul, like me," Friedkin once said of Vercoutere, "an experimenter and a perfectionist." In preparation for the August 1972 start date, Vercoutere assembled a zealous crew and moved his family into the basement of the 54th Street studio where they would be shooting in New

York. He and the team created, among other effects, three beds that would perform various movements; built Regan's bedroom on eight pneumatic wheels that could rock the set as if an earthquake hit it; and crafted a device that would thrash Regan around in the bed. "If I was the devil, I would get up there and thrash her," Vercoutere told Friedkin, "and Billy said, 'Go ahead and do it.'" It was he who, allied with Dick Smith, built the model of Regan with the spinning head. To give it a test once it was completed, Vercoutere drove around Manhattan with "her" sitting beside him staring out the passenger window. When they caught a driver's eye, they would spin the head and watch the person freak out.[7]

Owen Roizman was a natural choice as director of photography, having worked with Friedkin on *The French Connection*. Skilled at lighting and verité camera as well as glossy studio style, Roizman lost out on a baseball career after contracting polio, but was drawn to film through his father, who was a cameraman for Fox Movietone News. He began shooting commercials in New York and lensed one feature, *Stop!* (1970), that was never released, before coming to the attention of producer Phil D'Antoni, who was putting together *The French Connection*. When Roizman received an Oscar nomination for that Best Picture–winning film, his career was assured.

Production manager/first assistant director Terence A. Donnelly was also fairly new to features, having worked on *The Subject Was Roses* and *Midnight Cowboy* without credit before *Last Summer*, *The People Next Door*, and *The French Connection* put his name on the screen. After service with Friedkin on *The French Connection*, he was a natural choice to keep *The Exorcist* rolling.

One person sorely missing from the team was editor Jerry Greenberg. Greenberg had won an Oscar for the dynamic cutting in *The French Connection*, and Friedkin asked him personally to cut *The Exorcist*. All Greenberg had to do was call associate producer David Salven to set the deal. After several tries without response, Greenberg gave up and accepted another film, *Come Back Charleston Blue* (1972). When Friedkin heard this, he was incensed and dismissed Greenberg's explanation that Salven had never called him back. Believing he had been abandoned, Friedkin accepted the suggestion[8] of Nick Sbarro, his script supervisor on *The French Connection*, to hire Jordan Leondopoulos as editor. It was an odd choice given that Leondopoulos had no feature editing credits.[9] Greenberg went on to have a remarkable career (he died in 2017) but never worked with Friedkin again. Salven and Friedkin made five more films together. Salven died in 1991.

As it played out, Leondopoulos's efforts weren't enough to move the film along (he would be given the credit "supervising film editor"), so Friedkin brought in a team of additional editors—Evan A. Lottman, Norman Gay (for the hospital X-ray sequence), Bud Smith (for the Iraq sequence)—and a cadre of assistant editors—Michael Goldman, Ross Levy, Jonathan Pontell, and Craig McKay.

But all the behind-the-camera folk in Hollywood and New York would mean nothing if audiences didn't care about the people in front of the camera. Not only did *The Exorcist* demand skilled performances, each cast member had the additional burden of credibly selling an incredible story. Actors were of foremost importance; stars were not.

As soon as the film was announced, William Friedkin became everybody's best friend. Job solicitations arrived from costumer Donfeld; agent/manager Phyllis Rab, who represented costume designers Bob Mackie and Ray Aghayan and production designer Richard Sylbert, among others; extras who had worked for him on *The French Connection*; and clergy and laymen asking to be advisors. Patty Duke's agent, William Hirshan, even suggested her as an offbeat choice for Regan (Duke was twenty-five, Regan was eleven). To each of these applicants, Friedkin, often through his secretary, Judy Gold, sent gracious notes declining.[10]

Lou DiGiamo was in charge of casting the extras, and he threw a wide net. Terry Donelly's script breakdown was specific in how many people would be needed as "background" for Mrs. Karras's slum neighborhood, the foot of the Hitchcock steps, and Georgetown streets. DiGiamo's eye even found the perfect subway derelict in Vince Russell ("Can you help an old altar boy, faddah?"). Casting specialists Nessa Hyams and Juliet Taylor sent over lists of small-part players to be interviewed on April 21, 1972, at the Warner Bros. New York offices. Those up for the role of Sharon included Jill Clayburgh, Susan Sarandon, Gail Strickland, Diane Keaton, and Kathryn Walker. It wasn't until July 14 that Friedkin saw and settled on Kitty Winn, the same day that the director met Vasiliki Maliaros and hired her as Mrs. Karras.[11]

One casting decision would have an unforeseen impact several years later. For the medical test scenes involving the arteriogram and pneumoencephalograph at New York University Medical Center, the hospital's professor of radiology, Norman E. Chase, offered his team members for Friedkin to screen. Among them was Paul Bateson.[12]

If its heart was the love of a mother for her troubled daughter, the soul of The Exorcist was its targeted priest, Father Damien Karras. According to Friedkin, every male star in Hollywood, from Paul Newman to Jack Nicholson, desired the part. What he and Blatty wanted, however, was a real priest who could act. What they got was a man who was already troubled but had diverted his demons into drama.

"He came to see my play on Broadway," said Jason Miller,

whose *That Championship Season* had won the 1972 Pulitzer Prize. "I said, 'You want me to do the screenplay, right?' He said, 'No.' I said, 'What do you want?' He said, 'I want you to do a screen test as Father Karras.' I said, 'You *what*?'"[13]

"It was incredible," Friedkin said. "The camera loved him."

Miller, thirty-three at the time of the film, bore a Jesuit education and a brooding sensibility that Friedkin valued. Miller had studied English and drama and considered himself a writer rather than an actor. This would change.

Their first meeting didn't go well. Friedkin was trying to stifle the flu, and when Miller met him at his Sherry-Netherland suite, he found the director buried under a chemistry set of pills. Friedkin finally persuaded Miller that he was not a druggie, but Miller remained aloof, no doubt distracted by the acclaim his play was receiving. Not only that, Ellen Burstyn had rejected him as her costar, asking how her character could fall into the arms of a man who was shorter than she was. Friedkin held out for Miller, but there was a glitch. He had already cast Stacy Keach. "Pay him off" is what Friedkin told an astonished Warner Bros., and the Miller deal was done.[14]

Burstyn was also a tough sell, not only to the studio but to herself. She had come to notice from her Oscar-nominated performance in *The Last Picture Show* after drawing attention in *Tropic of Cancer* and *Alex in Wonderland*. A member since 1967 of the Actors Studio, where her mentor was Lee Strasberg, she had started as a dancer and model. She made her Broadway debut in 1957 and began the grind of television shows that were still being done in New York. Her preparation for Chris MacNeil was extensive. But she wasn't a star, and that's what Warners wanted, even if Friedkin did not. Friedkin held fast and inundated her with information.

"First of all, I read the book," she told an audience at the

Samuel Goldwyn Theater of the Academy of Motion Picture Arts and Sciences at a forty-fifth anniversary screening emceed by Friedkin. "And then, if you'll recall, Mr. Friedkin, we had a very long time before we started shooting, and you took me to the Metropolitan Museum to look at paintings. We played music together. You showed me photographs, including the Magritte that you used for [the shot of Merrin's arrival at the MacNeil home].[15] You showed me the books that had been written about the research that was done on the real case. You filled me with information and background and understanding, so I was well prepared by you by the time we went into rehearsal, so thank you, sir."

Nevertheless, rehearsal revealed something Friedkin didn't realize until he started shooting. "It was so well-rehearsed," he said, "that I could have put it on the stage. Then when we went to shoot it and we started doing it, it was like a play. They were so locked into their roles that they couldn't breathe and they were doing things like robots, the way I had staged it in rehearsal. So I said to the actors, 'Forget everything we've done, forget all the rehearsal, put all the scenes in your own words. You know your characters now, just go out and say it and do it. Just play it as you feel it.'"[16] Notwithstanding those instructions, what is in the film is what was in the script, only as though it's happening for the first time.

Burstyn, who said she stopped being a Catholic at the age of seventeen, was analytical about possession. "I know that it happened. I read the material on the actual case of the boy, but I know about history. There's that wonderful play *The Dybbuk*,[17] which is the Jewish version of *The Exorcist*, but older. Certainly there are many ancient writings about being possessed by spirits. I don't pretend to know. I only know that there's more to the universe than we have any idea about, and

I don't tie myself down to one belief system that says, 'Okay, this is the way it is.' . . . I don't rule out anything."[18]

And yet, consummate actress that she is, she developed a block over one line. In her final scene with Father Dyer as she and Regan prepare to leave Washington, her scripted line was "I believe in the devil." She staunchly refused to say the line, saying that it was too preachy. Even though it was just as assertive as Chris's dialogue in the novel, on hearing its delivery, Blatty agreed. "That scene was a show stopper, in the bad sense of the word," he realized. "My impression was we were stopping for a commercial."[19] And yet it was necessary, along with accepting Dyer's return of the St. Joseph medal, to show that Chris was open to accepting God. All that's said now is Dyer's "Why don't you keep this?"

Burstyn's most challenging scene was surely the one in which she asks Damien Karras to arrange an exorcism for Regan. Played on a footbridge and photographed with a telephoto lens to underscore their isolation, she starts off trying to be casual and ends up in controlled desperation. It is a tour-de-force performance playing three or more objectives at once. "I remember that day so clearly," recalls the actress, who was nominated for an Academy Award for her performance. "In the script it's 'Father, it's my daughter,' and I changed it to 'Father, it's my little girl.' When I saw Bill Blatty many years later, he said, 'You know, I always loved that line and I was always very proud of it, and then I was doing some research and looking at the original script and that's not what I wrote! I didn't write that line at all! *You* wrote it!' It came out of the moment, you know? When your child is in jeopardy, even if he's a grown man, he's your little boy. That just came out of me."

Amazingly, Burstyn had to later recreate her performance in a sound studio when Friedkin's demand for intimacy in the scene meant that he rejected the actual location recording because of its traffic noise, and would rather have just the actors' voices floating in a subjectively silent environment. Many actors resent having to recreate a performance in "looping." For Burstyn it was all part of the job. "When I think about it, I can be back in that place."

Max von Sydow arrived on the job with an unusual advantage: He was the living image of Pierre Teilhard de Chardin, the Jesuit priest whose archaeological expertise had led to the discovery of Peking Man in 1926. As a Darwinian (flying in the face of religious dogma), it was Chardin's scholarship, not his collar, that made him the model for Lankester Merrin. "My approach was colored by my, let's say, protestant upbringing," von Sydow said. "To me the devil has never been scary. I wasn't brought up with it. I was brought up with Scandinavian folk tales, and in those, the devil is ridiculous, always the loser. Of course I was totally aware of the fact that the priest believes [in Satan] and was modeled after Teilhard de Chardin."[20]

Internationally celebrated for his appearances in the films of Ingmar Bergman, von Sydow had just begun branching out into films by other directors, although *The Greatest Story Ever Told* (George Stevens, 1965) and *Hawaii* (George Roy Hill, 1966) had not made him a familiar face to mainstream American audiences. This, plus his austere, holy physical appearance worked in his favor. What worked against him was that he was not a Christian, something that gave him an acting block when they were filming the exorcism scenes. As Friedkin told a 1994 American Film Institute seminar, von Sydow was hung up on the line "I cast you out, unclean spirit." The scene wasn't working and neither man could figure out why. "Maybe I just don't believe," von Sydow said. "I don't believe it. I'm not a Christian, I don't believe in Christ."

"Max, you played Christ in *The Greatest Story Ever Told*," Friedkin said.

"I played Jesus, but I didn't play him as a Christian, I played him as a man. When I played him, he was not the founder of Christianity." The solution turned out to be the antithesis of von Sydow's matchless craft: He acted it from the outside, not the inside. It disappointed both men, but it got the job done.

Bravely playing a hack director modeled after British helmer J. Lee Thompson, Jack MacGowran, late of the Abbey Players, dared to be obnoxious as Burke Dennings. (At one point Thompson himself was considered for the part.) His lonely neediness—which Regan misconstrues for a romantic interest in Chris—leads to his murder, an event that brings Lieutenant Kinderman into the MacNeil universe. With relatively few scenes to establish himself, MacGowran took hold of Dennings and made each appearance memorable.

Having received acclaim for her performance as a drug addict opposite Al Pacino in *The Panic in Needle Park* (1971), Kitty Winn landed the serviceable role of Sharon Spencer, Chris MacNeil's assistant/secretary. In the novel, Sharon was into meditation and became suspect for introducing mysticism into the MacNeil household. The herring was so red that her backstory was almost entirely dropped from the script, although it would awkwardly resurface four years later in *The Heretic*. *The Exorcist* proved to be one of Winn's few feature films, the bulk of her career existing in episodic television despite strong reviews for her work. Like MacGowran, she does not earn a mention in Friedkin's memoirs.

Perhaps the luckiest casting decision was Lee J. Cobb as Lieutenant Kinderman, the *hamish* cop who lucks into the solution to Burke Dennings's murder even though it seems incomprehensible to him. Famed for originating the role of Willy Loman in Arthur Miller's *Death of a Salesman* on Broadway and reviled for naming names during the Red Scare, Cobb happened to be sitting a few rows away from Blatty and Friedkin in the audience of a play they were auditing in the San Fernando Valley. They didn't go with anybody from the play, but both men realized at once that Cobb should be their Kinderman.

The crucial role, of course, was Regan, which was the reason Mike Nichols had passed on making the film, because he didn't want its success to hang on the talent of an unknown child.[21] Friedkin and Blatty knew they faced a challenge and threw the casting doors open to Fate.

"We did not want a Hollywood child," Blatty kept saying, "we wanted a real child," and they sent casting director Juliet Taylor on a citywide search.

"There were thousands of girls twelve and thirteen years old who made tapes across the country," Friedkin recalled at the forty-fifth anniversary screening of his film at the motion picture academy, "and I saw several hundred of the tapes and I personally interviewed at least a hundred girls. There came a time when I thought we were not gonna be able to make this film with a twelve- or thirteen-year-old; it was impossible—a lot of reasons, not least of which was what was this going to do to a child after performing an experience like that? And I remember sitting in my office at Warner Bros. . . . having my head in my hands, thinking we're going to have to try and find some sixteen- or fifteen-year-old girls who look younger who can do this, when my assistant buzzed me and says, 'There's a woman out here named Elinore Blair and she doesn't have an appointment but she's brought her daughter, can you see her?' I said why not."

The daughter had been modeling and doing commercials in New York and was represented by an agent, but for unknown reasons, the agent had not submitted her for the role; her mother did that on her own. By the time the Blairs crashed Friedkin's office, Taylor had already vetted her and had given her a page of dialogue to use in an audition. The intervening years have brought slightly different versions of what happened next.

"It was like the worst language you could possibly imagine," Blair recalled. "I remember thinking to myself, 'How am I going to tell my mother?' So I didn't."[22]

Even at age thirteen (she would turn fifteen shortly after the film was released), Blair was uncommonly well centered. "I didn't grow up Catholic," she said, "I didn't know about the devil. That's the safety net. Why I was chosen to do the character, I think, was because it was never a monster for me." She was also trained to leave her acting on the stage and not bring it home with her.

Friedkin was sold. "The second Linda Blair walked in the door. I knew it was her. I just knew it. I believe it was the Movie God that brought Ellen Burstyn and Linda Blair to the film."

The next part of the meet-and-greet was more testy. "I asked her if she knew anything about *The Exorcist* book," Friedkin said, "and she said, 'Oh, yes, I read it.'"

"I said, '*You read this book?*'"

"'Yeah.'"

"I said. 'What's it about?'"

"She said, 'It's about a little girl that gets possessed by the devil and does a whole bunch of bad things.'"

"I said, 'Like what?'"

"She said, 'Well, she hits her mother across the face and she pushes a man out of her bedroom window and she masturbates with a crucifix.'"

In his memoir, Friedkin finishes the story: "I looked at

her mother. She seemed to realize her daughter was special. Linda was unperturbed.

"'Do you know what that means?' I asked her."

"'What?'"

"'To masturbate.'"

"'It's like jerking off, isn't it?' she answered without hesitation. Giggling a little. I looked again at her mother. Unflappable.

"'Have you ever done that?' I asked Linda."

"'Sure, haven't you?' she shot back."

"I'd found Regan."[23]

It's a wonderful anecdote, but it's not about Blair's audition. As Friedkin told Peter Travers and Stephanie Reiff in 1974, it's about "a really cute nine-year-old who seemed quite hip" when she auditioned for him, but whom he decided against using.[24] Indeed, as Blair remembers it, "I didn't understand what masturbation was at that age. I had no idea what it was until many years later."[25]

But Blair's audition wasn't over yet. Blair: "Then [Friedkin] would have me acting things out, like get on the couch and writhe in pain. Well, I was just embarrassed. And that's what he wanted—to see how stable I was. He realized I was very stable. I went to public school, I'm a Christian, and in my religion we never discuss the devil, so, to me, it was a fictitious character like people think of Frankenstein or something like that. It wasn't real to me."

Blair told Dick Smith the same thing during one of their daily four-hour makeup sessions. Recalled Smith, "One day I asked her, 'Linda, how does it feel when you have to say these lines?' She said, 'Oh it's not me, it's Regan.' She just divorced herself from this horrible character and even the language."[26]

Because Linda was a minor (deemed an "infant" under the law as she was born January 22, 1959), Elinore Blair and

Warner Bros. had to get confirmation from the court that she was stable in order to employ her for such a grueling role. At first the court objected that both sides of the deal (Warners and Blair) were represented by the same attorneys at the August 24, 1972, hearing, but they eventually permitted the hire, and thirteen-year-old Linda Blair became eleven-year-old Regan MacNeil at a salary of $1,400 a week.

Ellen Burstyn, who bonded with Blair during rehearsals and enjoyed a close relationship with her thereafter, recalls a very together young girl. "I was very careful of her and I thought Billy was," she says. "My vision of Linda during the film is her sitting in the makeup chair for three hours and she's looking at the mirror and behind her is a television set which she can see in the mirror and there are kids' cartoons on. She's being turned into this monster and she's watching kiddie cartoons!"[27]

Max von Sydow was stunned by the juxtaposition of Blair's innocence and her disgusting dialogue. On the first take when Regan tells Merrin to violate his own mother (but not in those words), von Sydow froze in shock at what he was hearing. That the most composed actor in the film was thrown by what was happening before him boded well for how audiences would respond.

Despite this, the rumor mill has persisted that Blair was psychologically damaged by the part. Nothing could be further from the truth. Indeed, she was protected not only by Friedkin and her own mother but by Ellen Burstyn.

"Ellen worked with her like a mother," Friedkin said. "Linda's mother was wonderful, but Ellen became a surrogate mother to Linda on the set, and the reason that Linda is so damn good in this picture is because Ellen worked with her and talked to her and embraced her and imparted all the incredible knowledge that she has as an actress."[28]

Although she was stilted in rehearsals, she loosened up in working with Burstyn. "She has an understanding of what this all is, but no real deep knowledge of how dirty and how vile it is supposed to be. Linda thinks that this all a game, and I intend to keep it that way."[29]

Supporting roles were cast with equal attention to what they could bring or what they could do, the two being separate attributes. Ever the documentarian, Friedkin enlisted William O'Malley and Thomas Bermingham, both of whom were ordained priests, to play Father Dyer and the university president (Karras's supervisor), respectively. Said Blatty about casting real clergy to play fictitious clergy, "You can't get that kind of sanctity from an actor." Thrilled with being able to cast a real priest as a movie priest, Friedkin enthusiastically thanked the Reverend John J. McDonald for making Bill O'Malley available.[30] O'Malley proved his mettle rehearsing a scene with Jason Miller in which Fathers Dyer and Karras get drunk with a purloined bottle of Scotch. The two men decided to forgo the Method in favor of the Creature. They were in Friedkin's office and, while Friedkin was gone, got plastered. When Friedkin returned and saw them, he said, "God, if I only had a camera."[31]

With the principal performers set, the preproduction activities continued with locking down of locations, building sets, and the myriad details that go into making a film. A cloak of secrecy descended over the production. News was controlled, if not quashed entirely, and the filmmakers focused on their craft.

With one exception. Bantam Books, looking at the novel's sales figures, wanted more and dispatched their senior editor in charge of movies and pop culture, Nancy Hardin, to speak to Friedkin and Blatty with an enticing offer: "Tell us how this movie got made."

At the time, Bantam had a reputation for bringing out "instant books" which would cash in on hot news items before they cooled. "They wanted to get out immediately to take advantage of it being in the news," Hardin says. "It didn't happen that often, but when *The Exorcist* was published as a novel it was a huge success and the upcoming movie was also perceived as going to be a success, so it was all hands on deck."[32]

The first negotiations were with Friedkin, from whom Hardin wanted a behind-the-scenes chronicle like the one he had written about *The French Connection* for *Action*, the Directors Guild magazine. He responded that he would get "everything I can get" to her, a remarkable job of multitasking as he was still shooting.[33] Two months later, however, Hardin pulled the plug on her own pitch by writing Friedkin's William Morris agent, Tony Fantozzi, that Crown Books/New American Library was bringing out a making-of book, "but I would like to see Bill do a broader-based book about directing in general going back to his days in Chicago."[34]

When the film was released and soared to box office heights, Hardin renewed her push for a book, this time turning to Blatty, who savored the opportunity to relate how he had been savaged on his odyssey from page to screen. For the next six months—between December 1973 and June 1974, the book's release date—Hardin would fly back and forth between New York and Los Angeles guiding the project, with Blatty as writer and executive producer Noel Marshall as cheerleader.

"He was very charming and very manipulative and was a driving force," she says of Marshall. At the time, Marshall was married to actress Tippi Hedren and lived with her on their wild animal rescue ranch just outside of Los Angeles.[35] His actual work on the film is obscure (Blatty doesn't mention him in his book), but Hardin says, "Boy, was he committed! He was 24/7. There would be calls at all hours to go over something. You'd want him in your corner." As for Blatty, who was dredging his memory about his novel and its tortured road to film, "It was hand-holding. That was a big job. He was so needy."

The resulting book, *William Peter Blatty on The Exorcist: From Novel to Film*, would include a (roughly) fifteen-thousand-word introduction, four-thousand-word afterword, Blatty's first-draft screenplay (the one Friedkin had rejected), and a transcript of the finished film. It would also carry his inscription: "I would like to express my deep gratitude to the talent and the intelligence of my editor on this book, Nancy Hardin."

But that's getting ahead of the story. During the summer of 1972 the novel continued to sell. All Friedkin and Blatty had to do now was deliver a movie that lived up to its immense and intimidating promise.

SIDEBAR

## Synopsis of the Film *The Exorcist*

*NOTE: As with the novel, a detailed synopsis of the original 1973 film will be helpful as preparation for discussing its sequels and prequels.*

In Northern Iraq, Father Lankester Merrin (Max von Sydow), a Jesuit priest and an archaeologist, supervises a historic excavation at Nineveh. He is shown a Saint Joseph medal that dates from the 1500s and has unaccountably been found in a pre-Christian site. More curious is that buried with it is a small model, encrusted in sand, of the demon Pazuzu.[1] What were these pagan and Christian symbols doing together in a pre-Christian dig? In the museum director's office a clock in the room stops when Merrin says, "There is something I must do," as he prepares to leave Iraq. Standing one last time at the edge of the excavation, Merrin faces off against a huge statue of Pazuzu. Nearby, two dogs growl and fight.

Dawn in Georgetown, a tony district of Washington, D.C. Actress Chris MacNeil (Ellen Burstyn) studies her script for a campus unrest movie titled *Crash Course* that she is filming on this location. Her concentration is broken by irregular rapping noises coming from the bedroom of her eleven-year-old daughter, Regan (Linda Blair). Later that morning she tells her butler, Karl (Rudolf Schündler), to check the attic for rats, and goes off to work.

On the Georgetown University movie location, Chris tells director Burke Dennings (Jack MacGowran) in no uncertain terms that she feels the scene is awful, while the movie's producer (William Peter Blatty) stands by. Walking home that night, she sees a brooding priest, Father Damien Karras (Jason Miller), in intimate conversation with another priest whose body language signals that he is troubled. She also sees groups of costumed young hobgoblins on the street because it is nearing Halloween.

In New York City, Father Karras arrives in his aged mother's cluttered apartment in Hell's Kitchen. Mrs. Karras (Vasiliki Maliaros) has injured her leg, and as Damien changes her dressings, he pleads with her to move from her solitary surroundings. She refuses. She recognizes that something is troubling him even though he has not spoken about it.

Back in Washington, Chris discovers a Ouija board and asks Regan why she has been using it. Regan tells her that she and "Captain Howdy" play with it. When Chris tries to touch the planchette, it flies away from her hand. It will be Regan's twelfth birthday on Sunday and she misses her father, who is in Rome.

That night Karras and his supervisor, Rev. Thomas Bermingham (himself), have beers at a campus pub. Father Karras, who is a psychiatrist counseling troubled priests, is himself troubled. He tells Bermingham, "I think I've lost my faith."

On Monday morning Chris awakens to find Regan sharing the bed with her. "My bed was shaking," the girl complains. "I can't get to sleep."

That same morning at Dahlgren Chapel on the Georgetown University campus a priest preparing the altar for services gasps in horror at a statue of the virgin that has been desecrated.

One afternoon in the charity ward of New York's Bellevue Hospital, Karras and his uncle (Titos Vandis) visit his mother, whose leg has necessitated her hospitalization. She asks him accusingly, "Dimmy, why you did this to me, Dimmy, why?" Later, Karras, ashamed that, with all his medical training, he cannot afford to give his mother the care she deserves, tries to work off his anger in a gym.

A cocktail party is in progress in Chris MacNeil's Georgetown house. Burke Dennings, typically drunk, insults Karl's Swiss heritage, calling him a Nazi. Father Dyer (Father William O'Malley, SJ) enjoys playing the piano and identifies Father Karras to an inquiring Chris. Suddenly Regan appears in the room. She looks coolly at one of the guests (an astronaut about to launch) and tells him, "You're going to die up there." Then she urinates on the rug.

After the party,[2] Chris bathes Regan, who asks, "Mother, what's wrong with me?" Chris tells her it's nerves and to keep taking the pills the doctor prescribed.[3]

After Regan has been tucked in, Chris pauses when a

sudden stream of screams comes out of her daughter's bedroom. Rushing in, Chris sees that the entire bed is wildly gyrating. She throws herself on the mattress but it continues to shake.

At night in the Jesuit residence, Father Dyer helps Father Karras get drunk with an "appropriated" bottle of good Scotch. Karras still feels that he should have been with his mother.

Chris's doctors are unable to diagnose Regan's malady. Even an arteriogram proves inconclusive. One afternoon, Chris's secretary Sharon Spencer (Kitty Winn) summons the doctors to the MacNeil home: Regan is having convulsions. When they arrive, Regan is violently bouncing on the otherwise motionless bed. Her throat swells to the size of a basketball, her voice changes into something ripped raw and bloody from the base of her spine, and she fights off the doctors saying, "Keep away! The sow his mine!"

Regan endures more doctors and more tests, all worthless to an increasingly distraught Chris. Returning one night to find Regan asleep in her bedroom with the windows open and the cold air blowing in, she confronts Sharon, who is just returning from filling a prescription, and admonishes her for leaving Regan alone. Sharon tells her that she had left Burke Dennings to babysit, but he must have departed. Moments later an assistant director appears to tell Chris that Dennings has died—fallen down the long flight of steps just outside the MacNeil house.

Under hypnosis, Regan reveals that Captain Howdy is inside her. Rather than speak when asked, Captain Howdy/Regan grabs the hypnotist's groin and forces him to the floor in agony.

The next morning Lieutenant William Kinderman (Lee J. Cobb) visits Chris on his investigation of Dennings's death.

He also speaks with Damien Karras, whom the detective's preliminary research has revealed to have written a school thesis on witchcraft. Kinderman feels that the desecration in the chapel and the manner of Dennings's death (his head twisted completely around) are the work of a devil worshiper and wonders if Karras, as counselor, knows a troubled priest who might fit this description. Despite Karras's stonewalling, he and Kinderman begin to develop a friendship.

Chris finds a crucifix under Regan's pillow. She confronts Karl, who denies knowing anything about it. Suddenly there are more screams from Regan's room and Chris rushes in. Speaking a stream of profanity, Regan is mutilating her genitals with the crucifix. When Chris tries to run for help, a heavy bureau slides across the floor under its own power to block her. Regan's head turns completely around and curses in Dennings's voice.

Regan's violent assault on visiting doctors, her self-injury with a crucifix, and a backhand to Chris finally convince the doctors that they can do nothing more for the girl. Dismissing psychiatry, one of them fancifully suggests an exorcism, not for religious reasons, but for its psychological effect. Chris is referred to Father Karras, who has training in both psychiatry and religion. She is also told that his mother has just died. Karras meets a haggard Chris and warns her that the Church rarely authorizes exorcisms but agrees to see Regan to collect evidence.

A series of encounters follows between Karras and Regan during which Regan, in declining health and worsening appearance, engages with Karras in badinage sophisticated beyond her years. At one point she says she is the devil himself. When sprinkled with fake holy water (which she doesn't know is fake), Regan writhes and speaks in tongues and multiple voices (Mercedes McCambridge). Chris confides in Karras that it was probably Regan who killed Burke Dennings. At last Karras is persuaded to attempt an exorcism, but realizing that he is too inexperienced to do it alone, he asks Father Bermingham for help. Bermingham summons Father Merrin from retreat. The elderly priest arrives at the MacNeil home, where the demon is waiting for him.

Merrin and Karras immediately begin the Roman Ritual of exorcism. Merrin proceeds as one who has done this before. As they repeat the ritual, Regan's bed shakes; IV bottles crash to the floor; the ceiling and door crack; and the room becomes cold enough to reveal people's breath. The exorcism is an ordeal that taxes Karras and Merrin's spirits and stamina. At one point the demon impersonates Karras's mother, asking, "Why you do this to me, Dimmy?" The young priest loses his composure and Merrin orders him from the room.

On the landing just outside Regan's room, both priests rest,[4] then Merrin goes back to resume. Karras enters shortly thereafter to find Merrin dead on the floor, having suffered a heart attack, and a freed Regan couched on the bed gloating. When Karras cannot revive Merrin, he lunges for Regan, beating her and daring her, "Come into me! Come into me!"

In a flash, Karras becomes possessed by Regan's demon and reaches down to strangle the girl. Somehow he regains control of himself and becomes momentarily de-possessed, seizing that moment to dive out the window. He tumbles to his death at the bottom of the steps at the exact moment that Kinderman arrives at the house.

Crowds form around Karras's body at the foot of the stairs. Father Dyer pushes his way through them and administers last rites to his friend.

A short time later, recovered and leaving Washington

with no memory of her ordeal, Regan says goodbye to Farther Dyer. Chris hands Dyer the St. Joseph medal that Father Karras had worn around his neck. As the MacNeils drive off for the airport, Dyer looks down at the steps where his friend died, turns, and walks away.[5]

## CHAPTER 5

# Shooting for Hell

Principal photography on *The Exorcist* began August 14, 1972, at Goldwater Memorial Hospital on Welfare Island in New York. It was the scene in which Karras visits his elderly mother in the charity ward where she was taken after the home treatment he gave her did not work. Karras's guilt becomes overwhelming at not being able to provide for her because of his priestly vow of poverty. Real-life priest William O'Malley, SJ, who portrayed Father Dyer in the picture, recited a blessing prior to the company making the first shot, just as Rev. Thomas Bermingham would later bless the shoot on the first day at Fox (Ceco) Studios. Depending on one's view of the power of prayer, the blessings either had no effect at all or greatly reduced the calamities that were to follow during the film's unusually long nine-month shooting schedule. The Reverend John Nicola, SJ, was retained as overall technical advisor and would also play an uncredited role as, of course, a priest.

Friedkin insisted on shooting on location in New York and Washington, D.C., rather than in the controlled confines of a Los Angeles studio. "I didn't want to get up in the morning and see mountains as I was driving to work to do what was supposed to take place in a Georgetown town house," he said. "I didn't want Ellen Burstyn and the others in the film to have to do it either. I wanted them to be more connected with the city kind of life."

But there was a more pragmatic reason for the move to

Manhattan. At the time, the child labor laws of California limited a minor's availability to four hours a day. Given that it took two hours to put on Dick Smith's demon makeup and another hour to remove it—not to mention compulsory schooling—this would have left little time for Blair to do any acting. New York's more liberal child labor statutes (or lack of them) made it possible to use her for a reasonable time period.

In terms of set construction, the entire interior of the MacNeil house had to be built with movable walls inside the Ceco Studios at 450 West 54th Street (the former Fox Movietone Studios, now Camera Mart). To create the intense cold of the "possession" bedroom, it was enclosed in a cocoon and drained of warmth by a massive $50,000 air-conditioning system which had the annoying habit of setting off the building's sprinklers at odd times, flooding the set. The air-conditioning, however, allowed the spectacular effect of seeing the breath of the actors suddenly appear when they moved from the warm hallway to Regan's cold room. (Today the breath could be digitally added in postproduction, as it was in *Titanic* and the prequel *Exorcist: The Beginning*.) After several hours' uncomfortable filming—Linda Blair was covered with electric blankets while she lay in bed—the temperature would invariably rise above breath-vapor level and require a complete shutdown until the air-conditioner could once more do its job. This took time and limited the company to two or three camera setups per day (eight to twelve are optimum).

To accommodate the various effects demanded in the script, Regan's bedroom had to be a world of its own. Production designer John Robert Lloyd—who had previously done Friedkin's *The Night They Raided Minsky's* and *The Boys in the Band*—apparently built it without knowing that it would have to accommodate the massive off-camera mechanical effects that Friedkin and Marcel Vercoutere had planned. Its reveal did not go well.

"I remember when Billy walked onto John Lloyd's set," assistant director Terence Donnelly said, "and I guess at that moment decided that John Lloyd was not going to be the production designer on the show. I can remember Billy just absolutely going berserk, and he . . . went off on John Lloyd. My feeling was, at the time, that this set is not really so bad. I mean the set actually worked very well and the floor plan that [replacement production designer Bill] Malley [later] used to complete the set was pretty much the same floor plan that John Lloyd had created to start with. I think Billy just wanted to delay the start of the movie because he wasn't ready to shoot. Often I've found, over the six movies I've done with Friedkin, there was always something that would come up when Billy wasn't quite ready to do something or he wasn't sure about something or he didn't feel like he had the actors tuned into a particular nuance of performance or whatever, I felt he would artificially create a reason to delay shooting."[1]

And delay it did; the production lost six weeks while Malley went to work as the new production designer, with Jerry Wunderlich as set decorator. Together they rebuilt the house interior to Friedkin's specifications. Malley would get sole screen credit (his first) as production designer.

The new team installed a number of devices. Small air vents were placed on windowsills so that curtains could blow even though the windows were shut. The bed was capable of being raised by a cantilevered device on the other side of the wall; its high backboard covered the slits. The mattress on which the terrified youngster would unaccountably bounce was fitted with false bottoms that could jerk Blair violently back and forth and, at times, appear to bat her into the air. Blair herself was fitted with a molded back brace, which, at one point, came loose and allowed the bounce device to injure her. Floors were raised to permit the camera to get low-angled views of furniture sliding around, pulled by hidden cables. Finally everything was poised for action.

Then one Sunday morning it all burned down. Only the night watchman was present, and he escaped safely, but $200,000 worth of fixtures had to be replaced. Everyone was kept on salary during the time it took to rebuild, driving up the budget without contributing to the completion of the film.

The film's most celebrated effect also proved to be its most troublesome: the pea soup scenes. Two forms of expulsion were required: The first was the shocker in which possessed Regan entices Father Karras to approach her and then lets fly at him, and the second was an extended spew during the exorcism itself in which the child endlessly regurgitates under Father Merrin's ministrations.

For the first, special makeup expert Dick Smith, working with mechanical wizard Marcel Vercoutere, created an appliance that ran thin tubes into the shadows in Blair's mouth where they would appear hidden, bent to aim outward. On a signal from Friedkin, the actress would lurch forward, open her mouth, and a technician would squirt a stream of warm pea soup. The effect simply didn't work; instead of a single projectile stream for the crucial shot, the green liquid exploded like a shaken soda can. What appears in the final film—a focused stream of green goo—was added in postproduction and is the only special visual effect in the entire picture (see sidebar at the end of this chapter).

The device did work, however, for the second scene in producing the copious amounts of vomit that seep out endlessly while Father Merrin blesses the girl during the Roman Ritual and bile overflows onto his vestments. It had to keep flowing so that it looked like more than a human mouth could contain.

"We could only do sixteen or seventeen takes before she started choking," Friedkin once joked.

In fact, it was this second scene—seventeen feet, eight frames, according to an editor's log—for which footage of Blair's body double, Eileen Dietz, was used. It was called "Green Vomit side-to-side During Exorcism."[2]

Blair and Friedkin developed a deep trust, and the actress always regarded Friedkin as her mentor.[3] But that didn't matter to the rumor mill which—without any basis in fact—circulated stories that the thirteen-year-old had, herself, become somehow "possessed" during the shooting and that she bore psychological scars. Anyone who knows the tedious process of filmmaking would recognize the ignorance of such assertions, but such talk fueled the public's morbid curiosity. It would also work against Blair and the film at Oscar time. Friedkin considered libel suits against those who said such things.[4] To quell rumors when the film broke internationally, Warner Bros. sent Blair on a world tour to show the press just how calm and together she was.

Vomit aside, three more noteworthy effects in *The Exorcist* were Regan's levitation, her 360-degree head turn, and her controversial crucifix self-mutilation.

The first was done with wires, although Friedkin at the time staunchly refused to admit it, hinting that it might have involved magnets, force fields, and even magic. In fact, while currently available DVDs and Blu-rays have had the wires digitally removed, an inspection of a 35mm or 16mm original print in its full-frame 1.33:1 aspect ratio clearly shows wires leading from Blair's harness into a slit in the ceiling of the set. (The projector's aperture plate cropped them from view theatrically.)[5]

Of greater artifice is the complete head turn, something that would have instantly killed Regan and, as reported by Lieutenant Kinderman, did in fact kill Burke Dennings.[6] Blatty objected to the effect. "As this scene was first shot," he wrote, "Regan's head turned 360 degrees. When I pointed out to Billy Friedkin that in such an eventuality the head would likely fall off and that *supernatural* was not synonymous with *impossible*, the head turn was modified in the editing room,[7] but the effect still gives you the impression that the head is going completely around. It's preposterous but, of course, a high-ranking executive at Warner Bros., when he heard from me, perhaps at a dinner party, that there had been a full 360 shot and I was the cause of pruning it, was outraged that I had caused the cut.[8]

"I still believed it to be excessive and unreal, but audiences loved it, proving me an idiot once again. Moreover, there is some factual basis for it. In the state of possession, and among hysterics, you will find one medical case after another in which the subject—no acrobat—was nonetheless able to perform such incredible physical contortions as bending over backwards and touching his heels with his head. What distinguishes possession—and pseudo possession—from hysteria in this context is that the possessed subject, when performing these actions, seems to be doing so involuntarily, for throughout he shrieks in pain."[9]

The third effect is the notorious crucifix scene. Blatty's challenge when writing the novel had been finding something so horrible that it would drive the unbelieving Chris to someone she once referred to as a witch doctor. After agonizing thought, he decided it would be having her witness her daughter hurting herself with the crucifix.

Although some viewers mistakenly believe that the girl is masturbating with the icon, she is, in fact, mutilating—stabbing—herself. Said Blair, "There was a box and a sponge with Karo syrup and red food coloring, and that was between my legs, so I just had to put the cross into the box."

Petite actress Eileen Dietz (then age twenty-nine) not only doubled for Blair in certain shots that appear in the finished film but served as makeup tester for Dick Smith. Confusion over who did what for whom would explode into a public relations and legal nightmare once the film proved a hit. The headlines that came to dominate the attention of critics and viewers were a constant frustration to Friedkin, who wanted to maintain the illusion of the supernatural. How far could he stray from reality and still suspend the audience's disbelief? Those who dared ask for details received what became known as his "Felt Forum speech":

> I went to New York's Felt Forum and saw the Great Rinaldi, who does a festival of magic and the occult, and he does this trick that he calls "the ultimate illusion," and what he does is, he gets this set, which is an operating room, and he wheels out a woman and says, "I'm going to saw this woman in half." And he brings out a huge, thick log and he tests it under a buzz saw. Zip! Boom! The saw goes right through these logs, breaks them up. Then he brings the woman out. He brings the saw down and runs it through the woman and blood spurts all over the place, all over the stage, the attendants, the whole damn thing, and it smells of death.
>
> And the audience goes, "Oh, my God, Jesus Christ!" And I dig this and they're sitting there in the Felt Forum in New York and you see the guts of the woman pour out, all the lights on the stage are

up. I'm staggered. Everyone is staggered. People are saying, "Oh, shit!"

Now he steps out and says, "Ladies and gentlemen, there may be doubters among you. I invite you to file up on both sides of the stage and review the remains." So everybody in the joint forms two lines and they're going up and I'm going up and when you walk by this thing, you're looking, and the woman's color has changed. She's got this deathly pallor. The guts are there. It stinks of death and formaldehyde.

But the closer you get, something looks wrong, you can't put your finger on it, and people are buzzing and guys are saying, "Aw, she's not really dead." Then then they all sit down again and the Great Rinaldi walks back out on stage and he says, "You're right. The woman isn't really dead. I am unable to kill a different assistant each night, for each performance. All I ask you is, Did the illusion work? Were you convinced?" To which he got a standing ovation. Now, that is a long way of saying to you, Did it work? Don't ask me how or why, but did it work? That's the only question, as a filmmaker, that I ask the audience.[10]

Other incidents were less operatic. One was designed to play a practical joke on the Warner Bros. executives three thousand miles away in Burbank. "On the Friday before the Monday that we were to shoot events at the MacNeil house beginning with the arrival of Father Merrin," Blatty recalled with a smile, "Billy and I were having dinner. Over the wine I said, 'Wouldn't it be funny if, instead of Max von Sydow showing up in the door, removing his hat, and saying, 'Mrs. MacNeil, I'm Father Merrin,' it was Joe Fretwell, the film's costume designer, who speaks with a southern accent?' And Billy said,

'What if it were Groucho Marx?' I said, 'Groucho is in town and he's a friend of mine. Would you actually do this?'" (Blatty had stayed in touch with Groucho following his appearance on *You Bet Your Life*.) Friedkin was game, and Groucho agreed to impersonate the exorcist provided it would be filmed on Monday; on Tuesday he was due to leave New York. "The plan was," Blatty explained, "that not only would he appear at the door, he would take off his hat and it's Groucho Marx. Jason Miller would precede Groucho into the room, and we have Eileen Dietz, as the demon, tied to the bed. And when she screamed a certain ten-letter obscenity, a duck would come down."

The gag was never shot—Blatty claimed that Friedkin "got psychosomatically ill that Monday"—but it shows the closeness that developed between the two men who remained friends for the rest of Blatty's life. The pair pulled another practical joke aimed at getting a studio representative off their backs, this one during a preproduction meeting. It became known as "the salad dressing story":

> Someone who had to do with production and budget, an old-line production man, was bothering Billy about whether he was going to be shooting day-for-night.[11]
>
> Something about the question outraged Billy, and he said, "No, we're just going to paint the windows black." From there he caught my eye and the man asked him another question, and I said, "Hold on a second. Before we get into that, you know what I'm talking about, don't you, Billy?"
>
> "Oh, yeah, that."
>
> "Well," I said, "let's get into it now. The salad dressing." I then preceded on a speech about Billy and me having a fight about cost-cutting. I, being

the producer, insisted that the crew have no choice other than vinaigrette and Green Goddess for the catered lunches, whereas Billy wanted them to have creamy Italian and vinaigrette, Green Goddess, and bleu cheese. Then Billy and I started to have a violent quarrel about this. It was reported and it sent tremors of anxiety through the executive offices because one of the many terrors—we were high among them—was that two strong-willed people could fall apart like this. Blatty and Friedkin fighting! They tried to mediate salad dressing! Think of what that tells you of what the executive mentality thinks about *our* mentality! That's much more revealing. I also remember when the first group of dailies came in and Billy had shot scatterings of autumn leaves. The critical comment from the studio was "I just looked at three hours of fucking leaves go by."[12]

One of the more legitimately controversial stories emerging from *The Exorcist* was about Friedkin's penchant for firing handguns to make performers show shock. Many directors create an environment where the performers can act as their characters do, but this generally doesn't involve small arms fire. With non-actors, however, additional measures are sometimes required. That doesn't justify their use, only explains it. This habit by Friedkin irked Jason Miller, who recalled telling the director to let him do his job and not use tricks. Max von Sydow took a more pragmatic approach. When he arrived on the set, he would say hello to everyone and then ask Owen Roizman, "Where did Billy hide the guns today?"[13]

Father William O'Malley, an experienced priest but a novice actor, was someone who needed additional motivation. According to Howard Newman, the film's unit publicist, when O'Malley had to play the tough scene where, as Father Dyer, he gave last rites to Father Karras, it was late on the fifty-first day of location shooting and the company had gone well into the freezing night in Georgetown. According to Newman in *The Exorcist: The Strange Story Behind the Film*, Friedkin wasn't getting the performance he wanted from O'Malley. Finally he took him aside:

> "Do you trust me?" asked Friedkin. The priest nodded. Friedkin stepped out of hearing range to talk with the sound man and the cameraman. He then came back to O'Malley and spoke to him quietly for a few seconds, again asking the priest if he trusted him. The priest assured him again without really understanding what the director was up to.
>
> Friedkin then nodded to the sound man, who yelled, "Speed," just as the cameramen boomed, "Rolling." With that, Friedkin hauled off and belted O'Malley right across the face. Stunned, the priest turned around and went through the scene a final time. With a trembling voice O'Malley absolved Karras for the last time, his hands shaking and tears welling up in his eyes. As Karras died, O'Malley threw himself down on the bloody corpse, sobbing uncontrollably. "Cut!" yelled the delighted Friedkin, who ran over to the shaken priest, grabbing him up in his arms and planting a big kiss right where he had struck him.[14]

Hitting O'Malley was an example of the same directorial expediency that Friedkin had used years before with Paul Crump. For decades, people have taken it out of context for its outrageousness not only as an example of Friedkin's anything-for-the-film ethos, but also for its subtext of a Jew-ish man letting a Catholic priest have one across the kisser. But it makes for a powerful screen moment, and O'Malley, in interviews, has long since given Friedkin absolution.

Assistant director Terence Donnelly was present for a stunt gone wrong in which the demon belted Chris, sending her across the room. "[Ellen] had a rig on. She also had a lot of padding on. We didn't have a stunt coordinator per se on the set. I'm not sure I can answer the question why. If that shot was to be made in a movie today, there would be all kinds of hell to pay if you didn't have a safety officer or a stunt coordinator on the set, but frankly, in those days, it just didn't feel like it needed any more tension. Ellen, obvi-ously, was not out of the loop. She was a part of the dis-cussion of how the shot was going to be made. She seemed quite comfortable with the padding that they had designed for her, and the rig that Marcel had cooked up to pull her back—literally pull her away from the camera so she ended up hitting the wall and the side of that dresser or piece of furniture there. It all worked exactly the way it was sup-posed to work and, if I'm not mistaken, we only did two takes of it. But Ellen was nervous about it. We were all ner-vous about it, but I don't think she had any big objections to it. And I don't think that she and Billy had any kind of discussions about it, but it was never a big deal."[15]

Afterward, Burstyn claimed that the stunt had wrenched her back and given her chronic pain. "It bothered me for many years," she offers as an update, "but it's been okay for between ten and twenty years because I've done much work on it and massage and so forth so that it's finally stopped giv-ing me trouble."[16]

Once production wrapped in America, the next adven-ture was shooting the prologue in Northern Iraq in which

Father Merrin confronts a statue of the demon Pazuzu. Unlike *Exorcist II: The Heretic*, the makers of *The Exorcist* were wise in never speaking the name *Pazuzu*. In fact, it isn't even made clear that Pazuzu is the possessing demon, although his presence, in the form of a sculpture of varying sizes, would imply so.

"The prologue shows that there is nothing more terrifying than evil when it is unavoidable," Blatty explained, reminding that his publisher had originally wanted to cut those pages. So did Warner Bros.—for budget reasons—but Friedkin and Blatty's insistence caused them to allow a trip to Iraq. Production manager William Kaplan was dispatched to the politically unstable but historically valuable locale and began to get it ready for Hollywood. There was a slight delay when the studio check for "location access" bounced and Kaplan found himself a "guest" of the Iraqi government, but that was quickly resolved.

"Bill Kaplan was a legend in most of Iraq as the man who was making sacrifices to a demon statue," Friedkin recounted glibly. "They thought we were a bunch of devil worshipers and were spooked by us!" This was the result of Kaplan's pursuit of the giant prop Pazuzu which had somehow been sidetracked during air shipment from Los Angeles and wound up in Singapore (*sic*). "It was packed in a ten-foot crate," Friedkin wondered. "How do you lose something like that?"

Billy Williams was the director of photography for the Iraqi sequences and recounts how they found the statue. He was supposed to meet Friedkin et al. in Iraq in March of 1973, but "so much had gone wrong and they were so far behind schedule that I didn't actually go until August. This statue was absolutely vital, and it was missing and nobody knew where it was. This was 1973, after the revolution in Iraq, and it was no longer possible to make an international phone call. David Anderson was the production manager. In order to make an international call he got on the train to Baghdad, and he flew from Baghdad to Beirut, and he made a call and they found this statue in Hong Kong. They'd forgotten to take it off the plane. Some days later it turned up and we shot the scene. It seemed to be quite extraordinary that in a film about exorcism the demon should disappear."[17]

While in Iraq, the "devil worshipers" were invited to a meeting with the Yezede, a sect that—according to Friedkin—were the "real thing."

"They're really very pleasant people," he reported, even if "they have some unusual customs. For example, they don't use any words beginning with the *sh* sound because the Arabic word for *devil* begins with that sound. Therefore, they never take the devil's name in vain! If words beginning with that sound are deliberately used in front of them, they are required to kill the person."

Friedkin took a meeting with, as he described, "some old guy who looks like Khomeini and had a thousand flies in his beard and you had to sit there and they told me going in, 'don't wipe the flies.' The flies are all over. 'Don't brush them away 'cause you'll embarrass him.' So if you want to meet this guy, use self-control."

The Iraqi sightseeing was balanced by the hardships of work. In the desert where they shot the scenes of Merrin confronting Pazuzu, the temperature rose to 120 degrees Fahrenheit. To accommodate the radical change in temperature from Regan's freezer-like bedroom to the Iraqi desert, Dick Smith had to change the chemistry of his appliances so they wouldn't melt on von Sydow's face. And because the company could only film in the mornings, before temperatures rose, the actor had a makeup call at 2:30 a.m. to be ready to shoot at sunrise.

Then there was the problem of getting two dogs to take direction while Merrin confronted the Pazuzu statue. "We were trying to get shots of vultures circling over Pazuzu's head," Friedkin recalled. "Every morning that we would shoot, we'd take along raw meat and set it by the statue of Pazuzu. And no vultures came. Then we wanted to get these dogs fighting, so we said, 'Let's throw the raw meat to the dogs.' They starved the dogs for three days, then threw them out. The dogs ran out—we're shooting—and the dogs sniffed the meat and walked away. It turns out that these dogs had never eaten meat; they ate bread. They're *vegetarian*."

But the dogfight that truly threatened the *Exorcist* company occurred within the warring factions of the Iraqi government.

"The country was in a state of flux," Friedkin said. "President [Said] Ahmed Hasan al-Bakr was out of the country holding meetings in Poland. The chief of the secret police, Nazim Kassar, tried to take over the country. He had a forty-man hit squad waiting at Baghdad Airport to assassinate the president. It turned out that the president's plane was four hours late coming into the airport. The hit team was in groups around the airport and panicked—thought it was a trap—and started to give themselves up. It wasn't a trap; President al-Bakr just decided to stay later. But when they gave themselves up, it turned out that Kassar was camped out around where I was shooting and the guys who were our hosts came in and said, 'We don't go out today.'

"I didn't know for a couple of days what the problem was. We were sort of confined in a house arrest while they tried to figure out what was going on. They rounded up the forty guys and they had a one-day trial. They were all tried in one day and hung the next. Took them two days."[18]

The power and beauty that the Iraqi sequences brought

to the film cannot be overstated, and it was Williams's job to capture that. "Initially I went on a long recce with the director to find the places to shoot these scenes of an archaeological dig, but we didn't find anything that was quite right until we came across a city called Hatra [in Eastern Nineveh] which was on the old trade route from India about three thousand years ago, and they were excavating this site and rebuilding the temple, a temple to the sun god. The Iraqi people were rebuilding this temple by going back to the original's quarry and cutting fresh stone and replacing what was missing. So we finally settled on this place called Hatra.

"I had quite a lot of interesting things to shoot out there," Williams continues. "One of them was in a souk, which is like an underground market with shafts of sunlight coming through and lots of activity with traders and so on, and Max von Sydow has to walk through this souk, and it was extremely contrasty. All we had were these shafts of sunlight coming through reading, I should think, about f/22—we were still using 100 ASA stock—and these shafts of light with dust making them show up beautifully. So I just got pieces of white card and put them on the floor out of picture to reflect light up from these beams of light, and in the foreground I put a bulb to illuminate some work that somebody was doing, and that about two, two-and-a-half stops under, and I shot it at f/3.5 and it came out. I was greatly relieved because they had a marvelous atmosphere."[19]

After Iraq came postproduction. The footage was edited in New York City by Bud Smith in the Warner Bros. office building located at—ready for it—666 Fifth Avenue. To those believing in the "Curse of *The Exorcist*," the address couldn't have been more appropriate.

# The Curse of *The Exorcist*

The notion that a curse befell *The Exorcist* has persisted ever since the picture went into production. It appears validated by the unusual number of accidents, deaths, and hinderances that took place while it was being shot and thereafter, and it fed the legend that this was a film that Satan, or whoever, didn't want made.

At the same time, the Hollywood publicity machine runs on such stories, and the experts promoting *The Exorcist* did little, if anything, to quell the notion that their enterprise had an evil cloud hanging over it. The big question, all these years later, is *How much of it was true?*

The answer is easy: *All of it.*

The more realistic question, though, is *Was it a curse or just statistics?*

*The Exorcist* was a film that made its own publicity gravy. By definition a story that mined the realms of superstition, religion, and sadomasochism, it was ripe for the rumor mill. Here are some of the major incidents that kept the wheels grinding:

- The MacNeil household interior, a set constructed at the 54th Street Ceco Studios in New York, burned to the ground (as previously noted).

- Jason Miller's five-year-old son, Jordan, was seriously hurt by a motorcycle during a beach visit; he recovered.

- Jack MacGowran died two weeks after his scenes were shot.

- Max von Sydow's brother died in Sweden during production.

- Linda Blair's grandfather died during production.

- A gaffer (lighting technician) lost a toe in an on-set accident.

- The film's budget rose from $5 million to over twice that.

- Linda Blair's pet mouse died.

- Ellen Burstyn injured her back when a stunt proved too harsh for her (as noted).

- The daughter of one of the limousine drivers, learning of the film's subject matter, began having hallucinations about holy objects and had to be institutionalized.

- A cemetery at Fordham University in the Bronx where deceased priests were interred was vandalized and its stones were split in half.

- As they left Iraq, Friedkin and his crew were held several hours at the airport in the wake of the failed coup against Iraq's leaders. Only after they left did they learn that the airport lounge in which they had waited was wired with explosives designed to kill the government cabinet as part of the coup.[1]

"Such negative energy in that film!" remarked Shirley MacLaine, William Blatty's California neighbor and the person on whom the character of Chris MacNeil was admittedly based. "Of *course* I was Chris MacNeil!" the Oscar-winning actress confirmed. "Bill used the French couple who ran my house in his book, he used J. Lee Thompson as the basis for the director, and the first séance I ever went to, he arranged in my house.

"He also," she added with an edge in her voice, "still claims the picture on the front of [the book] *The Exorcist* is not my daughter, Sachi [Stephanie Sachiko], but it is; he took it himself and distorted it photographically. Her friends used to ask her about it." Blatty repeatedly denied this claim.

The MacLaine/MacNeil comparisons extended, MacLaine said, to "Billy [Friedkin] came over to visit me. I'm making pancakes. He was getting down my movements so he could coach Ellen Burstyn on how to play me."[2]

Coincidentally, when Ellen Burstyn was hired to play Chris, her analysis of the character brought her to Shirley MacLaine. "Before I knew that Bill Blatty knew Shirley," Burstyn said, "once I started working on the character, I thought, *Well what kind of actress is she? What's her background? Did she study acting or what?* I said, 'No, I think she was probably a dancer and worked in the chorus line on Broadway and got seen and brought into films from that. Well, that's exactly the way Shirley's career started.'"

It was also how Burstyn's career began. Eventually the two actresses got together in Malibu where both were then staying. "We made a date to have dinner at one of the best restaurants in Malibu," Burstyn continues. "We could hardly eat dinner, we were so the focus of the whole room. But I found out that, from Shirley's point of view, Chris MacNeil was her role, and in her words, she referred to me as 'the one who stole that role' from her. But I don't think that Bill Blatty ever meant to cast her. I don't think he wrote it for her, which is the way she interpreted it, but that he used her as the model."

Burstyn and MacLaine share another characteristic: Both are deeply spiritual women. This raises the long-discussed matter of a curse that supposedly hovers over *The Exorcist*. MacLaine's notion of "negative energy" emerges in the film's numerous production delays and other unexplained occurrences. Some of them might have been anticipated, even if they couldn't be avoided: The groundbreaking nature of the effects—which had to be invented for the film but have since become industry standard—required a high level of research and on-the-job experimentation. But the others?

Was there a curse on *The Exorcist*? Tabloid reporters and internet cultists like to think so.

"No, I don't believe in curses," offers Terence A. Donnelly, the film's first assistant director and a veteran of over fifty films. "My explanation has always been, on a picture that goes fifteen, sixteen months, there's gonna be a certain number of anomalies that are gonna come up and, God knows, we had our share of anomalies. We had the fire; Max von Sydow's brother passed away in Stockholm the very night at he did his entrance scene in Georgetown; Jack MacGowran died two weeks after he finished his role. There was some stuff, but, again, the laws of probability satisfied me. I never felt like I had to look over my shoulder or anything like that. There was the missing statue of Pazuzu [that] ended up in Hong Kong. People will say, 'Geez, that was really weird.' Well yeah, it was really weird, but it wasn't cursed."

Burstyn believes otherwise. Her observations are persuasive. "I don't know that I would go along with that word [*curse*]," she avers, but adds, "When I attended that forty-fifth anniversary screening with Billy, we were asked questions afterward, and he was asked about all of the weird events that happened during filming and he said, 'None of that's true, it was all made up.' And I was shocked. I said, 'Really? We were on two different sets, then, because there were a lot of very strange things that happened.' I don't see how that could not be when we are talking about energy. We were calling on some very heavy energy. People might say dark forces, but that might be too dramatic. I don't think you fool around with those kind of energy fields without having some sort of manifestation, and we had a lot. It's not all made up. It's probably overblown in a lot of cases, but the set actually *did* catch on fire on a weekend when nobody was there.

"When I knew I was going to do the film, I [went] on a spiritual retreat and I spoke to a teacher about what I was going to do and he said, 'You'll have to protect yourself. I'll give you some prayers to do to keep yourself from attracting those kind of energies,' and he made a tape for me. I brought the tape and the recorder to my dressing room—we hadn't started shooting yet—and within three days the tape was stolen, along with the recorder. I told Billy and he said, 'Oh, we're going to hire a guard.' So he hired a guard to be at the studio when no one was there at night. A young black man. He got shot, mistakenly, by the police and got killed. Within two weeks, maybe less, maybe ten days. The police were called to a scene and it happened to be in the house where he lived. He was just exiting the house and was reaching into his pocket to get his keys and the police thought he was reaching for a gun and they shot and killed him.

"Some people do want to believe it," she says. "Billy started out telling a completely psychological story. He wasn't at all convinced it was metaphysical. And something happened early on, but Billy's response, as I heard him walking away from my dressing room, was 'Get Father Birmingham to bless the set.'" And he did.

If there was, in fact, any *Exorcist* curse, it settled upon those cheeky enough to challenge its supremacy. All three attempts to extend its legacy—*Exorcist II: The Heretic*, *The Exorcist III*, and *Dominion*—required extensive reshoots and re-edits that cost millions of extra dollars and still resulted in commercial and critical failure. Whether the same fate will befall the new trilogy, due to unfold in October 2023, is unknown.

## CHAPTER 6

# The Devil Is in the Details

There's an old Hollywood saying (Hollywood is full of old sayings) that a picture never looks as good as it does in the dailies or as bad as it does in the first cut. William Friedkin and William Peter Blatty had shot *The Exorcist* so well that the second half of that maxim didn't apply. They knew what they wanted. The trick was how to get it.

Returning to cutting rooms in New York after wrapping principal photography, Friedkin was as energized as everyone else was depleted. Looking forward to the intricate editing process, he also began investigating solutions to his most difficult postproduction problem: the vocal personality of the demon.

"You can't make demonic forces behave like Shirley Temple," Blatty had cautioned. "This is true or you're kidding yourself." During production, Father John J. Nicola, who was on the set to ensure authenticity—and who was opposed to the crucifix and church desecration scenes—offered the comment that the demon's obscenity during the exorcism itself was too tame.[1]

"Billy said to me one day out of the blue," Blatty recalled, "'tomorrow we're doing the scene. I want the most steaming, horrendous obscenities that you can give me.' And I handed him the pages like this—by one corner."[2] Interestingly, Blatty continued, "most of the obscenity that had to be looped or replaced with other language [for the TV version] related to the Ellen Burstyn character. About seventy-five percent of it was her dialogue, not the demon's, and quite honestly I was happier with the new lines that I wrote for the [TV version of the] demon's obscenities, because Billy had given Linda Blair, because she was a very young girl, free rein to improvise on the obscenity so that it would seem more natural to her, and thus what I feared during the exorcism scene was a grammar school kid's idea of steaming obscenity. It's always embarrassed me considerably, and I was very happy to have the opportunity to change it [for television]."[3]

Even with the filthier dialogue, it was apparent that a voice other than Linda Blair's would have to speak it; if not, as Blatty said, it would sound like a schoolgirl talking dirty, not the forces of evil.

*The Exorcist* soundtrack was to be mixed at Todd-AO in Hollywood, under the skilled supervision of Robert "Buzz" Knudson, who would win an Oscar for his work. In 1973, when the various dialogue, music, and effects tracts were to be mixed, audio techniques had not yet entered the digital age. In casting a wider net than Hollywood then possessed, Friedkin, as he had in the past, sought help from his cronies in hometown Chicago.

"We would listen to what was there and tried to substitute sounds for it that would aid and abet the horror of the possession at that particular time," explained Ken Nordine, Friedkin's friend from the days when both men worked at WGN-TV. Nordine, by then a successful commercial producer and highly recognized voice talent, says he "brought special equipment to play with and distort Linda Blair's voice."

"A lot of what I know about sound came from listening to Ken," Friedkin acknowledged, "so he was the first one I reached out for, and we paid Ken a lot of money to go out and experiment. He was going to go out and use computers to mix the voice with animal sounds and come up with that distortion. At a certain point, Ken played some tapes for me, and it basically sounded like Ken Nordine doing a demon voice. It was wrong. But what it told me—while I'm listening to this voice that is trying to sound demonic, which basically sounds comic—is that I had to go for a kind of unnatural sound. Neither male nor female. Otherworldly. But what is 'otherworldly'?"

Nordine recalled learning that his work had been rejected when he sent Warner Bros. a bill and the studio refused to pay it, "figuring they weren't going to be using anything." Nordine sued. Five years later it was settled with one important casualty: the Nordine-Friedkin friendship. "Bill was placed in the position, because of his relationship with Warners, that he had to take a deposition that was against me," Nordine said. "We had experts—voiceprints and all that—but, when you really get down to it, it was an episode in my life where I felt I should have gone to an exorcist myself to get rid of this evil that had been placed on me."[4]

Friedkin was open to any and all suggestions of how to create the demon's voice. What he didn't tell his team was that he had something against which to compare whatever they devised. According to editor Craig McKay, one day he took aside him and his two leading audio experts, Doc Siegel and Ron Nagle, and said, "'I'm going to give you a tape that's of the actual exorcism.[5] We're not going to tell you how we got it. And I want you to figure out how to create that sound, the exact sound that you hear.' And so I said, 'Okay!' And he wanted to be in on it. That's the kind of thing, [Friedkin] wanted to be in on things. So we started and then we tried to figure out how we could get a demon voice, because it was all going to be [dubbed later]. Billy told us we couldn't ever talk about the tape, which now I'm doing."[6]

As these were the days before digital manipulation, the

audio experts used a variety of analog tricks. "We would lower the pitch for the line, take the line again with the lowered pitch, and put it through a Chinese cymbal with a transducer on it," McKay explains. Doc Siegel was a mastermind at conjuring audio effects.

Eventually, to perform the voice of the demon, Friedkin turned to Mercedes McCambridge, the Oscar-winning actress whom he remembered for her mastery of the technique of dramatic radio. Associate producer David Salven located McCambridge—whose voice and career had both tasted hell—in a Texas stage production of *Who's Afraid of Virginia Woolf?*

"The minute she walked into my office I knew that was it," Friedkin said.

McCambridge insisted on suffering abuse while lip-synching the demon's voice. She smoked to excess, ate raw eggs and a pulpy apple, and even asked that her hands be bound with bedsheets, all in service of conveying such anguish that it would express a kinship with the possessed Regan MacNeil.

"It was her idea to drink," added Friedkin, noting that the actress was a recovering alcoholic. "She asked me to let her drink, which was a traumatic thing for her. She asked me to tie her to the chair, and I did. She was really up for shit and we tried everything. She did everything, and she was really incredible."

In addition to McCambridge's looping of Blair's on-set lines, Friedkin, Knudson, and their sound crew added the squeals of pigs being led to the slaughter, voices played backwards, different microphones, and various levels of distortion on the combined tracks. Friedkin used his own voice in some instances.

As the firm December 26, 1973, premiere date approached,

Friedkin had to seek help outside the Todd-AO facilities to complete the reel containing the exorcism itself.

"Reel eleven of *The Exorcist* was the motherfucker reel," he says. "We were so behind schedule that I took that reel over to Fox, to the boys that I did *The French Connection* with—Ted Soderberg. It took me one month just to mix reel eleven at Fox, and I was going to Fox in the morning for two hours, then I'd shoot over to Todd-AO in the afternoon, then back-and-forth for a twenty-hour day."[7]

Then there was the problem of the film's music. Friedkin's first choice was Bernard Herrmann, the feisty composer who had scored the classics of Orson Welles and Alfred Hitchcock. Living in England, Herrmann flew to Los Angeles to view a rough cut of *The Exorcist* and to meet its director.

"I want you to write me a better score than the one you wrote for *Citizen Kane*," Friedkin said, according to one story.

"Then you should have made a better movie than *Citizen Kane*," Herrmann replied, and returned to London.

Executive producer Noel Marshall then suggested Lalo Schifrin, the Argentinian pianist-composer who had become popular in Hollywood through such soundtracks as *Cool Hand Luke*, *Bullitt*, and television's *Mission: Impossible*. Friedkin had met Schifrin some fifteen years earlier when the musician had played with Dizzy Gillespie. Now the two discussed the score and, according to Friedkin, agreed on a sparse, atmospheric style, "like a cold hand on the back of your neck." Schifrin then went off to compose.

"Lalo came in and we went into a little projection room," said Bud Smith, who was again editing for Friedkin, for the first time since they had worked together making documentaries for David L. Wolper in the early sixties. "He wanted to play Billy what he thought was a theme and Billy said, 'I can't tell what this is. Go record it and then I'll know.' This was arranged. "What he was recording was this 110-piece orchestra playing Brazilian music for the score," Smith said. "Billy stopped him recording it right in the studio. I was trying to convince Billy to go ahead and record the stuff, and if we didn't want it we can let Warner Bros. use it for some other movie; he's gonna be paid anyway.

"He hated it," Smith said, quoting Friedkin: "'Get that shit out of my movie!' He took the roll of [sound] film, took it out in front of Todd-AO, right in the street, and just threw it into the parking lot and said, 'That's where that fucking music belongs. In the parking lot.' And that's the honest-to-God's truth." Smith later tried to place a little of what Schifrin had recorded in the MacNeil party scene, but Friedkin objected. His reaction to Schifrin's score reflects distaste and betrayal. "It was big, loud, scary, wall-to-wall, accent, accent, a guy picked up, accent, accent," Friedkin said. "I don't like any musical accents. It pained me to do it, but I would rather have Lalo Schifrin denounce me on the front page of the *Los Angeles Times* every day for the rest of my life than use one note of his score in my picture."

Eventually he licensed other music from records, and the cut from Mike Oldfield's *Tubular Bells* became as closely identified with *The Exorcist* as Strauss's *Also Sprach Zarathustra* had become with *2001: A Space Odyssey*. Friedkin had wanted a theme that sounded as innocent as a children's nursery song, as "Brahms Lullaby," but wasn't as well known or hackneyed. He found it while poring through the Warner Bros. music department auditioning hundreds of recordings that had been sent to the company for possible U.S. commercial release. One of them was an ET (electronic transcription) from the Virgin Group that perfectly fit the director's needs. It also met the public's taste; by 1992 some sixteen million copies of "Tubular Bells" had been sold worldwide.[8]

*The Exorcist* is as visually innovative as its soundtrack, if not more so, but how much of it was intended, how much was accidental, and how much is the stuff of scholarly navel-gazing is a fluid discussion. In their seminal analysis of the film, Tim Lucas and Mark Kermode[9] call it the "pink rose" theory, referring to something so obvious that people glom onto it as symbolism. As they write, pink roses were cited by author Wilson Bryan Key in his 1977 jeremiad *Media Sexploitation*[10] as appearing throughout the film: in a teapot in Iraq when the wall clock stops, held by Chris MacNeil when Regan urinates on the carpet, and in Mrs. Karras's apartment. It's the kind of sophistry that academics take pride in propounding and which makes artists roll their eyes.

Lucas, whose magazine *Video Watchdog*[11] positioned him as the authority on pre-1980 horror films (that is, before slashers took over the genre), is more accepting of filmmakers' use of symbolism. "I've known enough filmmakers to know that it is more conscious than they let on, sometimes," he says. "More often, their use of symbolism is unconscious, but that doesn't make it any the less from them; the heart sometimes has as much involvement in the writing as the brain, and the heart sometimes writes while the brain is sleeping. The most important thing is that a book or film is as many things as it has readers or viewers; we all bring ourselves, our experience, our baggage to the movies with us, and every response is probably more unique than we can discover in the course of going for a coffee afterwards. Is it possible to read too much into a film? Only from someone else's perspective. There are people who just go to the movies for a good time—it starts and ends there—but these people tend to be people who don't cultivate much of an inner life. I'm glad I don't just see *The Exorcist*—and indeed, a good many lesser films—just as entertainment."[12]

Key continues to deconstruct *The Exorcist*'s use of subliminal images such as single or double frame flashes of Captain Howdy (Eileen Dietz in test makeup footage), quick cuts of Pazuzu or the St. Joseph medal, and other visuals intended to convey emotion without necessarily clarifying meaning. It matters not that Key uses the wrong definition of *subliminal*, which, when correctly used, applies to something that is below the human threshold to notice, and a one- or two-frame shot in a twenty-four-frame-per-second movie is immediately noticeable. *Subliminal* conjures memories of an equally fallacious campaign in the late 1940s to sell consumer products by flashing words like "Drink Coke" or "Buy Camels" on a movie screen in front of unsuspecting audiences. The experience supposedly induced in the viewer an immediate craving for whatever was advertised. But because a one-twenty-fourth-second cut would have been instantly recognizable, a projection machine called a tachistoscope was used to flash the words at a rate between the eye's ability to see and the brain's ability to comprehend. There was never any substantiated proof that it worked for sales purposes, although it is used today for market research. Nevertheless, in the reactionary 1950s, it was banned.

A more accurate term than *subliminal* might be *flash frames*. These quick insertions have a history throughout cinema; among the most famous are the two red frames ahead of a suicidal gunshot in Alfred Hitchcock's *Spellbound* (1945, Hal C. Kern, editor), quick cuts of a concentration camp in Sidney Lumet's *The Pawnbroker* (1964, Ralph Rosenblum, editor), flashes of Mrs. Robinson's breasts and thighs in Mike Nichols's *The Graduate* (1967, Stan O'Steen, editor), and the one that most people credit with initiating their modern use, the flash-frame cuts in Alain Resnais's *Hiroshima, Mon Amour* (1959, edited by Jasmine Chasney, Henri Colpi, and Anne

Sarrite). Lucas and Kermode don't hop onto Key's wobbly bandwagon, but they do remark on the succession of comprehensible images that Friedkin and his editors use.

"For years, William Friedkin actively denied any knowledge of this subliminal image of Eileen Dietz as 'Captain Howdy' in *The Exorcist*," Lucas wrote in an October 8, 2007, blog comparing the flash frame in *The Exorcist* with those in Bergman's *Persona,* "but once the film came to home video and could be manipulated by those in the know, it became undeniable. (I should point out for the sake of interested historians that, even though Linda Blair's Regan refers to her inner voice/imaginary friend as 'Captain Howdy' in an early scene of the movie, the epithet is never heard again in the movie and never mentioned in relation to her demonic possession. It was actually me who first identified this face as 'Captain Howdy' in *Video Watchdog* #6, and I note with some pride that the ID has caught on.) [The image appears] on the cover of the first edition of Mark Kermode's BFI Modern Classics book on the picture; the face in the movie bears much the same pallid, ogreish look as Bergman's Devil."

Elaborating on this important point, Lucas says, "I truly believe that the real power of *The Exorcist* was in Friedkin's unprecedented uses of subliminal imagery and irrational sounds in a mainstream film, and also an ingenious ad campaign by Warner. When I had my first conversations about the movie with people back in 1974, I'd ask them if they saw the subliminal images during Karras's dream, and people thought I was kidding them when I told them you see the Devil's face. When videotape became available, I did a freeze-frame of that image off my TV screen (I had to shoot many, just to get maybe one print without a roll-bar across it!) to show people. When I asked Dick Smith about it during an interview he granted me for *Video Watchdog* #6, even *he* had no idea what I was talking about—and when I sent him photos of my grabs, he congratulated me on 'the acuity of [my] vision'! Because it was only then that he remembered doing some experimental makeups on Eileen Dietz that 'Billy must have' tucked away for special use. I printed the Captain Howdy image, as well as other similar images imbedded in early TV spots for the film, in our *Exorcist* coverage and I think it may be the first in-print acknowledgement of that image anywhere. I never saw it anywhere earlier, and afterwards it began showing up on fanzine covers, concert posters, all kind of places. Now, with HD, it's crystal clear."[13]

The imagery to which Lucas refers includes the meandering St. Joseph medal: its unaccounted presence in Iraq,[14] in Karras's intoxicated dream, around Mrs. Karras's neck, and finally around Karras's neck. It is his contention that, at the end, when Karras dares the demon to enter him, he only becomes vulnerable to possession after Regan snatches the medal away. Given that reasoning, it's tempting to wonder if St. Joseph medals work on demons the way garlic works on vampires. That said, it was Blatty's idea that Father Dyer handing the same medal to Chris at the end should signify her openness to accept Christ and, more than that, as a symbol that Karras lives. That idea sat heavily on Friedkin for twenty-five years until he restored the scene in 1998 to show it as Blatty intended.

An additional visual that enriches *The Exorcist* is the appearance of the demon's (Dietz's) face behind the dummy Regan in the head-turning scene. Lucas and Kermode learned from Dick Smith that this was created by optical effects innovator Linwood Dunn to add not only texture to the film but life to the inanimate model. Dunn is not credited. Kermode insists that this is also an optical effect like the vomit spew;

technically, it is a simple double exposure, not a matte shot that creates something that was never there.

Long before the complex sound work had begun, Friedkin had skidded through the original $12 million budget and the Warner Bros. executives were getting nervous. The firewall created by his *French Connection* Oscar was fast eroding, and the studio bosses wanted to know how much further into the financial hole he would drop them before *The Exorcist* was ready. They were riding him so hard that he refused to speak with them. That's where assistant editor Craig McKay came in.

"I was very young, very young at that point," McKay recalls, "and he said to me, 'Take the cut out to Warner Bros. Show it to the executives.' So I got on a plane with all the fiber cases,[15] went out to Warner Bros., got to the screening room, threaded up the film, and I'm waiting. They all know I'm there. All of these executives come in. Nobody says anything to me or anybody. They just walk in, sit down, they look like automatons. And Ted Ashley, who was the head of the studio at that point, said, 'Hi, I'm Ted Ashley. Your name?' I said, 'Craig McKay.' He said, 'That's right,' and then he turned to the suits and said, 'This is Mr. McKay, he is representing William Friedkin and he's going to show us the cut of *The Exorcist*.'

"He sat down and the lights went down and the movie came on. We ran the entire film. After the film was over, the lights came up. Not a word was said for a full three minutes, easily. Nothing. They just sat there in dead silence. And then, finally, Ted Ashley gets up and looks at me, points at me directly, and says, 'You go tell Billy Friedkin he's got carte blanche at the studio. He can do whatever he wants, fully. You go tell him that.' I said, 'Okay,' and they all left.

"So I get Billy on the phone in New York and he said,

'What'd they say?' I said, 'Well, they said you got carte blanche at the studio to do whatever you want to finish the film.' He goes, 'Good. Fuck 'em.'"

It was at this point that Friedkin (with the consultation of Warners executive John Calley) began removing sections of the film that William Peter Blatty would ride him about for the next twenty-five years.

Terence Donnelly, who worked with Friedkin on half a dozen films as first assistant director or production manager, has perspective on the Friedkin-Blatty partnership. "Bill Blatty was a really nice man and I think a very talented writer," he says. "He and Billy got along professionally okay, but I don't believe they really liked one another very much. Although it didn't really show, they were both very careful to maintain a social distance, as it were, but Blatty was not acting like a real producer. Perhaps because he might have been, like many of us, scared to death of Billy. Not wanting to get in Billy's way. I think Blatty just sort of laid back a bit."[16]

As the Boxing Day release deadline neared, word began seeping out of the editing room that there were disagreements between director Friedkin and writer-producer Blatty. "There came a certain point where I was barred from the postproduction by Warner Bros.," Blatty confirmed. "First Lalo, then me!"

Yet Craig McKay says, "I never saw him in the editing room. I think I saw him in Billy's office one day." Was he ever barred? "Not that I know. He might have said [it] to Blatty." When David Salven was called upon to squash Blatty's contention that he was barred from the set, he explained that the film was in postproduction, where there are no sets. "Billy simply told Blatty that he didn't want Blatty around him," Salven said.[17]

To a press starved for official news of the production, this morsel became a feast. First the *Hollywood Reporter* quoted

Blatty as saying that Friedkin had barred him from the set and was suing both him and the studio over credits. The next day, Friedkin said that Blatty's suit against Warners was "to get his profit position improved." Not content to have won the he said/he said, Friedkin asked his business manager Ed Gross and attorney Gerald Lipsky to demand a retraction. By January 1974, when the film had become a monster hit, all talk of litigation had ended.[18]

Despite the he said/he said in the trades, Blatty and Friedkin both denied any real conflict. "I was sick in bed with hepatitis anyway," Blatty says. "There was no point in barring me. But they didn't want me around. Billy showed me the first cut; it was a masterwork. Really, a classic film." Then, he added slyly (in the 1988 interview), "Which I don't think the version we've all seen is."

Blatty had several concerns, among them clarifying the target of the possession. The text makes Karras, with his crisis of faith, appear to be the victim. Yet the demon's line to Merrin, which was cut, "This time you're going to lose," referencing their African encounter twelve years earlier, targets him. Another problem arose in the "the devil does commercials" scene in which Blatty and Friedkin determined that Ellen Burstyn's personal rejection of religion was making her delivery of the line disingenuous. They never did solve that one.

But the greatest difference was what became known as the "stairwell" discussion between Merrin and Karras over why the demon attacks with such ferocity. It was this scene that Blatty argued was essential to the preservation of the religious content of the picture. "If it were merely the artistic considerations," Blatty asked, "why would [Friedkin] choose to create great gaps in the carpentry of the story?" Friedkin's response was more direct: "I am not making a commercial for the Catholic Church." This was ironic, considering Chris's notion of commercials for the devil.

The first fine cut of *The Exorcist* ran two hours and twenty minutes. Anxious about hitting a more commercial two-hour running time, Friedkin reduced its length, as noted above. Blatty was not pleased. "[Warners] knew I would explode over the cutting of the twenty minutes," Blatty said, steaming. "I'd seen only one version and approved one version, and I guess someone wanted to prevent trouble."

Blatty maintained for years that his purpose in writing both the novel and the film was to demonstrate how faith can help mankind conquer despair. He used the illustration of the possession not as an example of the torment that one demon could cause one little girl, but as a warning that the forces of evil could instill doubt of the Almighty in those around the girl.

"The point was to make us despair at our own humanity and to make us feel so bestial and vile that, if there was a God, He could not possibly love us," Blatty often said. He believed that the moral center of the film—contained in long dialogue stretches that Friedkin removed—would have allowed the audience to wallow in the shock and obscenity so that they would afterward consider the question "Why?"

"And that, I think, is what removes it from possibly the level of a truly masterful film to what is only a superb thriller," he stated at the time. This discussion began when Friedkin and Blatty were shaping the shooting script and would continue for decades. At the time of the preview that Blatty saw, however, it was in the film. Why, then, did Friedkin cut what Blatty felt was a remarkable longer version into a more commercial two-hour length?

Blatty has the answer: "Billy didn't know he had a hit. Apparently audiences are either so wrapped up in the story or so heedless of story in films of these kinds that they never notice."

Both men continued for years to ride each other about the final exchange between Chris MacNeil and Father Dyer involving Father Karras's St. Joseph Medal, which Regan had clutched in her hand before Karras gave his life for her. Blatty wanted Chris to keep the medal; Friedkin refused and had her hand it to Dyer.

"I think Bill's wrong," Friedkin insisted. "You get a sense of the rhythm of a picture and those scenes were out of rhythm. They were the author's message. I shot them, had trouble getting them to work on the set, finally thought they were badly done. I didn't know what to say to the actors. I took them out."

There was one more hurdle: the advertising. Just as people would come to insist that *The Exorcist* was merely a horror film, the Warner Bros. advertising department in 1973 had to be educated that it was more than that. The poster that is now world famous—Merrin standing beneath a street lamp as Regan's bedroom window casts a beam of light on him—was not the studio's first choice. As Friedkin recalled years later, "I saw it in the Museum of Modern Art in New York, it's called *Empire of Light* by René Magritte. It's a very simple, realistic landscape except the top half of it is sky, daylight, and the bottom half of it is a house at night lit by a streetlamp. And I had that in mind, I actually had chosen the house to sort of match the Magritte painting. While I didn't make the sky a daylight sky, I did put up the streetlamp and I did have a shaft of light coming out the window. The scene took a full day and night just to light, and then we shot it the next night. It became the ad because the original ad was a drawing of a little girl's hand holding a bloody crucifix and the caption, 'For God's sake, help her.' They showed me this ad and I wanted to choke everyone in the room. I had to be physically restrained. I said, 'You can't. First of all, this is a cheap horror film piece of shit ad and, second, you don't use God's name in an ad. You don't use God to shill for your movie."[19]

With all of that as prologue, *The Exorcist* hit the screens on time the day after Christmas 1973. Everybody expected it to do well. What nobody expected it to do was change history.

SIDEBAR

## A Word about Authenticity

Director William Friedkin's insistence on the reality of everything happening before the cameras without using optical effects was more than an application of his celebrated documentary style. It had everything to do with physical perception. If a film has been manipulated with optical effects, even if they are flawless, the human eye and brain know they are being fooled, particularly if what they are seeing is beyond the realm of reason. They may not know *what* is wrong, but they will know that *something* is wrong. This is why modern CGI-laden films can be emotionally unsatisfying. No computer-generated image is perfect—or, perhaps, it is too perfect. The primary challenge that Friedkin and his team of conjurers had to meet was the audience's suspension of disbelief.

They did it by telling the truth.

Friedkin was determined to achieve realism. "When I signed on to do the film," he said, "I decided to try to abandon all technique. I did not want the audience to be conscious of the camera at all. Owen Roizman lit it very dramatically but very naturally. *The Exorcist* is made by a director [and novelist] who believe this is happening. 'We're not kidding, folks,' is the attitude that we took. This is all weird stuff, strange behavior, but we believe it."[1]

Consequently, everything that happens in front of the cameras really happened. The bed really shook. Regan really levitated. Furniture really moved. Doors and walls really cracked. They did this for reasons other than demonic possession, but they really did it—all through mechanical and makeup effects.

The reason they look real is because Friedkin demanded a "first generation" look; that is, everything appeared on a single, original camera negative unsullied by optical effects, multiple exposures, or lab work—all captured on the original negative.[2]

"I know of no way to achieve these things with opticals," he said in hindsight. "Today they would be a piece of cake. Today they can make you believe that the *Titanic* is sinking. In those days I could not, with an optical, make you believe the bed was thumping on its own. It had to happen on the set. It was a case of trial and error."[3]

The visual authenticity extended even to the release prints used in the premiere bookings that were very likely struck off the original negative. This imparted unmatched image clarity and resolution. It was, in a sense, HD before HD, and audiences responded viscerally.

Something else that has gone almost without notice, however, was Friedkin's canny use of a magnetic soundtrack, at least on some of the release prints in the film's initial engagements. At the time, traditional 35mm prints had optical soundtracks that employed the "Academy curve,"[4] which resulted in a limited frequency response in playback of approximately 80 Hz to 8 kHz and a dynamic range of 50–60 decibels.

Magnetic tracks were already known to have superior quality in stereophonic theatrical presentations (like home recordings on tape versus 78s). They were widely used in the 1950s and 1960s, in the heyday of widescreen road shows, but their use had diminished by the early 1970s. Friedkin's decision to use a monaural magnetic track for select prints of *The Exorcist* permitted a wider frequency range of 50 Hz to 10–12 kHz and an increased dynamic range of some 15 decibels. This enabled the track to reproduce sounds from whispers to demonic thundering, not only in terms of clarity and low background noise but in sheer volume. It was still monaural, so audiences didn't hear anything directional. Instead, they felt it.

"The entire *Exorcist* was looped,"[5] Friedkin told the New York Film Academy in 2016, "including the dialogue, and not just the demon voice, everything, because there were some things that I wanted to be spoken so softly that, in those days, the microphone would [pick up the air conditioner]. I wanted pure silence in *The Exorcist*."[6] A mag track, with its low background hiss, was the only way to get it.

*The Exorcist* was released at the end of 1973 in the era before Dolby and digital audio became the norm. As such, the film's clarity and stunning range of sound, coupled with the integrity of its images, gave it astonishing credibility, even if audiences didn't know the secrets behind what they were experiencing.

SIDEBAR
───

# Karras's Death

No aspect of *The Exorcist* has been as controversial or as misunderstood as the ending in which Damien Karras throws himself out of Regan's bedroom window to meet his death at the foot of the Hitchcock steps. William Peter Blatty was always careful to use the terms *gives his life* rather than *takes his life*, and *sacrifice* rather than *suicide* to describe the act. It was a theme to which he would return, with more specificity, in *The Ninth Configuration*. But its portrayal, first in the book and then in the film, has been a matter of unnecessary conjecture since 1971, not for reasons of philosophy but for reasons of clarity.

In the novel, Karras's leap through the window happens offscreen, so to speak. As Chris and Sharon are waiting downstairs:

> "No, I won't let you hurt them! *You're not going to hurt them! You're coming with . . .*"
>
> Chris knocked her drink over as she flinched at a violent splintering, at the breaking of glass, and in an instant she and Sharon were racing from the study, up the stairs, to the door of Regan's bedroom, bursting in. They saw the shutters of the window on the floor, ripped off their hinges! And the window! The glass had been totally shattered!

For his fortieth anniversary edition of the novel in 2011, Blatty tried to erase all doubt about what happened by adding a descriptive paragraph following Karras's dare to the demon to "take me":

> The next instant Karras's upper body jerked sharply upright with his head bent back and facing up to the ceiling, and then convulsively down and forward again, with the Jesuit's features twitching and contorting into a mask of unthinkable hatred and rage, while in strong, spasmodic jerks, as if pushing against some unseen resistance, the Jesuit's large

and powerful hands were reaching out to clutch the throat of a screaming Regan MacNeil.

This puts into prose what audiences saw in the film. Had Blatty written it that way in the first place, there mightn't have ever been a question. From his script:

> The demon—in Karras's body—had moved to kill Regan; but Karras has won control now long enough to reach the window, rip the shutters off their hinges and leap out.[1]

The scene was not shot exactly as described, but it is nevertheless indisputably clear: After Karras challenges the demon to "take me, come into me," his face adopts the mime-like "Captain Howdy" look and he leans over to strangle Regan, who cowers on the floor in front of him, apparently de-possessed. But then he rises and his normal face returns, at which point he throws himself out the window.

Examinations of all versions of the film clearly show that he is not possessed when he sacrifices his life. Still, this has not been enough for fifty years' worth of audiences who have, at various times, asked the following questions:

- Where did the demon go?
- Why did it take only seconds for the demon to possess Karras when it took it weeks to possess Regan?
- Why can't the demon repossess Regan?
- If the demon's target was always Karras, doesn't Karras's death fulfill the demon's plan?
- Why did Merrin and Karras have to go through so much trouble to exorcise Regan when all either of them needed to do was tell the demon to "come into me"?

The answers depend on whether one believes in demonic possession in the first place.

To the first question, the demon goes back to whatever limbo world in which demons live.

To the second question, as Blatty stated, the point of Regan's possession was to make those around her doubt the worth of man and the existence of God, so the slower, the better.

The third question feeds off the second; there is no reason why the demon cannot repossess Regan, but it does not need to do so now that Karras is gone. "In the book they actually do ask that question," says Mark Kermode. "In the book, Karras directly asks Merrin 'Once the demon's driven out, what's to keep it coming back in?' and Merrin replies, 'I don't know, and yet it never seems to happen. No, never.'"

In question four, Karras foiled the demon's plan by his act of sacrifice. This would become a major plot point in Blatty's novel *Legion* and his film *Exorcist III*.

The answer to question five is almost the same as that of question three, except that it would have turned a feature movie into a short subject.

The cumulative power of viewing *The Exorcist* may explain why the ending, as plain as it seems to be, nevertheless baffles some people. But it also breaks down upon closer examination and defies logic, even for those who may believe in possession. Tim Lucas, who made a close study of the film for his and Mark Kermode's 1991 paper, says, "There is a flash of the demon as it enters [Karras] and he defenestrates himself while he contains the demon, but the questions that follow are one of the reasons why the film is great. The movie intends to open discussion, not kill it, and my own reading is just my own. Speaking for myself, flesh and spirit are divisible if integrated on our present plane of existence. Does

Karras really believe that he can contain another's spirit and use that vehicle to destroy it? I don't think Regan actually becomes the demon when it possesses her; I think it inhabits and uses her. Accordingly, I tend to think Karras kills himself and the demon simply moves on, perhaps having achieved its real purpose. Once he is dead, and forgiven his earthly sins at the bottom of those stairs, Regan is safe. The demon doesn't need or want her; Regan was a means of getting to Karras and the bonus point of Merrin. But Karras performs the ultimate good of saving the girl and putting an end to his own pain."

"Billy and I thought we made the ending perfectly clear," Blatty maintained, "that it was a triumph of good over evil, that it was Karras's love for this child that caused him to break out of the demon's spell for one split second, long enough to go out of the house, which is the only thing he could do to save the child's life, because, in another two seconds, the demon would be in possession again and he'd kill the girl. At least fifty percent of the people who have seen the motion picture never get that out of it; and they thought it was a triumph of evil over good and they thought it was a downer. So I put in the medallion along with the music that goes with it to tell you that viscerally, emotionally, you're supposed to feel good now, it is a happy ending, you should be elated."[2]

Mark Kermode echoes Blatty's frustration. "I do remember Bill Blatty saying to me sometime afterwards [that] he was sitting around, having a dinner with one of the executives and he said, in this very Bill way, 'We were congratulating ourselves on how well we had done. And I said, "You know, the one thing I did think is, I wish some people didn't think that the demon threw Karras out of the window," and the executive went, "He didn't?"' Bill went, "No! No! No! He doesn't."' Imagine the frustration if you were Bill Blatty."

Some viewers regard Karras's death as suicide rather

than sacrifice, a notion Blatty emphatically rejects. "A man gave his life for a stranger," he said. "He exemplified what he preached. It was a Christ-like action and better to salvage his integrity than to preserve his life, surely."[3]

Friedkin further and forever muddied the waters in Alexandre O. Philippe's landmark 2019 documentary *Leap of Faith: William Friedkin on The Exorcist*, an intimate colloquy in which the director clears the air about his most famous film. Interviewed over three days in early 2018, with three more days of pickups and recordings over the next year, Friedkin seems freer and more exuberant, perhaps because his *Exorcist* "conscience," William Peter Blatty, died in 2017. Synthesizing nearly fifty years of experience, feedback, and contemplation, he says:

"First of all, I find it improbable that a character could call upon the devil to enter him or her. The devil does what the devil wants to do. If you look at the scene and analyze it, the demon enters Karras because Karras invited it to come in, and he's beating up this little girl, which is an evil act. . . . And at that moment you see, for a split second, his features change and become demonic and he sees his hands about to go around the little girl's neck to strangle her to death, which is probably the demonic impulse. And then [his features] un-change. The demon is not in him. And specifically at Blatty's request . . . we go back to Karras as Karras. I would have kept the demon features on Karras throughout, and Bill said, 'No, you have to go back to Karras's own features in the act of saying *No* so that he makes the conscious decision to do it. Otherwise it's the demon that has triumphed.'

"But it isn't even clear to me as I sit here why in the hell that happens. Why the demon decides to pay attention to Karras and leave the little girl and go into him is a question, but then I believe that the entire possession of the little girl is directed at Karras's weakness and potential loss of faith. Are we to say that he regained his faith in that final moment with the demon? That's what Blatty is trying to say. . . . I think if there's a weakness in *The Exorcist* it's that. . . . It doesn't appear to have been a problem for the millions of people who have seen the film."[4]

"I don't know that it doesn't make sense," argues Mark Kermode, a self-confessed "*Exorcist* nerd." "I think it's clear, and when Billy says that it's confusing, I don't know why because what happens is this: Karras comes in, he finds Merrin dead. In the film, Regan's sitting on the bed giggling. He grabs her and he starts punching her, saying to the demon, 'Come into me, take me.' And then we see a shot of *her* unpossessed face, and a shot of *him* reeling backwards and then coming back possessed. The possessed Karras reaches out to strangle Regan, but then Karras overcomes the demon and shouts "Nooooo!' and throws himself out the window. The demon is within him and he's actually wrestling with the forces of evil. He has suppressed the demon within his body. The demon has left Regan's body, gone into his body, but he has overcome it and he jumps with the demon out the window. And as to the question of why the demon doesn't just fly back out and go back into Regan, the rule is that once a demon is cast out, it doesn't go back in again. Where's the ambiguity?"[5]

## CHAPTER 7

# All Hell Breaks Loose

If *The Exorcist* had squabbles among its own people, it was nothing compared to what happened among the general public. On opening day, December 26, 1973, people queued to see the film, often in lines winding around city blocks in freezing weather.[1]

Not everybody had to wait for opening day. Those with industry connections, whether executive or usher, have stories. "I first saw it under extraordinary circumstances," recalled horror film expert Tim Lucas, who was seventeen at the time and working as the editor of the film section for a local entertainment paper, the *Queen's Jester*. "The manager of the Showcase Cinemas in Springdale, just north of Cincinnati, called on the afternoon of December 24, 1973, to tell us the print had arrived and to invite us to a special midnight screening the day before it played anywhere else in the world. I had been exposed to no pre-publicity images, as Warner Bros. strictly forbade this. We arrived a few minutes late and were ushered into the theater just as the Iraqi runner came up to Father Merrin with the medallion he had found. Huge curving screen, full surround sound, and most of the seats were empty so we all spread out and sat well apart from one another. It was one of the greatest movie experiences of my life, no question."

Like the rare others who saw the film before it opened, they had no idea what would follow. On December 26 the rest of world started buying tickets.

And throwing up.

Psyched to near-hysteria by the long waiting lines and ignited by the power of the film itself, audiences savored the cinematic roller-coaster ride. And, as on a real roller coaster, some got sick. Surprisingly, it wasn't at the scenes of possession.

"At the first public press preview in New York City I stood throughout the film at the back of the theater, behind the audience," said Blatty, wryly claiming to be "the only person who knows" why people got sick at his film. "At a certain point a young woman came up the aisle and, walking by me, was a little unsteady and I heard her saying, 'Jesus. Jeeeesus,' and I thought, 'Oh boy, we're dead. She hates the picture.' But I marked the point at which she left. And that's the point at which *everybody* got ill and at which I always have to lower my head: It's when they're giving Regan the arteriogram and the needle goes into her neck and the blood comes out. *That's* the moment it's always been."[2]

Michael Finlan, an usher at the Boston theater playing the film, differs. "Ninety-eight percent of the people who got sick were men," he recalls, a number and gender closer to reports from the studio.[3] While audiences were getting sick at *The Exorcist*, the filmmakers were getting rich. And that's when two hitherto unheralded people stepped forward to claim their share. The first was Mercedes McCambridge, who, in an impassioned interview with Charles Higham in the *New York Times*, accused Friedkin of denying her an agreed-upon screen credit. Friedkin fired back that McCambridge's contract did not call for a credit and that he'd wanted to give her one but Warner Bros. prevented it. The settlement was to add the words *and Mercedes McCambridge* to subsequent prints.

Then Eileen Dietz, the woman hired to serve as Linda Blair's camera double, said on the syndicated *The Mike*

*Douglas Show* that she, not Blair, performed the possession scenes.[4] Warner Bros. and Friedkin vehemently disputed her claim and called on film editor Bud Smith to measure those few shots in which Dietz doubled Blair. "It came out to 133 frames," he reported, or about six seconds.[5]

"Eileen Dietz did some acrobatics that we experimented with but are not in the picture," Friedkin added, perhaps referring to the spider walk.

"I know what I did," Dietz countered. "I did every possession scene in the film." She later petitioned the Screen Actors Guild, asking them to invalidate what she called a "gag clause" in her contract and for "guidance from the Guild regarding what I considered to be 'an extraordinary escalation of doubling.'"[6]

The Dietz-Friedkin dispute grew, with Dietz charging that Friedkin had promised to end her career. Protective of Linda Blair and his film, Friedkin issued a public statement[7] through Warner Bros. following a tense meeting in his office with Eileen Dietz Elber and her husband Richard in early 1974. "There is no other way to put it," he said unequivocally. "Miss Dietz's statements are absolutely untrue. First, I did not at any time, in any way threaten her, or tell her she would never work again. . . . I told her, and her husband-manager, in the presence of David Salven, associate producer, and Noel Marshall, executive producer, what I repeat now, and what Miss Dietz knows—that every member of the cast and crew could refute her statements and that the studio and Miss Blair's representatives would inform the Screen Actors Guild that she was attempting to lay claim to Linda Blair's work. She gave no answer. Her husband attempted to provoke me to raise my voice or make a threat; I did neither. And the meeting was over." The company also procured statements from Jason Miller, Dick Smith, and Marcel Vercoutere, if not others, that Blair alone performed the scenes.

On March 1, 1974, Friedkin's attorney Gerald Lipsky asked the Screen Actors Guild to arbitrate the dispute.[8] In her March 4 rebuttal, Dietz said that she "did not want to minimize the talents and abilities of Linda Blair's debut performance" and that "an arbitration proceeding would only serve to generate more publicity" as Oscar balloting approached.

Two weeks later, Lipsky suggested to Friedkin that taking out an ad in the trade papers thanking Dietz for her help in making the film "could take the steam away." In the end, Friedkin opted to do nothing, but suggested that Linda Blair fight it on her own.[9]

Dietz's IMDb listing shows dozens of post-*Exorcist* roles and more than two dozen (at this writing) in planning or postproduction. Her mini-biography carefully says that she portrayed the demon who possesses Regan in *The Exorcist*. Her public statements, in Friedkin's opinion, "cost Linda Blair her Oscar."

As for the infamous projectile vomit scene, studio lawyers revealed that in the shot of Regan spewing pea soup it was actually Blair who leaned forward and mimed throwing up while the stream of green was added afterward in a matte shot, the sole lab optical in the film (any others are dissolves and superimpositions, not mattes). A frame analysis of the scene reveals the same thing. Nevertheless, in 2012, Dietz published *Exorcising My Demons: An Actress' Journey to The Exorcist and Beyond* (written with Daniel Loubier; CT: Author Mike Ink) and repeated her 1974 charges, including, "If you see Regan vomiting, then that's me, but if you see her after the vomiting then that's Linda." She also reported Friedkin had repeatedly fired guns to startle people, made numerous retakes, hid rotting meat on the set to irritate the actors, and didn't know the proper anatomy for the crucifix scene. "You have to remember that Linda Blair was just 12 so it wasn't possible for a child to film stuff like the crucifix masturbation scene or the fistfight with Father Karras, especially not back in the 1970s. That's where I came in."[10]

Beyond the McCambridge-Dietz controversies there appears to have been an organized movement against *The Exorcist* within the industry. George Cukor, one of Hollywood's most respected traditional directors, was dead set against *The Exorcist* receiving any recognition at all from the filmmaking establishment. According to those who heard the elder Cukor wax against the picture, he called the film "an abomination" and said "if this thing wins an Academy Award it's the end of Hollywood."

Cukor had directed *Travels With My Aunt* the same year as *The Exorcist,* and it had not fared well at the box office. Word was getting around town that Academy members were splitting into two camps. One indication of rough seas came when the Board of Governors of the Academy of Motion Picture Arts and Sciences decided that no film was worthy of an Oscar for Best Special Effects at the 1974 ceremonies. Director Tom Gries defended Friedkin's film in a meeting at which Cukor assailed it. Sources say that when *The Exorcist* won the special effects vote, rather than give it the award, the whole category was nixed for that year.

At a DGA luncheon for directors of the year's Academy foreign language film nominees, Friedkin recalls being greeted by Cukor, who suddenly began spontaneously denying rumors that he had been bad-mouthing *The Exorcist*. Friedkin was amazed that Cukor would even acknowledge them. "He came up to me and absolutely copped out on it," Friedkin said. "The only other thing I remember was the Directors

Guild awards, which I was favored to win. I remember seeing that, when they announced that George Roy Hill had won for *The Sting*, Robert Aldrich, who was president of the Guild, was standing on the stage, smugly nodding his head and clapping, and there was a wave you could see. I saw it in Aldrich and there were other guys around the stage who were sort of nodding in assent and, in a sense, breathing a sigh of relief. It was that moment that made me feel that a bunch of people did get together and influence votes away from my film."

William Peter Blatty added an equally bizarre note to Friedkin's story. "It may not even be connected," he revealed in the compelling way he had of making everything he said sound mysterious, "but only one director other than Billy Friedkin ever contacted me and/or met with me about his desire to direct *The Exorcist* and that was Bob Aldrich. The only one."

If some remembered, others forgot. *The Exorcist* was nominated for seven Golden Globes and won four. It then was announced in competition for a staggering ten Academy Awards. On April 2, 1974, the difference between the Hollywood Foreign Press, who had voted the Golden Globes, and what was then the three thousand Academy members who chose the Oscars became apparent. Buzz Knudson and Chris Newman won the Academy Award for sound and William Peter Blatty accepted his for adapted screenplay. Everything else seemed to go to *The Sting*.

Critic (and later music producer and discoverer of Bruce Springsteen) Jon Landau, on the NBC *Tomorrow* show after the Oscar telecast, opined that Friedkin's behavior had hurt the film: "I also have an intuitive feeling—again, that's all it can be—that Mr. Friedkin himself worked against the acceptance of the picture. I think that he added a certain unpleasantness, apart from the movie itself, in his interviews and in his way of handling himself."

Friedkin did not appreciably alter his conduct following the Oscar snub. According to Hollywood etiquette, he didn't need to. *The Exorcist* was becoming one of the top-grossing motion pictures of all time. It is still one of the few R-rated releases in that impressive group. It has been given several theatrical reissues and is represented by several home video editions, whereas *The Sting* is barely remembered. People continue to quote the most memorable lines from *The Exorcist*, and if pea soup is served at a dinner party someone is likely to make an *Exorcist* joke. At last count the film has grossed between $230 million and $441 million (depending on the source) on a $12 million investment.

William Friedkin became affected by the film as time went on. Attending a Catholic Communion service, he was so moved that he accepted the Eucharist, an act that a horrified Blatty told him was blasphemous for someone who was not baptized, let alone wasn't Catholic. Over the years, Friedkin has been variously quoted as saying that he accepted the divinity of Jesus and on May 1, 2016, he journeyed to Italy, where he accompanied Father Gabriele Amorth to an actual exorcism. Writing about it that October in *Vanity Fair*, he described the ritual in as much detail as he had fabricated for his 1973 film, only this time as reportage. He later produced a documentary about his pilgrimage, in 2018, titled *The Devil and Father Amorth*.

William Peter Blatty's spiritual trajectory was more consistent. A passionate, compassionate, thoughtful man, he was a strange combination of Jesuit scholarship, comic sensibility, and old world charm. In an expansive and relaxed mood during a wide-ranging interview about the mystery of faith, he spoke of a different ending he had always wanted to add to *The Exorcist* even though he knew it would be impossible to shoot.

"Over the years," he began, "I kept saying [to Friedkin], 'Your failure to include the epilogue in the film, which was in the novel to help people feel that everything was really all right, that somehow and in some way Karras lived.' I said, 'Everybody takes it as a downer, Billy. They don't understand Karras's last act of self-sacrifice, they think the demon carried him out. Not your fault, not mine, just a shot at that moment. But to leave it with Father O'Malley standing at the top of the stairs looking for all the world as if his life has just ended is such a despairing moment!'

"'Then,' [Friedkin] said, 'we should have another ending.' And he came up with the idea of Karras walking up the Hitchcock steps smiling. But we don't know if he is, or is not, Karras. I said, 'Let me play with that,' and I went off and I wrote the six-page epilogue on that theme: Karras is not dead. In it, Father Dyer is at Saint Andrew-on-Hudson years later, he's reading, a retreat at dawn. A jogger comes along. The jogger falls in beside him; he is a rough-and-tumble type and ignores Dyer's obvious need for silence so he can read. Instead, he tries to engage him in conversation. And as he talks—and what we're really talking about is the problem of evil—very gradually we notice a subtle change in his voice and then finally you realize that it's the voice of Damien Karras! And then you play off Dyer looking at someone whom you don't see. But you'll *know* it's Damien Karras! He says, 'Don't you know me, Joe?' And suddenly his vision begins to go this way and then up—he starts looking up—and you continue to hear a voice saying, 'We are the light, Joe.' And up here there are millions of white lights in the daylight sky. Everywhere. That's what I wrote. I get a rush of emotion just remembering the moment. Billy—I'll never forget it, in my house on Canon Drive, in the screening room. He read it, and then the hand holding the papers dropped to his side. He said, 'Oh, God, I feel the weight already.' What he meant was that he knew he was going to direct it, he was going to shoot it, and he felt the weight of all the work and the decision and the importance of having the shooting absolutely clear, falling upon him.

"Now, we began, and my source is Billy. He went to Warner Bros. and they changed his mind. They told him it would take $400,000 to shoot it and John Calley—I don't know if it was John Calley—someone, perhaps all the executives—said, 'Look, you don't tamper with success.'

"We were talking about a new ending for a rerelease, a year later. And Billy, I remember, must have been persuaded by them because he said there were all sorts of flaws in Hitchcock's pictures, but he never went back and corrected them. Someone at Warners had favored excising the epilogue in the first place. He took a look at the rough cut and Father Dyer came to the steps and looked down and he said, 'That's the end of the picture.' And I have asked time and again, if it's only for the collectors in the videocassette edition, put together the original full-length version."[11]

Blatty's wish would be answered, but it took decades and a whole separate adventure to make it happen.

SIDEBAR

## The X-orcist

While the film was bei ng edited, the U.S. Supreme Court in *Miller v. California* issued a ruling on obscenity using the amorphous grounds of "community standards" to define what Justice Potter Stewart once said he'd know when he saw it.[1] The June 21, 1973, decision said that the First Amendment did not protect obscenity, which they then defined using three standards:

1.  Would the average person in a community think a work appeals primarily to prurient interests?

2.  Does the work depict or describe things explicitly forbidden by state law?

3.  Does the work, taken as a whole, lack serious literary, artistic, political, or scientific value?

While, in theory, all three standards had to be met in order for a work to be judged obscene, that didn't stop various localities from bringing action against movie theaters, and Warners girded for local challenges. Few came; some exhibitors, notably those in Boston and Washington, D.C, circumvented possible battles by self-applying an X rating and restricting attendance to people over the age of seventeen (when they remembered to monitor it). To forestall action against the studio, William Friedkin and others testified before a congressional subcommittee on obscenity that the SCOTUS ruling would have a chilling effect on artistic expression and that "the jails of this country are going to wind up with a larger talent roster than MGM had in the forties."

They had reason to worry. In 1968, Jack Valenti, head of the Motion Picture Association of America, had liberalized the industry's self-censorship program into a letter-based rating system that would warn parents and exhibitors of film content. Almost immediately, two Warner Bros. films, *The Devils* and *A Clockwork Orange*[2] (both 1971), self-applied an X-rating, meaning that no one under seventeen could be admitted to see them. Would *The Exorcist* similarly suffer?[3]

Fearing the worst, the studio screened a rough, unmixed

edit of the picture for the Classification and Ratings Administration (CARA) of the MPAA, which, on October 3, adjudged it "tastefully rendered," did not request a single trim, and allowed it to go out rated R, "no one under 17 admitted without a parent or adult guardian." The studio had an inside advocate in Dr. Aaron Stern, a New York psychiatrist who, while it would be unfair to say he was allied with the studios, was not above being their paid consultant after he left office in 1974.[4]

Nevertheless, some exhibitors, mindful of *Miller*, self-applied an X when they played *The Exorcist* in its initial engagements. Some allegedly made their own trims, causing Warner Bros. to advertise that when the film opened in suburban theaters after its exclusive opening runs, it would be shown "uncut." Today, of course, it is available streaming and on home video, where anybody of any age can see it.

SIDEBAR

## Mrs. Warren's Profession

In early 1974, shortly after *The Exorcist* opened in Boston, the exhibitor Sack Theatres was indicted by the attorney general of the Commonwealth of Massachusetts for "obscenity, blasphemy, and corrupting the morals of a minor."[1] The minor in question was the daughter of Mrs. Rita Warren of Brockton, Massachusetts, who had brought her young Teresa to the R-rated film with the clear intention of creating controversy, if not getting the film banned outright under the state's outdated (but at that time still on the books) blue laws.

Warren, born in Italy in the days of Mussolini, reportedly had had encounters with Nazi soldiers and found that Jesus gave her the faith to resist. Emigrating to Massachusetts in

1947 as a war bride, her marriage didn't last, but her commitment to religion did. She first drew attention in the Bay State in the 1970s for trying to bring prayer back into public schools.

Whatever possessed Rita Warren to bring her underage daughter to see *The Exorcist*? And if her accusations were genuine, why was she never prosecuted for child endangerment?

It was a grandstanding move, of course, designed to capture headlines by latching onto the hottest movie in America, one that had stretched the MPAA's rating system. Warren, the president of a nonprofit group calling itself Youth of America, Inc., had been joined by a Reverend Lee and a handful of supporters who threatened a courtroom riot unless newly appointed judge Joseph R. Nolan issued the indictment after a previous judge had declined on obvious First Amendment grounds.

The hearing before Judge Theodore Glynn on Wednesday, February 17, 1974 was brief: All charges against Sack Theatres were dismissed. Pundits took pleasure in noting that Massachusetts gave up Mrs. Warren on the first day of Lent.

The crusading zealot was not to be silenced. In the 1980s she moved lock, stock, and Bible to Washington, D.C., where she became known as "the Jesus lady" for her Capitol Hill demonstrations, some twenty of which resulted in her arrest. She usually brought along a life-size mannequin of Christ beside which she eagerly posed for tourist photos.

She died on September 1, 2020, at the age of ninety-two and was survived by the same daughter, Teresa Pepin, whom she had exposed to *The Exorcist* so many years before.

The antiquated Massachusetts blue laws stayed on the books until November 26, 2003, when then Governor Mitt Romney signed them out of existence.

## CHAPTER 8

# Second and Third Thoughts

Tere exist today four *Exorcists*: the original (1973), the *Special Edition* (1998), *The Version You've Never Seen* (2000), and the *Extended Director's Cut* (2010). Who knows, there may even be a fifth in 4K by the time this book is published for the film's fiftieth anniversary. Which is the real *The Exorcist*? The answer speaks not only to the importance of the home video market but, more significantly, to the friendship between the director and writer and the complex relationship they had over the years with their most famous work.

Home video had long since become a major ancillary revenue stream in 1981 when *The Exorcist* was released on both VHS and Betamax after making its American network television debut in 1980. Its videotape and subsequent laserdisc releases were all mastered from the original 1973 theatrical release, although the TV version required edits such as trimming the crucifix mutilation scene and changing the nature of the vandalism to the statue of the Virgin in Dahlgren Chapel (as a safeguard, these had been double-shot during production). It was Blatty's privileged access to Georgetown that had enabled the location shooting in the chapel, but that doesn't mean it sat well with the crew. "As an Irish Catholic kid," recalled assistant director Terence Donnelly, "I had sixteen years of Catholic education and, as I was shooting that scene, holy shit."[1]

Not surprisingly, when it came time to dial down the demon's dialogue for a network TV sale, edits were required by the CBS Program Practices Department. CBS vice president Alice E. Henderson sent two-and-a-half pages of changes in a December 6, 1979, letter to Friedkin. In addition to deleting numerous uses of "fuck," "chrissake," "God damn," "Jesus," and the ever-popular "Your mother sucks cocks in hell," the censor also required removal of the shot of Regan urinating on the carpet (use audio only), all blood from the arteriogram, almost all of the crucifix scene, and asked the director to "lose the second spewing shot" of vomit. Because no alternate takes had been made during production, the replacements were done editorially and in a looping session.[2] Rather than approach Mercedes McCambridge, Friedkin opted to use his own voice saying, "Your mother still rots in hell" and "Shut your face, you faggot" (apparently *faggot* wasn't considered offensive on TV at the time). The cuts reduced the running time from 122:00 to 117:50.

Otherwise, for twenty-five years, whenever it was reissued or booked into revival houses, *The Exorcist* remained *The Exorcist*.

The game changed in 1995 with the introduction of digital versatile disc (DVD) technology. The clearer image, digital audio, and greater running time of DVDs meant that longer films didn't have to be speeded up or put onto two tape cassettes or laserdiscs; they could fit onto a single DVD. It also meant that special features such as behind-the-scenes documentaries, video essays, interviews, and commentary tracks could be included as value-added elements.[3]

It also allowed directors to revisit their films and restore footage that the studio had originally removed for various reasons (running time, nudity, violence, focus group meddling, etc.). By the 1990s, expanded and—especially—unrated DVD "director's cuts" had become a marketing incentive. They also sidestepped the Motion Picture Association of America's mandate that no two versions of the same film could be in the marketplace at the same time.

But director's cuts were still a matter of controversy among film scholars and filmmakers: Which version, exactly, was the one that history was supposed to judge?

"The film, when it's born, is about the only shot it should get," said Robert Altman. "I think it's interesting, and I think in many cases you see that it's a better film when cut in a different way. The stuff that was added to *Lawrence of Arabia* certainly helped it. But these are all afterthoughts. I don't plan on that; I don't save footage thinking, 'Oh, well, someday we'll put it back in.' You have your fight at the time."[4]

Martin Scorsese—whose *New York, New York* was truncated by the studio and later restored—had a similar take. "Why would you want to add footage? You'll ruin the whole rhythm of the movie if that's the rhythm you decided on. Why would a major director release a major film and then put out a restored director's cut? Or a director's cut? Or a director's cut with extra footage? They really mean three different things." Nevertheless, he was sympathetic with the need to go back. "Sometimes when you're finishing a film the madness of the moment takes over and things get cut or misplaced or you panic or studios get nervous—I don't know what happens—but you make a sacrifice and you think it's the right way. Afterwards, in certain cases, you say, 'Let's put it back together and release that version; that was probably the best version.'" Still, he cautioned, "*More* is not necessarily *best*, believe me."[5]

And yet fervent fans of particular films crave more of what they liked the first time. Director's cuts—perhaps they should be called "expanded versions"—of such films as James Cameron's *Aliens* (1986), *The Abyss* (1989), and *Terminator 2: Judgment Day* (1991); Peter Jackson's *Lord of the Rings* trilogy (2001–2003); and Ridley Scott's *Blade Runner* (1982) have all benefited from added footage. With some films, however, such as Steven Spielberg's *1941* (1979), more is not necessarily better, it's simply more.[6]

Which leads to *The Exorcist*.

Strictly speaking, the 1973 version of *The Exorcist is* the director's cut. William Friedkin, having just won the Oscar for *The French Connection* and buttressed by his close working relationship with the film's producer, William Peter Blatty, held enormous sway over any attempts by Warner Bros. to make changes prior to release, including for MPAA rating purposes. And yet even Friedkin, despite his clarity of vision, was uncharacteristically vulnerable to suggestion during the tense postproduction process.

"The original cut of *The Exorcist*, Bill Blatty and I disagreed on," Friedkin recounted for a screening audience at the Academy of Motion Picture Arts and Sciences in 2018.[7] "I cut a number of scenes out, more than twelve minutes' worth, from the original version of the film for two reasons. One, I showed it to a man who was an executive at Warner Bros. then, called John Calley.[8] He was sort of head of production, and I showed the work print[9] of the film to him and he had what I thought were some very good suggestions. A couple of scenes he said, 'I don't think you need that, I think that's over-statement.' When he first said that to me I said I respected John Calley, but who the hell is he? I mean, I've lived with this film now for well over a year, I won an Academy Award, what is he, telling me how to change my film?' But I went home after this meeting and I started to think about everything that he had said, and I went into the cutting room the next day and I tried all of the changes and cuts that he suggested and I thought it was a better film, and so I went out with it that way."

William Peter Blatty, who had been led to believe that the work print cut was the one that was going to be released, was not pleased, and stayed unpleased for decades.

"For years," Friedkin confirmed, "Blatty was angry about that, and for a long time he didn't even speak to me. But whenever he did speak to me, he'd say, 'Billy, you cut the heart and soul out of the movie. And I would say, 'Bill, you're a sore winner. The movie's out there. It's a success. The success keeps growing. It's the gift that keeps on giving as far as you're concerned and you're telling me that I was wrong?' And then many years went by, actually, from the year 1974 [*sic*], when the film came out, and the year 2000. Blatty and I had resumed our very close friendship. He called me one day and he said, 'Bill, would you consider looking at the footage you cut? I'll look at it with you. We'll look at it on an editing machine at Warner Bros. where they have it stored. Will you just look at it and see if you could restore it and put it into a new version of the film?' And I did this as a favor to Bill because I love Blatty and I respect him and he gave me the best piece of material that I've ever received. I said okay and we went into Warner Bros. and I looked at all these cut scenes. I looked at the shot of the girl walking backwards down the stairs which we couldn't use at the time because the cable showed, because it was so bright."[10]

Two years earlier there had been another player in this gambit: Mark Kermode, Friedkin's close friend and England's top film critic. When Kermode and director Nick Freand Jones got the go-ahead from the BBC to produce what became the documentary *The Fear of God: 25 Years of 'The Exorcist'* to mark the film's silver anniversary in 1998, they enlisted Friedkin's permission to track down the missing footage. At the same time, Friedkin had informed Warner Bros. that he would consider creating an expanded edition of his film if the studio thought it commercially viable and would pay for it themselves. Several meetings in Burbank and, eventually, a trip to the Kansas salt mine where the studio stored its celluloid legacy uncovered that much of the deleted footage was there but some of its matching audio was either lost or had been misfiled.

"There was a bunch of stuff that existed in work print that we couldn't find a matching negative," Friedkin reported during his motion picture academy presentation. "But I wasn't gonna stick in a work print which is scratched and splotched; I wasn't gonna try to integrate that into a brand-new print of the movie. There was a scene at the Arlington Memorial in Virginia. Ellen takes Linda, her daughter, while they're in Washington, on a tour of various landmarks. She takes 'em up to the Tomb of the Unknown Soldier and watches the ceremony. And that scene was shot just for the line where little Linda says to her mother, 'Mommy, why do people have to die?' I thought it was wonderful to see this ceremony celebrating the death of the American soldiers who died in various battles and the little girl not understanding death [but was] concerned about it. I would have put that moment back in the film but we could not find the soundtrack."

Another reason may have persuaded Friedkin to consent to revisiting his film: At the time, William Peter Blatty was rumored to have agreed to write a three-hour television miniseries of *The Exorcist* that would include all the parts of his book, including the subplot about Karl's daughter and the religious philosophy that he had missed in the movie. While, of course, the language and violence would have to be toned down for the tube, the philosophy would remain intact, and that was what Jesuit scholar Blatty had so fervently urged Friedkin to preserve.[11]

The holy grail was the "spider walk." In 2000 a version

was released that included the famous "spider walk" scene in which Regan descends the stairs from her bedroom head-first and upside-down, her legs and arms bent backwards like a spider. Who performed the spider walk? Over the years it had been confirmed that Dietz, who was Linda Blair's makeup double, appeared in the bedroom possession shots where Blair's face was not needed, such as her hand grabbing the shrink's crotch, the crucifix entering her nightgown, and clawing the air backlit against Pazuzu. Dietz also wore white makeup as Captain Howdy in test footage. But the spider walk remained forgotten until *Exorcist* devotee Kermode opened that can of worms by showing the footage in *The Fear of God.*

"There are two people that did the spider walk and there is more than one version of the spider walk," Kermode reports. "There is Linda Hager and the other one is Ann Miles. Here's what happened as far as I understand. Linda Hager was working with Marcel Vercoutere, who had established this rig. And I think some filming [was done] with Linda Hager coming down the stairs. Then a few years ago, someone called Ann Miles got in touch with me through the BFI and said, 'I did the spider walk, and here are some photographs of me doing the contortion.' And I think that's her in *The Version You've Never Seen* when the mouth opens and the blood comes out, because she said something like, 'I recognize my own teeth.' But if I remember rightly she also said that she didn't use the rig. Now here's the thing: There's more than one version of the spider walk, as you know, because there's the version that we did in *The Fear of God* when she comes down, she flips over, out of the rig, and then she goes on all fours. Then there's another version, a much shorter version, which is in the [expanded] film. All I can tell you for a fact is that, as far as I know from all the research that I've done, both Linda Hager *and* Ann Miles did stuff on the spider walk, and I don't know which one is in the finished film. It may be a combination of both of them, but I don't know. What I do know is that you could see, in the version that we used in *The Fear of God*, the wires. So whoever is in that is somebody that is doing it in the wires. One of them is using Marcel Vercoutere's rig. So ultimately, it was never Eileen Dietz. She never had anything to do with it. Linda Hager and Ann Miles are the two people who may actually be on screen. All the 'missing scenes' that we used in *The Fear of God* were reconstructed from scratch by Nick Jones and myself with BBC editor Jan Beas working from videotape dupes of takes which Bill Blatty and myself pulled (at some length) from the Warner Bros. archive.

"The hardest thing was finding the sound," Kermode continues, "some of which I located after days of shuffling around in huge cardboard boxes which were gathering dust in the Burbank vault. Nick and Jan and I then reconstructed the scenes working from Blatty's script, but clearly our edits were just done as demos—not the way Bud Smith or Jordan Leondopoulos would have cut them. That's probably why the spider walk looks weird [in the documentary]—we didn't have all the takes of that scene to hand, and that really was the best we could do. It doesn't stand up to intense scrutiny because any lengthy shots of the rig make you realize how it's done."[12]

Reconstructing the scene was its own adventure. In January 1998 Kermode flew at his own expense from England to Warners in Burbank, California, for a confab with the studio's then head of distribution, Barry Reardon, and to screen what had been uncovered. As stated above, much of it had been intentionally shot MOS (silent) or the sync tracks were lost or unusable, such as the Dyer/Kinderman *Casablanca*-esque epilogue that was drowned by traffic noise and never looped. What was discovered, however, was the long-sought-after "spider walk" footage that had never been edited and existed only in rushes. Significantly, Kermode reported, this involved a stunt performer hanging from a ceiling rig for the walk and replaced by Linda Blair right-side-up flicking Dick Smith's extended tongue appliance in search of Kitty Wynn's heel.

When Friedkin decided that the newly found footage could not be polished in time to be included in the 1998 rerelease he was planning, he allowed Kermode to use it in *The Fear of God*. Friedkin later constructed the sequence himself from several different takes and sweetened it with sound for the anniversary release.

In general, the expanded DVD and Blu-ray versions contain two types of visual additions: added footage and new optical effects. Each changes the film in significant ways.[13]

The four most substantive examples of the added footage are:

1.  Regan's first medical examination, the one Chris refers to when she tells her daughter, "It's like the doctor said, it's nerves." Now we see the actual exam during which Regan becomes agitated and profane.

2.  The "spider walk" sequence.

3.  The stairwell respite during the exorcism in which Father Merrin explains to Father Karras that the demon's intent is to make us ask ourselves how God could love such bestial creatures as mankind.

4.  The ending in which Chris returns Father Karras's St. Joseph medal to Father Dyer, followed by Lieutenant Kinderman and Father Dyer walking off together.

The optical effects, which were introduced for the new editions, include:

1. Superimposing Mrs. Karras's face on a window in Regan's bedroom.

2. Flashes of the white-faced demon ("Captain Howdy") appearing on the walls of Regan's bedroom. This is the Eileen Dietz makeup test footage created by Dick Smith.

3. Additional flash frames of the demon Pazuzu.

The effect of the reinserted footage and added visuals is profound: The former amplify and clarify the meaning of the film while the latter undercut its power.

The spider walk is, arguably, the most controversial addition. There is a solid reason why it was taken out of the original film. First, as Blatty stated in an on-camera discussion with Friedkin for the 2000 DVD edition,[14] the spider walk, coming immediately after Dennings's death, creates dramatic moments that happen too close to each other. It was a failure of writing, he admitted. Friedkin relished Blatty's confession but added that, regardless, he wasn't able to get the right reaction shot from Ellen Burstyn and Kitty Wynn, so he didn't have the footage to construct the scene anyway. Both men, however, miss the more obvious point: When Chris sees Regan coming down the stairs upside-down, it's obvious that the child is possessed, or at least beyond traditional medical help. Chris would have immediately given up taking the girl to more doctors and jumped right to exorcism. This adds to Friedkin's contention that, by the time the film had been playing for two weeks, everybody buying a ticket would know that Regan was possessed, and all the buildup would be unnecessary, if not coy.

Director of photography Owen Roizman had a more pragmatic reason. "When we did that spider sequence originally, it was so tricky," he said. "You had to have a pretty well-coordinated person to do that, and of course, putting the person on wires helped because you couldn't do it without the wires. It didn't make the movie because of the wires and so, in the 2000 release, they were easily able to take those wires out with CGI and so Billy decided to use it in the rerelease."[15]

Tim Lucas agrees that the spider walk upsets the storyline. "It's too big a shock or change too soon. There is a point in the film when Karras enters the room and finds Regan greatly changed, and it should occur just before that, to mark that she is getting worse and harder to restrain. I'm not sure exactly where the scene is placed now but I'm against the shot as a whole. The special effects are too obvious, she looks mechanical coming down the stairs, and the final upside-down shriek with blood coming out of her mouth crosses a line—too much, too soon. It weakens what comes after, which is quite strong in its original sequencing."[16]

The most important moment that Friedkin had cut and that Blatty was pleased to see restored was the discussion on the stairwell between Fathers Karras and Merrin during a break from the Roman Ritual. "Why *this* girl?" Karras asks. "It makes no sense."

"I think," Merrin sighs, "the point is to make us despair. To see ourselves as animal and ugly. To reject the possibility that God could love us."

This, to Blatty, encapsulates the meaning of the film. To Friedkin, it was best left implied and did not need to be stated. Blatty and Friedkin argued about it even on the set as it was being shot.

"The point is to make us despair," Blatty stressed, "to make us feel that humanity is ultimately vile, ugly, bestial, putrescent—so much so that, if there were a God, He couldn't possibly love us. To me, that speech was so important because, on a practical level, it would permit each member of the audience to not hate himself for enjoying some of the more horrific moments. It would explain things like the green vomit spewing, everything, all that horrific stuff.'"

Restoring it was the outcome of a change in Friedkin's thinking. "I felt that that statement of what it's all about was inherent in the whole film. Bill always felt that it needed to be stated. I said, 'Bill, I can't include it because the whole movie is saying that.' I really put it back for him, because I feel, and felt, that I owe him a lot. He wrote this thing, he created it, he gave it to me, and as I got older, I have become somewhat less arrogant and I felt that he should have the version of the film come out that he wanted.[17]

"For twenty-five years," he continued, "Bill Blatty would hock me every day about the twelve minutes I took out of it. And I love Bill Blatty. He passed away [in 2017]. I loved him and I wanted him to be ultimately happy with the film. So I asked him to come out to California. We went to Warner Bros. and we looked at the footage that I had cut. And after I saw it with Bill on a Movieola, I remember putting my arm around him and I said, 'Well, Bill, I finally understand what you were getting at,' and I added the twelve minutes back. The studio wanted to call it a director's cut, but it's not a director's cut, this is the original cut of the film that I showed to Bill Blatty."[18]

While he was at it, Friedkin made other changes. "I even did other things with the film, like I added some subliminal cuts. And I added, at the end of the final scene, which I cut out, a scene between Kinderman, the detective, and Father O'Malley, where they're talking outside the house after the family has left—"

Blatty: "—but we were unable to retrieve proper dialogue of Kinderman's voice, Lee Cobb's voice, when he says, 'I think this is the beginning of a beautiful friendship.' That hurt a bit, but we've got a good piece of it, and Karras lives on. He lives! A relationship continues!"

Honoring Blatty was a respectable reason to restore the dialogue scenes whose loss the author had lamented. Adding visual effects was something else. As established earlier, the power of *The Exorcist* lies in its documentary reality and its remarkable soundtrack. The cause is subtle but the effect is powerful: At the time the film was made, CGI wasn't even a gleam in Hollywood's digital eye, and the use of traditional optical printers to combine separate elements would have degraded the quality of the image. The only way to shoot the possession effects, therefore, was to make them actually happen in front of the camera. Through the makeup artistry of Dick Smith and the mechanical wizardry of Marcel Vercoutere, that's exactly what happened, allowing Owen Roizman's photography to keep its first-generation clarity. Whether the audience knew it or not, they felt it, and the original crackled with reality because everything in it looked the same to the audience as it did to the camera. It was all part of a symphony of brilliantly coordinated mechanical—not visual—effects. And this is why optically adding demonic faces on walls or splicing in flash frames moves the picture into the realm of a typical horror film. Perhaps Friedkin thought it would spice up dull (?) sections for jaded modern audiences. Instead, it's a gimmick that takes away more than it adds.

Agrees Tim Lucas of the changes, "I found them vulgar and laughable, and not in a good way. They destroy all of the original film's subtlety."

Ellen Burstyn agrees. "I like the original the way it was," she says. "I haven't paid a lot of attention to the changes. I didn't see it again for many years; I saw it at the forty-fifth anniversary screening in Hollywood. I just like the original, I was fine with the original and didn't need the improvements."

Alexandre O. Philippe, who came to know Friedkin during a series of intense interviews for *Leap of Faith: William Friedkin on The Exorcist*, considers the revised version "more of a Blatty cut, in the sense that he saw it as a way to bring back things that were important to Blatty that were not part of the original cut. Then, of course, when he was caught in that moment, he started playing with it and adding a few things. We can probably look at it and see things that were not necessary, and I can probably agree with you. But Billy was also very clear to me that they were going to make a lot of money, and who could say no to that?"[19]

*Exorcist* scholar Mark Kermode is more forgiving. "The first thing to say," he agrees, "is that it is not the director's cut. If anything, it is the writer's cut." He is not bothered by the addition of optical effects. "I quite like the idea that there are these little tweaks. What Friedkin has done with those additions is to tweak the original, but he hasn't substantially done very much." Kermode notes the addition of the demonic faces on the wall but adds, "and of course there's the face of Karras's mother in the [bedroom] window, which I know is a source for some controversy. There are a few other fleeting inserts, too; to be honest, they don't bother me. I always thought that the way that the film was, was perfect, but he's doing what anyone else would do. He's going back in and thinking, 'Why don't I just . . . ?' The impressive thing is, Friedkin keeps the tinkering very low. But I'm reminded of something that Bill Blatty said to me. He said, 'I have a worry that the film works and I don't really know why it works, but I know it works and there's a part of me, as much as I want all this stuff to be in there, there's a part of me that worries that if we do anything to it, it will stop working.'"

By way of noting the risks in tampering with success, there is a unique film called *The Mystery of Picasso* (Henri-Georges Clouzot, 1956)—unique in that it is the only motion picture to be declared a national treasure by the French government—in which the famed Spanish painter creates twenty pictures in real time as the camera watches. Clouzot and Picasso used a translucent screen so that the artist could work on one side and the camera, watching from the other, saw nothing but the brushstrokes materialize. The effect is mesmerizing; Picasso is so skilled that he can, with a single curved line, for example, evoke a woman's reclined form. As he fills in details, the entire painting emerges.

But soon something becomes awkwardly apparent: Picasso overworks his canvases. Where minimalism would have sufficed, he keeps adding stripes, dots, curlicues, and other details until the electricity of his original inspiration is smothered in filigree. Why didn't the greatest painter of the twentieth century know when to leave well enough alone?[20] Similarly, why didn't Friedkin?

*The Version You've Never Seen* is not a "director's cut" in the sense that prevailed at the time it was released. The "director's cut" of *The Exorcist* is *The Exorcist*. If anything, *The Version You've Never Seen* was Friedkin's rethinking of his original in the same way that George Lucas returned to *Star Wars* when technology allowed him to fully realize his vision (and the public has been debating his wisdom ever since).[21]

Why did Friedkin make the cuts in the first place? His reasoning goes to the mindset of a filmmaker, even one who has just won an Oscar: "That first cut was about two hours and fifteen minutes and frankly it bothered me that it was so long. Your mind may be going with it, even your heart may be going with it, but your ass gets tired! I didn't know it was going to be a hit!"[22]

"Would the film have done as well at the time with all these scenes in it?" Friedkin asks rhetorically. "We'll never know that. The film did great at the box office every time they release it in no matter what version. And, of course, the DVDs have been successful, and Blu-ray is the best format that has ever come out, as far as I'm concerned, for viewing a film in the comfort of your own home. I've heard little details of sound effects in the Blu-ray that I've never heard, that I didn't even know were in the track. Little details or little tickles or noises that we built in which is now all high-definition digital track you hear that I don't even remember we built in.

"So there are all these versions of it and I now tend to believe with Blatty that the best version, the most complete version, is the 2000 version, *The Version You've Never Seen*."[23]

And there's an important footnote: Unlike the *Star Wars* trilogy, which has compiled a litany of complaints from fans over the years because of George Lucas's repeated meddling and the longtime unavailability of its first-run versions, the original *Exorcist* has never been out of release, thanks to its evergreen status in a succession of home video technologies.

"I think that if you've made a film and it's your film and it's your vision, you have the right to do that stuff," Mark Kermode argues passionately. "Because I don't hold with the absolute text version. I think it's one of the really interesting things about *The Exorcist* and *The Exorcist: The Version You've Never Seen*. They quite legitimately sit side by side. They are tonally different films, and what's really remarkable about it is how fairly minor changes alter the tone of the film. And this is a version of what you're saying. The difference is, I don't think it's for the worst. I think it's different. And I think one of the things that is different is when in the film, in *The Version You've Never Seen*, when it has this space to breathe, you feel that—this sounds terrible—you feel the humanity of it. In the little additional moments, in which the film feels like it exhales slightly. You feel like you are actually spending time with the characters rather than being hurled headlong through the film. And this is not a criticism of the original. I still think it is the greatest film ever made."

SIDEBAR

## The Versions Are Legion

*The Exorcist: The Version You've Never Seen* was released to selected theaters on September 22, 2000, and on home video on December 26, 2000. Approximately twelve minutes of footage was added that had been excised from the original's December 26, 1973, release. New computer-generated optical effects were also added. On October 11, 2011, an "extended director's cut" was released on home video. This version was almost exactly the same as *The Version You've Never Seen*, with the exception of an image of Pazuzu that was removed.

1.  The film now opens with an establishing shot of the MacNeil home in Georgetown panning right to the streets, showing the neighborhood as eerie music plays.

    *Comment:* By preceding the Iraq sequence, this shot throws emphasis on the as-yet-unidentified MacNeil house and, by virtue of its juxtaposition with the Iraq scenes, implies a connection that should not be made until the bishop's orders call Father Merrin back from his retreat. Ironically, its presence validates the early studio note, "Why are we in Iraq when the story takes place in Georgetown?"

2. Trying to reach Regan's father in Rome to speak to her on her twelfth birthday, Chris no longer tells the telephone operator, "I've been on this fucking line for twenty minutes."

3. Regan's first hospital medical exam is added, during which she acts resistant, then fights and swears at Dr. Klein and the attendants. This is what Chris refers to when she later tries to assure Regan, "It's just nerves."

   *Comment:* Other than creating a minor continuity gaffe, the removal of the first exam scene was a wise decision because, as the filmmakers well knew, everybody in the audience already knows that Regan is possessed, so why delay the obvious?

4. When Chris returns from location and prowls the house, the new versions add flashes of a demonic face on the walls (except in the extended director's cut).

   *Comment:* As stated elsewhere, the insertion of optical effects dulls the documentary-like feel of the film and mitigates its credibility by making it look like a horror movie.

5. The "spider walk" scene is inserted after Chris learns that Burke Dennings is dead. It was originally capped with Regan pursuing Sharon to the front door licking at her with a dark, distended tongue, but that footage was deemed unusable (although it appears in the special Blu-ray features).

   *Comment:* As stated elsewhere, although Friedkin and Blatty acknowledge that the sequence posed a narrative construction problem, the larger justification for its removal remains that, after seeing it, Chris would have instantly ditched the idea of seeing more doctors.

6. Regan subliminally morphs into the demon (Eileen Dietz) for a few frames before grabbing the hypnotizing psychiatrist's crotch.

7. At a listening station, Father Karras continues to play the tape of Regan speaking in tongues. Then he celebrates Mass.

8. Before entering Regan's bedroom to begin the exorcism, Father Merrin asks Chris for Regan's middle name ("Teresa"). Could this be an allusion to Mother Teresa? He also accepts a drink, saying, "Fortunately my will is weak." This line will be used again in *Dominion*.

9. The crucial dialogue is restored between Fathers Merrin and Karras in the stairwell outside Regan's room explaining why the demon possesses people.

10. Karras's mother's face appears superimposed on Regan's bedroom window just before Father Karras throws himself through it to his death.

11. The jump cut between the possessed Karras and the un-possessed Karras ("Come into me, take me") when he pulls himself away from strangling Regan has been smoothed somewhat by CGI morphing.

12. As Chris and Regan prepare to drive to the airport at the end of the film, Father Dyer now hands Father Karras's St. Joseph medal back to Chris. This suggests that he knows that she is ready to accept belief in God.

13. Father Dyer and Lieutenant Kinderman walk off together at the end. Only the rough production audio recorded on location exists of their *Casablanca*-esque exchange (in which Kinderman tells Dyer, "This looks like the beginning of a beautiful friendship"). Neither

Lee J. Cobb nor Father William O'Malley recorded it in postproduction, so restoring it had to be abandoned.

*Comment:* John Calley was right in suggesting the removal of this coda. As Friedkin told Kermode, "He said the conversation between Dyer and Kinderman didn't work because they had no history, so the scene has no weight. For him, the movie ended with Dyer looking down the steps where Karras had died." The carry-over of losing this scene is that Kinderman and Dyer never meet in the film, so when they are shown as being best friends in *The Exorcist III*, there is no backstory to warrant it.

14. The original monaural soundtrack has been remixed into stereo.

15. An additional sequence that had been shot of Chris and Regan taking a sightseeing tour of Washington, D.C., ending at Arlington National Cemetery, could not be restored.

   *Comment:* There was no audio with which to edit and insert the sequence in the expanded editions, but the original reason for excising it remains valid: It was a long way to go just to hear Regan ask, "Mother, why do people have to die?"

## CHAPTER 9

# Exorcist II: The Heretic

**E**xorcist II: The Heretic was very likely doomed from the start, although, ever since its troubled 1977 release, its director, John Boorman, has been saddled with the burden of having made what many people—including William Friedkin[1]—call the worst movie of all time. It may be near the top in a crowded field of contenders, but what it really is, is an example of the Hollywood system running amok with no one to press the panic button.

Nominally, *Exorcist II: The Heretic* is a philosophical contemplation on the nature of good that had the misfortune of being a sequel to the most famous film ever made about evil. Had it been called simply *The Heretic* as originally planned it might have escaped comparison, but it wasn't, and it didn't. It does have its defenders; Martin Scorsese, for one, regards *The Heretic* more highly than *The Exorcist*. "I like the first *Exorcist*," he has said, "because of the Catholic guilt I have, and because it scared the hell out of me. But *The Heretic* surpasses it. Maybe Boorman failed to execute the material, but the movie still deserved better than it got."[2]

What it got was nearly total rejection by critics and audiences. To use one of the film's own lines, *The Heretic* was brushed by the wings of Pazuzu. It was born in cynicism, executed in confusion, and released in fear. The tragedy is that, even if *The Exorcist* had never been made, *The Heretic* would still be a disappointment.

After the enormous and unexpected success of *The Exorcist*

(nearly $200 million gross in its first release[3]), a sequel was a foregone conclusion. In the early seventies, however, sequels never did as well financially as the originals.[4] For this reason, Warner Bros. wanted to do it on a tight budget. Their first idea was to use outtakes from the 1973 milestone plus as many of its cast members as they could persuade to join the enterprise. But first they had to get permission.

William Peter Blatty used to joke that he was to blame for *Exorcist II: The Heretic* (which from now on will be called *The Heretic* unless otherwise required), but on a realistic level, there is no way he could have anticipated it. Before film studios became "communications conglomerates" and entered the rights aggregation business, it was not unusual for writers to retain ownership of their work, especially if they had a good agent. Blatty, thanks to the power of his bestselling novel and the fact that his Hoya Productions[5] was a production partner, had negotiated a separation of rights agreement with Warner Bros. that gave him control of any sequels. At first he and Friedkin were asked if they wanted to encore their blockbuster, but both declined, with Friedkin adding that he was dissatisfied with his share of the profits from the first one, although he would be happy to produce but not direct its offspring.[6] As for Blatty, he also threatened to sue, but settled for what he called "a dizzying amount of money" to grant sequel rights to the studio. He later blushed and said, "I didn't know that all that money would compensate for Richard Burton saying, 'I've flown this route before on the back of a giant grasshopper.'"[7]

Frank Wells, the head of Warner Communications, the studio's parent company, made the deal with Blatty and turned the project over to studio president John Calley. Calley then chose Richard Lederer as producer even though Lederer had never produced a movie before. It was a calculated business decision; Lederer happened to be one of the most talented advertising and marketing executives in the industry, but he had risen as high on the corporate ladder as he could go and there were rumors that he was looking to take his skills to another studio. A University of Virginia graduate, Lederer served as an army cryptographer in World War II before joining the advertising/publicity department of Columbia Pictures. In 1950 he switched to Warner Bros., where he worked his way up to executive vice president of worldwide advertising and publicity. Considered a marketing genius (as well as a battle-hardened survivor of the Warner Bros./Seven Arts and Kinney International mergers in 1966 and 1969, respectively), Lederer supervised successful campaigns for *Bonnie and Clyde*, *The Wild Bunch*, *My Fair Lady*, and, of course, *The Exorcist*. He also helped filmmaker John Milius (writer, *Apocalypse Now*) develop his screenplay *The Life and Times of Judge Roy Bean* into a record-setting spec sale in 1972. By the mid-1970s, however, Lederer was getting itchy for greener pastures (he would, in time, go on to head ad-pub for Zoëtrope and Orion Studios), but in 1976, desperate to keep him in house, the studio anointed him producer and handed him the biggest plum in their garden.[8]

It was arrogance that made Warners think they could churn out any old follow-up to *The Exorcist* and people would come. At first, said Lederer, they wanted to manufacture "a low-budget rehash—$3 million—of *The Exorcist*, a rather cynical approach to filmmaking, I admit, but that was the start."[9] The story idea at the time was to have another priest investigating the MacNeil exorcism and the deaths of the two priests who officiated. When Blatty and Friedkin declined to participate, Calley conferred the scripting prize upon William Goodhart, a fifty-year-old playwright who'd had one play produced ten years earlier (*Generation*)[10] from which he'd subsequently written a screenplay adaptation. He turned in a two-page precis which impressed Calley enough give John Boorman a call.

Goodhart had been struck by Teilhard de Chardin's spiritual and evolutionary writing. It was a highly intellectual approach to which Boorman would have to find a visual equivalent and Goodhart a narrative one. The two men embarked on a location scout ("recce" in the parlance) to Africa, and Boorman looked forward to shooting and editing in his home country of Ireland.

Boorman was no stranger to *The Exorcist*; in fact, he was an enemy. In 1971, Calley had sent him Blatty's book with an offer to direct, neither knowing nor caring that Blatty wanted Friedkin. "As the father of several daughters," Boorman said, demurring, "I thought the book was about torturing a child" and he found it abhorrent.[11] Regardless, he took the job of directing the follow-up.

"I think John Boorman really did not want to make this picture and he had shame about that," said Louise Fletcher, who costarred in it. "I think everything he tried to do was to expel everything that people might think of the other movie. He felt he had two strikes against him starting out and that he was going to be a big loser. He was getting paid very well, but that was the only way he was winning."[12]

*Exorcist* scholar Mark Kermode agrees. "Boorman had basically gotten to do it by saying you have to repair the damage done by *The Exorcist*. Firstly, the idea that *The Exorcist* caused damage that needed repairing is, you know, let's take that into the parking lot. Secondly, it is recorded that John Boorman had not only turned down an inquiry about whether or not to make *The Exorcist*, he said, 'Not only do I not want to make this, I don't want anyone else to make it either.' Okay fine, so the sequel is being made by somebody who thought the original shouldn't have existed. Well, if you are that person, you have absolutely no right to march in with your meddling boots on and go, 'Okay, well, that was just a horror film.'"

Boorman and Goodhart's partnership quickly soured; Boorman found Goodhart resistant to his ideas, and after Goodhart turned in his December 22, 1975, 121-page third draft screenplay, the two ceased working together. At this point the filmmaker contacted Rospo Pallenberg. Even though Pallenberg would rewrite the script with Boorman, Goodhart would receive sole screen credit.

Goodhart's screenplay had been titled *The Heretic* for the specific reason that it was about a heretic, Father Philip Lamont, a disciple of Lankester Merrin who challenges Church dogma on the interdependence of good and evil. Philosophically, the film was a separate vision and should have gone in that direction without being burdened with sequel responsibility. At the time, sequels had names, not numbers, and it was up to the advertising department to educate the public. Not until *The Godfather Part II* in 1974 did numbers begin to routinely appear on titles. *The Heretic* was caught in the semantic bind. On November 11, 1975, in the trades it was called *Exorcist, Part II*.[13] Three days later it was changed to *Exorcist, Part II, the Heretic*.[14] Three months later it was being called *The Heretic: Exorcist II*,[15] but by that fall it had settled into being called *Exorcist II: The Heretic*.[16]

The identity crisis infected directors, too. Despite Boorman's claim of being the first asked by Calley, *the Hollywood Reporter* announced on June 11, 1975, that master editor Sam O'Steen (*The Graduate*, *Rosemary's Baby*, *Chinatown*) was attached to helm the project, and *Variety* repeated it on September 24, 1975. Trouble is, no one had ever actually signed O'Steen to the job, and on November 11, 1975, *Variety* announced that John Boorman would direct. The start date, according to *Variety* of November 7, 1975, would be January 3, 1976 with a budget of $8 million, "considerably below the $12 million cost of the first" film.[17]

Early versions of the script reportedly began with Lieutenant Kinderman continuing to investigate Burke Dennings's death, but when actor Lee J. Cobb died on February 11, 1976, that approach had to be abandoned. Other members of the original cast proved elusive. By 1975 Ellen Burstyn had achieved star status and an Oscar for *Alice Doesn't Live Here Anymore* (1974). Jason Miller, Jack MacGowran, and Max von Sydow's characters were all dead (as was MacGowran himself). The only other major survivors were Regan (Linda Blair), Father Dyer (Father William O'Malley), and Sharon (Kitty Winn). The studio announced that Linda Blair would again appear as Regan MacNeil.[18] Jon Voight, who had starred for Boorman and Warners in the unexpected hit *Deliverance* (1972), was announced that same month as the eponymous priest[19] then fell out when he and Boorman had philosophical differences.[20] Christopher Walken was considered in April,[21] as were David Carradine and George Segal. At one point a sex change was discussed and the names Ann-Margret and Jane Fonda (who had famously turned down *The Exorcist* as "capitalist ripoff bullshit") were considered.[22] As for Dyer, by then William O'Malley had long since gone back to his day job. In late April, Richard Burton was in.[23]

Burton's casting was significant. Over the previous ten years, a string of financial flops—some of them with his then wife Elizabeth Taylor and some on his own—had damaged his screen career. A film he had started shooting in 1974, *Jackpot*, ran out of money and was never completed. By summer 1975 he and Taylor were, in the words of the industry, "lobby attractions"—that is, stars who are recognized in theater lobbies by fans who do not then go in to buy tickets. Entering a sanitorium to detox from his alcoholism (he was going through two bottles of vodka a day), Burton accepted a bizarre offer from a German dentist named Wolf Vollmar to shoot a film titled *Abakarov* in Israel. When Taylor, likewise unemployed and by then divorced from Burton, agreed to come back and costar with him, the tabloid industry practically hemorrhaged. The gig fell through but, along the way, Burton reclaimed his self-confidence as a man and as an actor and remarried Taylor.[24] It was their second marriage. It lasted nine months, but the residual publicity made Burton bankable enough to appear in *The Heretic*, after which he returned to Broadway in 1977 to star in *Equus*, an event which professionally eclipsed that same year's *Heretic* gambit.

As stated, John Boorman was formally announced as director on November 11, 1975,[25] and thereafter a cast. In addition to Blair and Burton, Louise Fletcher, who had just won the Best Actress Oscar for *One Flew Over the Cuckoo's Nest*, was named as psychiatrist Dr. Gene Tuskin, a part originally written for a male.[26] This enriched the story, making it not only about faith versus reason but male versus female. "I just came in and made it about me, that's all," Fletcher says. "I didn't change anything except the clothes." (Chris Sarandon was still being considered for Tuskin as late as the seventh draft on March 16, 1976, but Boorman thought him too introspective.) Hiring people from the first film was essential for the sequel's pedigree; Kitty Winn would return as Sharon Spencer, Chris MacNeil's assistant. Von Sydow joined the cast after considerable wooing by Boorman. He would appear in flashbacks.

Von Sydow and Blatty had remained friends, and as *The Heretic* filming dragged on, Blatty gave the Swedish star a call. "I was living in Los Angeles at the time," Blatty said. "I had run into Max somewhere and said, 'Max, come out to the house for dinner on Sunday.' He said, 'Zat's all right; zat's the last hour ve're going to shoot.' Then Max called during the day and said, 'Bill, I am not going to be able to make it. Ve have to shoot today. Ve are going to shoot long and I vill barely be able to make it to the plane back to Sweden.'

"'Oh, Max, I'm so sorry. I was looking forward to it.'

"'Me too.'

"'Max, before you go, while I have you on the phone, may I ask you a question, please? In the scene'—and I begin to describe the scene in the script that I had read in which the saintly Father Merrin as a young man is knocking out 35mm shots for a research paper he's doing while a fifteen-year-old boy is being consumed by locusts. The kid [Kokumo] is shrieking in agony, according to the script, and the saintly Father Merrin is standing there knocking off 35mm shots for his research paper. I'd no sooner got the words out: 'Max, is there still a scene in the picture where he was—'

"'Bill, I had to do it. I didn't want to do it. I never wanted to do it, but Bill, I had to think of my family. They gave me soooo much money to do it. I'm sorry. I'm sorry.'

"I said, 'I gather this scene is in.'

"Max said, sadly, 'Yes.'

"And the other lovely story about that," Blatty merrily continues, "that I was just so crazy about, true story. I had heard a rumor—you see, all I had was rumors—that they were going to do the locust scenes on the backlot of Warner Bros. and that they had imported hundreds of thousands of locusts in tiny cages. So I was talking to a friend of mine at the studio and I asked him, 'Is it true?' and he said, 'Bill, Bill, Bill, Bill, how long have you been in this business? You're a professional. You know the stories and the rumors, the idiotic mix. I cannot believe it. It was *tiger moths*, not locusts. We sprayed them to look like locusts. They're much cheaper than locusts.' That's the true story!"[27]

The January start date was pushed to March, then to May, as script changes continued. "They rewrote it once, they rewrote it twice, they rewrote it five times," says Linda Blair. "The movie we set out to make never happened. Too many cooks spoil the brew and in this case it's what affected this movie. It was not the film we signed on. We all left with great disappointment, I believe."[28] A May 12, 1976, 100-page draft by William Goodhart and Rospo Pallenberg was issued, followed by a 102-page "final" draft dated July 26 with Goodhart's name and no mention of Boorman or Pallenberg.

"We had a lot of changes with Rospo [Pallenberg] working all along the way," recalls Fletcher, "but it wasn't a whole new script. I remember reacting badly to certain things I had to say over and over again, but at least I only had to say Pazuzu once at the end."

What had attracted Boorman to the project was his and Goodhart's belief that great good attracts great evil, and that the next stage in the evolution of mankind was bringing the minds of the world together to form a godhead. The idea may have been that of Teilhard de Chardin, but it had been more popularly espoused by science fiction writer Arthur C. Clarke in his 1953 classic, *Childhood's End*. Specifically, de Chardin thought that mankind was at the verge of a next step in evolution that would bring him spiritually closer to God. Citing evolution—which, at the time, was opposed by the Church—positioned him as a heretic (like both Merrin and Lamont). Clarke, in his novel (one of the inspirations for the film *2001: A Space Odyssey*) has alien overlords come to earth to shepherd mankind into his next stage of development, but at the cost of human individuality. When the overlords are revealed to look like Satan, Clarke posits that humans have a "genetic memory" that stores images of everything from the Creation onward, including the expulsion of Satan from Heaven, only these images are confused, creating a barrier between good and evil that will have to be unified if mankind is to survive in his new form.

Boorman became so infatuated with the concept that he brought in a succession of psychiatrists, hypnotists, ESP gurus, and other consultants to work with the cast. There were visits to hospitals and clinics. He demanded authenticity in casting the extras, going out of his way to hire special needs children for Dr. Tuskin's ward and to seek out authentic African, as opposed to African-American, performers for the African sequences.

Filming was originally to have commenced in November 1975 and wrap in February 1976, but when the script wasn't ready, Guy McElwaine, who had replaced John Calley as Warners' production chief, changed the schedule to April. Even so, *The Heretic* didn't roll until May 24, 1976 at the Burbank Studios. The first scene, set in Dr. Tuskin's clinic, involved Dr. Tuskin helping a deaf girl hear again through what are perhaps cochlear implants. It's a joyous scene made even more so by Fletcher, whose parents were deaf. "I'm pretty sure that John Boorman was aware of that and we maybe even discussed it," says the actress. "I'm sure we did, and discussed the possibility of doing a scene like that. I loved doing that. I thought my part was a very nice part."

The company then moved to Penn Station in Newark, New Jersey, and New York City for six weeks.

Originally there was to be extensive location shooting in East Africa, for which the crew received travel vaccinations—everyone except Boorman, for unspecified reasons. (This would become a problem down the line.) When budget constraints prevented an African sojourn, the fictitious

Ethiopian village of Jepti was constructed on Warner Bros. soundstage #16, augmented by miniatures and Albert Whitlock's masterful matte paintings. Rospo Pallenberg, acting as second unit director, did go to Africa to shoot background plates and aerial sequences for process shots involving flying with the locust demon Pazuzu.

Other production compromises worked to the film's advantage. When the Galleria apartment complex in New York City withdrew its permission for the company to shoot there, the production team erected Regan's penthouse atop the high-rise Warner Communications building on Fifth Avenue in Manhattan. This allowed complete design control, and production designer Richard Macdonald, art director Jack T. Collis, and set decorator John P. Austin created an environment that seemed airy yet was confined by mirrors. Boorman's notion was that Regan should be free to fly with Pazuzu, thus the vertiginous openness of her living accommodations.

As with the original, Linda Blair's age (she was then seventeen) brought her under the jurisdiction of California's child labor laws. Unlike the original, however, the makers of *The Heretic* couldn't flee to New York to avoid them, so Blair was limited to an eight-hour day while shooting in the Golden State. This added $1 million to the budget.[29]

There was also a four-week delay when producer Richard Lederer went through open-heart surgery two weeks into production, another when Louise Fletcher had to leave to be with her husband, producer Jerry Bick, who was having chest pains, and yet another when Kitty Winn had gallbladder issues followed by Louise Fletcher having the same problem. Finally, there was a month's delay when unvaccinated director Boorman contracted valley fever (coccidioidomycosis), an airborne fungal disease, after returning from Glen Canyon,

Utah, whose Boulder Dam and Lake Mead doubled for some of the arid African locations.

"John Boorman didn't like the earth that they brought from somewhere to make Ethiopia look like Ethiopia," Louise Fletcher said, "and he kept complaining about the color and they kept bringing different types of earth from other digs. Finally he caught valley fever from choosing this earth and blowing it around. Valley fever attacks your vital organs and you can die from it. He was at UCLA Medical Center for a good long time. He finally was back after several months' hiatus and looked like he was out of the woods and [we] kept going and going." Then she added, "Nobody gets paid for all that time."

Boorman's illness allowed Pallenberg, in concert with Calley (who had returned to Warner Bros.), to rework the film's ending, which would be a final showdown between Regan (by then repossessed by Pazuzu) and Father Lamont. Shooting resumed on August 9.

Richard Macdonald's production design, in spiritual alliance with Boorman's ideas, posed photographic challenges to director of photography William A. Fraker. Dr. Tuskin's clinic, in particular, was a labyrinth of glass partitions, each pane of which had to be angled so as not to reflect lights or the camera crew. Fraker hung a bottle of Maalox on the camera for when the tension got to his stomach, and his assistants kept it filled. The hive of glass and rheostat-controlled lights, totally lacking in patient privacy, was a miracle of design. The limitations turned into advantages that added to the film's mood of fantasy and unreality. Of course, this placed it further from the documentary realism of the original.

The final three weeks were spent destroying the house on Prospect Street made so famous in *The Exorcist*. When the Washington, D.C., neighborhood of Georgetown denied the filmmakers access to the actual *Exorcist* house, Boorman built the entire façade inside a soundstage, complete with the top of the Hitchcock stairs, iron gates for the taxi to crash through, and a breakaway house that would rend and crumble on cue.[30] By then the pressure was on as Burton had to be in Canada no later than November 1 to start shooting the film version of *Equus*. By the time principal photography was completed on November 5, 1976, the budget had swollen to $14 million.[31] Editing proceeded through Christmas in Boorman's Ireland home, far away from Warner Bros. supervision. The unrealistically early February 1977 target date for a locked print in advance of the film's scheduled June 13, 1977, theatrical release had long since become a memory.[32]

What happened between those dates is part of the legend of *The Heretic* because, even before it premiered, the studio was already planning retakes. They knew they had a stiff. When Blatty asked Joe Hyams, the studio's national publicity executive, how the film was going, he was told it was "very attractive," "and when all you can do is compliment the art direction," Blatty said, "you've got a problem."[33]

At a press conference on May 20, 1976, before shooting began, Richard Burton (accompanied by Fletcher, Blair, and von Sydow), swore his devotion to the project. "I'm not doing it for the money," he told a room of cynical reporters. "I'm an agnostic who doesn't believe in anything, but as one gets older, the Devil invades your mind through all kinds of channels. I've had one supernatural experience but it would take me four hours to explain it to you." For his part, the sardonic von Sydow noted that there "are more believers in the Devil in California" because "the Swedes from my country are terrible skeptics."[34]

Blair, who had looked forward to working with Burton, was pragmatic. "I didn't want to do the demon makeup again for two reasons," she told Barbara Pallenberg for the "making of" book. "First, I was afraid my face would die. I'm very lucky it didn't the first time. And I knew I didn't have to do it again; my position had changed. I think John Boorman and Billy Friedkin are both geniuses. John, I think, will be more visual and not into the performances, and I do like help with the performance. Billy was my first teacher and I would really like to work with him again."[35]

Despite the studio's efforts, the film grossed $5.8 million over its June 17 opening weekend in 725 theaters in the U.S. and Canada,[36] and Warner head Terry Semel said it toppled more than 150 previous Warner Bros openings.[37]

When the reviews hit the street and audience blowback started, however, the box office fell 60 percent. Perhaps the most devastating review came from an exhibitor who said, "Theaters need two lines for *Exorcist II*: one to sell tickets and another to give refunds."

Among the first disappointed viewers was William Peter Blatty.

"I never saw John Boorman," he said. "I never saw one clip of that film until I went to a theater," after which he notably called it "the worst movie ever, ever made." He then added, with a twinkle in his eyes, "There have been many efforts to top it since then. I had a friend—who shall be nameless—a pirate [who sent me] a copy of the script, *which I could not believe* [italics Blatty's]. And I called Dick Lederer and said, 'Don't ask me where I got it. I have what purports to be a copy of the script,' and I went through it. 'Is there a line of dialogue that sounds like this . . . ,' and I went through spotting it and he said it was the final script. Now my worst fears had been aroused and I said, 'You're not going to shoot this.' And I'll never forget Dick's words. He said, 'They (*they* meaning everybody at the studio) think it's a masterpiece.'

"I saw it opening night in Washington, D.C.," Blatty continued. "From reading the script I had circled the lines where I turned to my wife and said, 'This is where the audience is going to go up and never come down.' I was absolutely right. It was when they put the helmet on Regan MacNeil. Because up till then people sitting next to me were going [he stifles a giggle] but they suppressed it. We were in a silly mood, but when the helmet went on, worlds collided."[38]

A gloating William Friedkin (who had earlier seen parts of the film while visiting a lab) told an audience at the Chicago Critics Film Festival of a different kind of reaction at a sneak preview before a test audience:

"These executives drove out to Pasadena in their big limousines and they were all dressed up and they went into the theater, which was packed, turn-away crowds. Before they went into the theater they told their limo drivers, 'Look, we're gonna be in there for about two hours and twenty minutes, maybe more. You guys go on down to the end of the block,' there were some fast-food joints. . . . The executives go into the last row. Ten minutes into the picture, a guy stood up in the audience. He stood up and he looked around and he said, 'The people who made this piece of shit are in this room!' And somebody else said, 'Where? Where are they?' Ten or twelve people get up and he says, 'They're all back there!' Now, these guys got up, the heads of the studio, they got up, they ran out of the theater. They get outside, no cars. The cars are all down at McDonald's. And they were chased down the street. That was the first public reaction to *Exorcist II*."[39]

"The thought was that a sequel would do good business," says Tim Lucas, an expert on the horror genre. "I saw this film at a night-before preview and the audience started laughing at the movie well before I was inclined to. It was like people had been hired to sit in the audience to ruin it. I don't think it's a good movie, but I know people who respect it, who have sought out the different versions, and their findings strike me as valid, just not mine. Their experience isn't mine."

On their March 4, 2012, website *Money Into Light*,[40] John C. Kerr and Paul Rowlands cite examples of dialogue that turned audiences against it: endless repetitions of the name Pazuzu (the original film never spoke it), phrases such as "I have been brushed by the wings of Pazuzu," and lines like "If Pazuzu comes for you, I will spit a leopard" did the trick. And if they didn't, this nonchalant exchange between Regan and the autistic Sandra Phalor (Dana Plato, uncredited) in Dr. Tuskin's office sealed its fate:

> SANDRA: "What's the matter with you?'"
>
> REGAN: "I was possessed by a demon. Oh, it's OK. He's gone."

Before the first weekend was over, the studio was telling exhibitors that they would be sending them a new edit.[41] Boorman at first suggested the cuts by phone from Ireland but then returned to Los Angeles for hands-on work.[42] At first he resisted, but when Warner Bros. showed him the damage that had been done to the Bruin Theatre in Westwood Village, Los Angeles, by rioting UCLA students, he changed his mind and watched his film with an audience. Whatever they laughed at, he cut. Some of the excised footage made it into the final version eventually released on home video, some did not. Among the revisions was a prologue explaining how Father Lamont (Richard Burton) had been shaken by the botched exorcism in South America; more dialogue between Cardinal Jaros (Paul Henreid) and Lamont about Merrin suddenly falling into disgrace; and the victim of an auto accident asking Dr. Tuskin for help. Bizarre scenes of Linda Blair rehearsing a school tap dance number were cut, as was a scene in which Lamont rebukes a bus driver for taking a dinner break. A three-minute shorter version was announced for American bookings after the June 17 opening.[43]

They say that nobody sets out to make a bad film, but what were they thinking?

"The nature of evil is investigated in the film," Boorman says, "but the notion is that goodness competes with evil and, in the context of the film, helps to drive it out, and I think this is perhaps why the film was rejected by so many people because they went to see it hoping to see more of the same and were frustrated to discover the film was not about evil, it was about goodness. In many ways it was a disaster and it took a long time before the film could be understood for its own sake rather than as a sequel to *The Exorcist*. And it certainly was a very painful experience for me because I felt that I had put a lot of very good work into this film and had something important to say, yet it was rejected by audiences."[44]

Admittedly, Boorman is an acquired taste. In his first feature, *Point Blank* (1967), he turned the revenge genre inside-out by making a violent art film that has withstood the test of time (and a 1999 remake, *Payback*). His 1972 *Deliverance*, whose unexpected success no doubt endeared him to Warner Bros., is a hallmark of intelligent tension and exquisite violence. *Hope and Glory* (1987), his nostalgic piece about World War II, is perhaps his most accessible film, and *The General* (1998) is an uncompromising character study of a gangster. But he can be wildly inconsistent; despite its cult following, his 1981 *Excalibur* is a near-incoherent retelling of the Arthurian legend; his 1974 post-apocalyptic science fiction feature *Zardoz* is a stylistic and dramatic mess; *The Emerald Forest* (1985) is an idea looking for a plot; and then there's *The Heretic*.

A visual director, Boorman had little to do with his actors. Certainly Richard Burton (who had begun drinking again as the shoot dragged on) didn't need to listen to him, not that he had much to say anyway. "He didn't make contributions that I know of," Louise Fletcher revealed. "If he didn't like something he would say that he didn't like it, but he didn't say that often. Once he talked to you and he knew what you were doing, he just let you be. He just let me be. I didn't have any problems with him at all. I remember once or twice he wanted more intensity and he would ask for that in a very straightforward way. I never had a problem with him or longed for another director. I felt comfortable in my role and I didn't have any deep frustration or questions except, 'When is this movie going to end?'"

In the final analysis, the explanation may simply be that Boorman had a grand vision but lacked the basic filmmaking skill to achieve it.

"It may have been that a Catholic or a Jewish director approaching the topic, that's typecasting," Blatty said analytically, "but with a Protestant, the more trouble you're going to get into. He simply didn't understand the difference between *supernatural* and *impossible*."[45]

The core of *The Heretic* lies in its optimistic belief that great good attracts great evil and that the former conquers the latter. Thus Regan, who, in the sequel, has the ability to cure an autistic child by simply starting a conversation with her, is seen as a magnet for Pazuzu, the demon that possessed her four years earlier (and who possessed Kokumo in Africa).

That concept, in particular, may have been the death of *The Heretic*, according to Mark Kermode. "*The Heretic* trashed *The Exorcist*," he says. "How? Simple. In *The Exorcist* a young girl is possessed by a demon. In the novel, Father Karras says to Father Merrin, 'This makes no sense. Why this girl? Why?'

And Father Merrin says, 'The target is not the girl. The target is us, it is everybody else in the house.' Then along comes *Exorcist II: The Heretic*, which is both a prequel and a sequel. We have young Father Merrin in Africa doing an exorcism and the demon's target is actually very specific: . . . a new breed of people who are super-good and have to be targeted by the demon Pazuzu. So originally it's this young boy in Africa and then it's Regan MacNeil. Actually she's part of a new super-species. So the target *is* her after all. It makes no sense and it completely contradicts everything that *The Exorcist* is about."[46]

Speaking of Pazuzu—and that's the problem: Speaking of Pazuzu—the constant repetition of the name, most awkwardly in the magnificent diction of Richard Burton, becomes a punchline. Other plot contrivances complete the disaster: a helmet that can synchronize brain waves, enabling one person to enter another person's dreams (this was seven years before *A Nightmare on Elm Street*), that looked like an old Buck Rogers prop; a possessed Regan (doubled by Karen Knapp) who looked nothing like Linda Blair; and flying over the African Savannah staring up the ass of a locust. None of these can be seen with a straight face.

Blair reported that Boorman at first wanted everyone in the cast to be hypnotized.[47] The cast pronounced that a nonstarter, despite Boorman having hired two experts, Dr. William Baumann and Henry Prokop, to advise. Blair also refused to submit to the grueling regimen for demon makeup, for which Dick Smith was again engaged, so Knapp appears as the demon. She shares the screen with other characters in flashback using a classic cinematic device known as "ghost glass" in which action on a tandem set is reflected in a piece of glass set at an angle so that the camera can look through it and see both images at once. It takes coordination on the part of the performers to "meld" into a single shot, but its great advantage is creating the appearance of an optical effect without losing a generation of film clarity.

Scott Michael Bosco,[48] the project consultant for the Shout! Factory Blu-ray release of the film, intelligently defends the movie in his commentary, although it is often at odds with Boorman's own commentary. Bosco offers a wealth of persuasive observations including controlled color palette, the importance of flashing lights and mirrors to signify psychic linkage, and the use of music and sound effects. The most crucial element is that such various times as Lamont's encounter with the grown Kokumo, the use of the synchronizer, and the ending in Georgetown, take place in an alternate reality. All of these, he explains, demonstrate that Boorman was not haphazard in his design and creation of the film. And yet several times he laments that the audience didn't notice them, that the symbols may have been too obscure, and that viewers couldn't make connections. What this implies—and it's what doomed the film—is that, regardless of Boorman's intent, he lacked the ability to present his vision in a way that people could understand. In movies, as in life, if you want to be subtle, you have to be obvious about it.[49]

The synchronizer, which looks like the Pushmi-Pullyu of desk lamps, was one of the reasons Boorman wanted to shoot Goodhart's script in the first place. "When I finished reading Bill Goodhart's screenplay," he said at the time of production, "my hands were sweating and I was terrified but immensely stimulated by the ideas it contained, particularly the idea of exploring the possibility of a world mind. The last few years there's been an explosion of research into these ideas of ESP and thought transference and related phenomena. In our script we have what is really a logical extension of this research, very close to what is being done. It's called synchro-nized hypnosis. We have the psychiatrist and the priest, each in their way concerned about this girl who is possessed by two forces, one of good and one of evil, which are warring within her."[50] It sounds so touchy-feely that all the film needs to finish being its own satire is Uri Geller, and guess who shows up on a background TV broadcast bending spoons.[51]

Boorman was earnest in his optimistic belief that good and evil can coexist in a world that is evolving into a new era, as de Chardin theorized. What ultimately sinks its presenta-tion in *The Heretic* is not that it took its subject too seriously but that it didn't bring the audience into the loop. The power of the original film lies in its documentary style and William Friedkin's obsession to make every unreal moment look real, from the acting to the supernatural effects. John Boorman decided to make *The Heretic*'s unreal story even more unreal by stylizing it. While this created beautiful images, it bled the picture of the authority of reality. Audiences who had been made cynical by war, Watergate, assassinations, and the Me Decade weren't up for New Age mumbo-jumbo.

"Why is it we like to be frightened and horrified by a movie?" Boorman had asked rhetorically while making his film. "I think it releases something—our deepest fears, our most horrifying nightmares are exorcised by the process of watching and being tortured, perhaps, by a film. But I think what we've done is something more because out of this hor-ror and tension and fear and terror emerges the possibility of the human race rising to something better."[52]

"They thought it was going to be a big deal," says Linda Blair. "*The Exorcist*, nobody knew and it became the phenom-enon that it is, and so I can only say to people [that] if you find anything in [*The Heretic*] to enjoy, great. And if you don't, I get it. But I didn't write it and I had nothing to do with putting it together. I did my best and that's all you can do."[53]

In hindsight, the ambition was there but the craft was not. It had an interesting premise but presented it so incompetently that it became its own satire. But the real crime of *The Heretic* is that it cheated its audiences of what they had come to expect from seeing *The Exorcist* four years earlier. The irony is that, if anyone knew how to give the public what it wanted and how to sell it to them, it should have been publicist-turned-producer Richard Lederer.

How does Boorman feel about it now? "Perhaps too many ideas," he admits, "but I think interesting ones, and something that you could only have done on film to tell this strange story. Perhaps I put too many ideas together, but I tried to join them up into a coherent whole."[54]

Once released, *The Heretic* drowned in its own ambition. Grossing just shy of $31 million worldwide on a final budget of $14 million,[55] what should have been a slam-dunk at the box office turned out to be a pretentious disappointment that chilled the franchise for thirteen years. It also scared distributors worldwide away from horror films, traditionally a bread-and-butter genre.[56]

"We're victims of audience expectation based on the first picture," Boorman told *Variety*. "The sin I committed was not giving them what they wanted in terms of horror. There's this wild beast out there which is the audience. I created this arena and I just couldn't throw enough Christians in it." As to the artistic pretentions of his film, its director maintained, "I am bored by naturalism. The problem for people going to this [is] that they expect the other reality and in the present climate—you see it in in *Star Wars* which is a brilliant but mindless film—people resent being asked to contribute anything. I thought I produced a film which was thoughtful and beautiful and involving."[57]

"The failure of the film was too painful for me," Boorman admitted years later. "In fact, I wouldn't really work for a couple of years and I came back into filmmaking making *Excalibur*, which was an even more difficult film to make than *The Heretic*. But I have no regrets about this."[58]

As for Max von Sydow, who had been bewitched into returning as Merrin, he said, "I have to admit I never saw *The Heretic*." The he added, with a twinkle in his blue Swedish eyes, "There weren't many who did."[59]

## Synopsis of *Exorcist II: The Heretic*

Father Philip Lamont's (Richard Burton) faith is already shaky as he enters a home in a South American village to perform an exorcism on a local girl who, although she has the power to heal the sick, is also possessed by a demon. Drawn to this fascinating duality, and inspired by the writings of Father Lankester Merrin (Max von Sydow), Lamont fails in his task when the girl sets herself afire. Despite this, or perhaps because of it, Lamont is assigned by Cardinal Jaros (Paul Henreid) to investigate Father Merrin, whose death four years earlier exorcising Regan MacNeil (Linda Blair) has brought him under Vatican suspicion of heresy for believing that great good attracts great evil in the form of a personified devil, something from which the Church is trying to distance itself.

Lamont seeks out Regan, now seventeen and living in New York with Sharon Spencer (Kitty Winn) while her mother, actress Chris MacNeil, is away on a movie shoot.

Since the exorcism, Sharon has become a mystic and is slavishly devoting herself to Regan's wellbeing. Regan is also being supervised by Dr. Gene Tuskin (Louise Fletcher), a psychiatrist who is developing a way to meld two minds through a flashing hypnotic device called a synchronizer. With this, she wants to probe Regan's memory, believing that the girl was never really possessed and it was all in her mind. Lamont's insistence that the girl was indeed possessed leads to an immediate conflict between him and Tuskin that wavers as Lamont realizes he can use the synchronizer to learn from Regan the circumstances of Father Merrin's death. There is also an element of precognition involved.

Regan and Tuskin link through the device. The visions summon the demon (Karen Knapp), who appears in a present flashback and grabs Tuskin's heart. Realizing that something is amiss, Lamont dons the machine's headband and saves Tuskin. Still, Tuskin refuses to believe in demonic causes, citing psychiatry rather than religion.

When Dr. Tuskin blocks his investigation, Lamont visits the abandoned Georgetown house with Sharon, who remains haunted by her experiences there and refuses to enter Regan's former bedroom.[1]

Back in New York, Dr. Tuskin finally agrees to allow Father Lamont to couple with Regan on the synchronizer. Instead of seeing visions of Regan's exorcism, however, Lamont is transported to the past on the back of the locust-like flying demon Pazuzu to an African village of Jepti built atop mountainous buttes. There he witnesses Father Merrin exorcising a young Ethiopian boy, Kokumo (Joey Green). He sees that Kokumo has the power to fend off swarms of crop-eating locusts, and this power of good, coupled with the boy's vulnerability to possession, reinforces Lamont's theory that great good attracts consummate evil.

Lamont declares his intention to journey to Ethiopia for real to find the now-grown Kokumo, but is denied permission by the cardinal. Lamont defies His Excellency and makes the trip anyway. He finds his way to a Coptic church in the clouds atop staggeringly steep rock columns. When he has a vision (thanks to Pazuzu) of where an earlier man fell to his death, and tells the others, he is damned as a Satan worshiper by the priest and stoned by the congregation. After nightmarish hallucinations and an encounter with Muslims who think he is seeking a prostitute, he finds the adult Kokumo (James Earl Jones), a scientist who is studying how to prevent locust infestations by breeding "good" locusts with "bad" ones.

Meanwhile, in Tuskin's psychiatric clinic in New York, Regan strikes up a conversation with an autistic girl (Dana Plato), something none of the doctors has ever been able to do, and cures her. Dr. Tuskin warns Regan to be careful of her ability to get inside the head of other people, regardless of the benefits.

Lamont's investigation proceeds. He learns that Father Merrin agreed with the Jesuit scholar Teilhard de Chardin, who believed that psychic powers (such as those shared by Regan and Kokumo) were a gift that could unify the world's people, but it would do more harm than good if people were not prepared to be unified.

Lamont, now possessed by Pazuzu, brings Regan from New York to Georgetown to close the emotional circle. They take the train while Sharon (likewise possessed) and Dr. Tuskin grab a commercial flight in pursuit. Pazuzu tries to delay them by causing a traffic accident as they head to the airport and turbulence when they are airborne. On the train with Regan, Lamont becomes more obsessed.

Arriving at the Georgetown house, Lamont goes to the upstairs bedroom where Regan was once placed in restraints.

There he finds another Regan (actually the demon Pazuzu) who changes from her grotesque possessed persona into that of a seductive teenage Regan offering him unlimited power. Although he is at first tempted, he is brought back to reality by the actual Regan, who in fact remembers everything about her possession. Lamont physically grapples with Pazuzu/Regan as locusts violently attack the house, and the building begins to crumble around them. Real Regan fends off the locusts by using the same incantation that the young Kokumo used, while Lamont kills Pazuzu/possessed Regan by reaching into its chest and yanking out its heart. (By now Regan and Pazuzu are split.)

While this is going on, Sharon and Dr. Tuskin arrive in a taxi from the airport. They and the driver crash through the gate, killing the driver and pinning Dr. Tuskin in the backseat. Sharon extracts herself, but as Dr. Tuskin watches helplessly, she sets herself ablaze on leaked gasoline, in service of Pazuzu. She dies, charred, in Dr. Tuskin's arms as Regan and Lamont emerge from the house. Dr. Tuskin now believes in possession as she watches Lamont and Regan walk into the sunrise to search for the next stage of human evolution.

SIDEBAR

## The Two *Heretics*

John Boorman's original cut of *The Heretic* is believed to have run two-and-a-half hours, but sadly, it was not preserved. In deciding what to delete from what was his 117-minute first theatrical version, later cut to 110 minutes, Boorman attended a public showing of his film at Westwood's Village Theatre (with a notoriously testy UCLA audience), on Sunday June 27, 1977, and cut whatever made that audience laugh. The result, with a little new footage, was the version that replaced the original version in American theaters and was used for distribution internationally.[1] There was also talk of a 102-minute version (unsubstantiated). What follows refers only to the two currently available versions[2] and is not a full account of the differences between them. A more complete account is available on IMDb.

- An introduction using stills and outtakes appears at the start of the cut version.

- The first tap dancing scene with Regan is gone, but the second one, in which she is psychically linked with Lamont in Africa, remains, coming out of nowhere.

- When Lamont visits the cardinal in the Vatican, they stand before an immense mural of the Crucifixion. In the longer version, when the cardinal's attendants leave the room, they do so by opening a hidden door in the rear end of a horse. That shot is gone from the cut version.

- In the longer version, the mother of the autistic girl cries with joy at her cure. It is quite touching. That shot is gone from the cut version because it drew laughter.

- In the cut version, Tuskin and Sharon no longer stop to help the car accident victims they encounter en route to Washington National Airport.

- A close-up is inserted into the cut version showing the taxi driver bleeding and twitching after crashing into the Prospect Street gate.

- In the cut version, Father Lamont is no longer seen physically seducing the demon Regan.

- The cut version flashes on outtakes from *The Exorcist* showing Linda Blair in full demon makeup.

- In the longer version, Lamont and Regan survive the collapsing house together. In the cut version, Lamont disappears below a crumbling floor and is never seen again.

- At the end of the cut version, Regan emerges from the rubble to look enigmatically at Dr. Tuskin. There is a freeze-frame, the screen goes white, and the end credits appear.

## CHAPTER 10

# The Exorcist III

The first rule of *Exorcist III* is: You do not talk about *Exorcist II*. The second rule of *Exorcist III* is: Which *Exorcist III* are you talking about—*Exorcist III-A* or *Exorcist III-B*?

Based on William Peter Blatty's 1983 novel *Legion*, *The Exorcist III* is a supernatural murder mystery in which Washington, D.C., police detective William Kinderman investigates ritual murders that appear to be the work of the long-dead Gemini Killer who is apparently still alive and inhabiting the body of Kinderman's equally deceased friend Father Damien Karras. The only explanation, as hard as it is for the unbelieving (read: irreligious) Kinderman to accept, is transcendence, that is, an experience beyond the rules of the physical world.

The *Legion/Exorcist III* odyssey began on July 24, 1980, when Blatty gave an expansive interview to *Variety*'s Stephen Klain in connection with the impending release of *Twinkle, Twinkle, "Killer" Kane*, set to open August 8. In point of fact, it would be the film's second release, the first having been a disappointing February 29 release under the title *The Ninth Configuration* (and a distributor switch from Warner Bros. to United Film Distribution). Blatty told Klain that *Legion*, the book he was then writing, would not be a sequel, although it would continue to follow the exploits of Lieutenant Kinderman.

"I'd always intended to build future novels and, in fact, had considered producing this story before what became

*The Exorcist*," he explained. "There are no exorcisms, no levitations, and no furniture flying around, though, to me, it is infinitely more terrifying."[1]

It would take ten years for Blatty to realize his dream. Along the way it would become a nightmare.

Finding a concrete story to support his philosophical ideas was Blatty's first challenge. Another exorcism wouldn't do, even if that's what everyone expected of him. And there was still the carrot of a real sequel dangled over his head by Warner Bros., whose scar tissue from *The Heretic* had healed over the previous decade.

Several challenges presented themselves at this early stage. As they had with *The Heretic*, Warners wanted a true sequel that might use outtakes from the original film to extend the story. Blatty insisted, however, that it would not involve Regan MacNeil since the whole point of her possession was to attack not her but those around her, and her character was no longer necessary. The relationship between Kinderman and Dyer seemed viable inasmuch as there was footage between Lee J. Cobb and William O'Malley, except Cobb, who had played Kinderman in 1973, had died in 1976 and O'Malley, who appeared as Dyer, had left the boards and returned to the cloth.

After *Exorcist II: The Heretic* came and bombed in 1977, Blatty had miraculously retained sequel rights. It was later in the seventies that the idea for *Legion* entered his mind. He and William Friedkin were at a home screening on the Beverly Hills circuit, and the writer casually pitched his Gemini Killer idea to the director. Friedkin immediately tapped another guest, producer Jerry Weintraub, on the shoulder and said, "Listen to this." Nothing came of it, although Weintraub tried, to no avail, to talk Friedkin into directing the movie for United Artists, where he had a deal.[2]

In 1979 Blatty wrote and directed *The Ninth Configuration* (released in 1980). When *Legion* was published in 1983, he first showed it to producer Steve Jaffe, who optioned it and brought it to producer Carter DeHaven. Why the man behind the mega-hit *The Exorcist* would choose to bring its official sequel to independent producers and not to a studio is not known, although Warner Bros. was then in the process of merging with Time, Inc., and Blatty's champion John Calley was long gone. For a time Lorimar Productions was interested.[3] Finally, DeHaven roused interest from Morgan Creek Entertainment.

Morgan Creek was a new player. Formed in 1988 by director-producer Joe Roth and Baltimore automobile businessman-financier James G. Robinson, it was named after Roth's favorite film, Preston Sturges's 1944 classic *The Miracle of Morgan's Creek*. Flush with money from their 1989 production *Major League*, the company formed output deals with various distribution companies, but primarily Twentieth Century-Fox. For a moment it was even hoped that William Friedkin could be enticed to direct the movie. He could not.[4]

"We were all together," Blatty recalled of his interactions with Friedkin, "until one night when Billy invited me over to his apartment in New York and he cooked a roast and he told me that he didn't want to do anything with knives anymore. I don't know where knives came in with *Legion*, but he was pulling back. We were ready to go, so I thought I'd better do it."[5]

Blatty, in comments withheld until now, offered a more detailed chronicle of the *Legion* backstory. After years of their well-known differences on the changes that had been made to *The Exorcist* after Blatty had approved what he thought was the final cut, he and Friedkin were united on doing *Legion* together. "I had this put together at Hemdale with him directing and . . . I asked him if he would like to read my latest draft of *Legion*. He took it with him and he came back the next morning and said, to speak fairly accurate quotes, 'It's great, oh God, it's terrific, goes like a bat. . . . I finally see what you were trying to do. The light has finally dawned. I finally see what you were doing. It's fabulous.' Now I'm back in Los Angeles and we're making the deal [Blatty pulled the film away from Hemdale and was meeting with producer Jerry Weintraub] and we're talking about the script and Billy now needs a rewrite." Blatty was stunned that Friedkin, who had just made a string of less-than-challenging films like *Deal of the Century, Rampage*, and two *C.A.T. Squad* TV movies, would suddenly dig in on a script by an Oscar-winning screenwriter. Then it struck him. "When this picture was called *Legion*," he realized, "the screenplay is brilliant. When this screenplay or film is called *The Exorcist: 15 Years After* or *The Exorcist* anything, it's not brilliant because it does not fulfill the expectation of the audience that there is a child in trouble. In other words, it's a remake."[6]

Previously, Friedkin had given a quote to columnist Joyce Haber, "Not for any price would I do a sequel to *The Exorcist*. Not for 100 percent of the profits, nor was I asked by Warners."[7] Technically he was correct; he was asked by Blatty and Weintraub, not the studio.

"That is the truth," Blatty reacted. "When it concerns himself, Billy is a one-man *Rashomon*. He tells himself four different stories about his own personal responses to absolutely anything, and he searches for the truth. But when it comes to his profession, films, Billy is brutally honest, even when that honesty is detrimental or pejorative to his own reputation."

Thus, sans Friedkin, *The Exorcist III* was anointed the

"official" sequel to the 1973 original.[8] Morgan Creek announced a May 12 start date with a production budget of $13 million and P&A (prints and advertising) allotment of another $10 million. It was to be called *The Exorcist 1990*.[9] Much more than the title would change.

Throughout production, the shadows of both *The Exorcist* and *The Heretic* dogged *Exorcist III*. During on-set interviews, Blatty repeatedly stressed that it had nothing to do with the first film, although its protagonist was the same Lt. Kinderman who had been in *The Exorcist*.[10] The confusion was complicated by Kinderman's recasting with George C. Scott.[11] "George had some things to overcome," Blatty said. "George did not believe in God. George didn't want Kinderman to be Jewish. I had a mild confrontation with him one day about that. He said, 'You sneak it into the rhythm of the dialogue.' Which is true."

Jason Miller was a different case. Blatty sought him to reprise his role as Damien Karras, but according to published reports, he had "a schedule conflict." This was a cover story; sadly, over the decade and a half since *The Exorcist*, Miller had become an alcoholic and was unable to memorize lines or sustain a performance.[12] Assuming the role of Karras was Brad Dourif.[13] Asking a younger, physically different person to take over an iconic role that was so closely identified with another actor was a risk, but Blatty felt that Dourif's superb craft would wipe the slate clean. There was one thing all the filmmakers agreed going in. As Dourif reported, "The concept was that *Exorcist II* never existed."[14]

Principal photography began on June 5, 1989, on location in the Washington, D.C., neighborhood of Georgetown (this time the residents approved the shoot) and in interiors at Georgetown University, before moving to the Dino De Laurentiis studio in Wilmington, North Carolina, in early July 1989. They wrapped there in mid-August.[15] There had been a glitch when actress Sylvia Sidney began shooting scenes as Kinderman's mother-in-law, Shirley, but left on hiatus to make another film. When she didn't return, claiming that she hadn't been advised that she was needed, she was replaced by Barbara Baxley, some of whose scenes awkwardly appear to be pickups shot without regard to screen continuity.[16] Eileen Brennan was first engaged, then disengaged, as "Nurse X," for which Viveca Lindfors was finally cast. There is also an in-joke in the casting: Actress Lois Foraker plays the role of "Nurse Merrin."

Blatty had no significant interference from Morgan Creek during the shoot. This was to change after Blatty and editor Todd Ramsay delivered their cut. To say the least, the film was not well received by James G. Robinson or the early test audiences who got a look at it.[17] Blatty had indeed shot his script, which was an internal psychological/spiritual thriller about a man whose belief in reality is shaken by exposure to forces beyond his comprehension. The problem, the company realized, was that a film with the word "exorcist" in the title needed an exorcism in it. To rectify this, Robinson committed another $9 million for rewrites and reshoots which Blatty, per his contract, was compelled to perform (although he would later state that "an art director" set everything up and all he did was say the directorial command, "action").

This is when Jason Miller's schedule suddenly "opened up" and Morgan Creek insisted on hiring him. The company's April 2, 1989, announcement said that he would return, not as Father Karras but as "Patient X, a man with an important clue about the identity of a ritualized serial killer."[18] This decision, while understandable commercially, threatened the integrity of Brad Dourif's singular performance. Could Dourif be cut out and Miller replace him? No—Miller, by this

time, was unable to memorize the Karras/Venamun monologues that Dourif had so compellingly delivered. Blatty hit
upon the idea of intercutting Miller's Karras with Dourif's
Karras using the contrivance that Kinderman sees one and
then the other. Dourif reshot his scenes to accommodate this
decision. When Miller was engaged, Blatty compassionately
guided him line by line through his performance.[19]

Says Dourif, demonstrating every actor's method of making a villain sympathetic, at least to themselves, "The character I was playing was kind of stuck between worlds and was
consumed with getting revenge. But he had lost it. The way he
had been treated is what had really driven him crazy, made
him evil, but he was really very human."[20]

For the crowbarred-in subplot, Nicol Williamson was
hired to play "Father Morning," a priest who reads signs that
an exorcism is needed and heads to Patient X's cell to perform
it. This triggers a confrontation in which Patient X hand-
ily repels Morning with a display of blood, animal sounds,
and lighting effects having nothing to do with the Kinderman narrative. But it was indeed an exorcism, or at least an
attempt at one, and Blatty rewrote the ending not only to
bring the Karras and Morning threads together, but to forge
a more assertive ending.

The intercutting is a noble gambit that works intellectu-
ally but not dramatically. Although Kinderman seemingly
follows the thread between Miller and Dourif, the audience
has to keep adjusting. It would have been helpful if there
were more cutaways to Kinderman reacting to the Dourif/
Miller switches, but that would have undercut Dourif's powerful monologues. The encounter climaxes with Kinderman
pinned to the wall of cell eleven while holes are blown in the
floor below so he can get a glimpse into Hell—all played in
his mind—until Father Morning recovers enough strength

to distract Patient X, peel himself off the ceiling, and release Kinderman. Blatty also rewrote his ending so that Karras, momentarily freed from possession[21] by the Gemini Killer, begs Kinderman to kill him. In response, Kinderman asks Karras to pray for him. Like the one between Father Dyer and Chris MacNeil at the end of *The Exorcist*, perhaps this hopeful last exchange suggests that Kinderman is ready to accept God.

Shooting the new footage and special effects did not go well. Second unit production manager Ronald Colby—who called Blatty's cut "leaden and without redemption"—handled the reshoots. A complex merging of visual and mechanical effects that should have taken twelve weeks to do properly was scheduled for only three. Moreover, one of the camera operators hired to shoot the footage lacked experience to the point where most of the shots of Greg Cannom's special makeup effects (the heads popping out of the floor from Hell) could not be used.

That said, it was a heroic effort by Morgan Creek to salvage what they feared was an ineffective film.

*The Exorcist III* opened as America's number one box office attraction on August 17, 1990, at the tail-end of Hollywood's lucrative summer playoff season. Released by Twentieth Century Fox, its opening gross was $9,3121,219. By the second week, receipts had dropped precipitously. Its eventual worldwide gross is $39,024,251.[22]

The theatrical cut enjoyed wide availability on home video in each successive technology: VHS, laserdisc, and DVD. The Blu-ray revolution, however, provided new opportunities. On October 25, 2016, Shout! Factory released a two-disc Blu-ray collector's edition of *EIII* containing both the theatrical cut and a new director's cut that had been reconstituted from 35mm trims, outtakes, and VHS screening tapes of dailies that had been made during production. Although visual and audio quality of this found footage was significantly reduced, it allows a strong flavor to emerge of what would have been a far more contemplative film that articulated Blatty's fascination with good, evil, and transcendence.

Mark Kermode stood with Blatty when Morgan Creek offered him the opportunity to reconstruct his version. The two men had worked together to publish his *Exorcist* and *Legion* screenplays (UK: Faber and Faber, 1998) and now Blatty asked Kermode to supervise, if not exhume, his original version of *Exorcist III* based on whatever materials he could turn up for Shout! Factory release.

As Kermode and Shout! progressed, Blatty became suddenly indecisive. "Bill was changing his mind about certain things, particularly the prologue," Kermode recalls. "At one point, there was a version which had a prologue that established Dourif as Karras. We see Karras go out of the window and down the steps from the end of *The Exorcist*, and he is then seen in the morgue as Dourif. They found the footage and for a long time that was in and then Bill decided he didn't want it in after all. But the version that Shout! put together was pretty close to what Bill had originally wanted to do and pretty close to what he showed to Morgan Creek executives when they gave the floor to a secretary who stood up and said, 'What the hell has this got to do with *The Exorcist*?' and they said, 'Exactly. You have to have Jason Miller. It has to have an exorcism and that's the beginning and end of it!'

"Bill was then in this kind of quandary, which was he could either just say, 'I'm not going to cooperate,' in which case somebody else would do it, or he could try and find a way of working it, in which case he still had [final] cut. And the thing that it is important to remember is that, even in the studio version of *Exorcist III*, it is still Bill. He did write the new ending. He did direct the new ending. You know it is still his film, but it isn't the film he set out to make. The film that he set out to make is the director's cut version, and I think this is a superior and more coherent work. I think that the end of *Exorcist III* makes no sense. I think the whole Nicol Williamson thing is just pish and tosh. But that was Bill trying to save a project."

Deconstruction of both versions raises interesting issues. This is hardly the first time that Kinderman, an assimilated (if not completely lapsed) Jew, has confronted such strange goings-in. Fifteen years earlier, his investigation into the death of Burke Dennings led him to conclude, not by evidence but by inductive reasoning, that the film director died at the hands of twelve-year-old Regan MacNeil, although how this might have happened escaped him and he could not pursue the case to closure. (In neither book nor film does Kinderman actually observe any effects of Regan's demonic possession.) *Exorcist III*'s main problem, however, is that there is no mystery. The villain—the Gemini Killer—is identified and confesses early on. If there is a mystery, it lies in explaining how Gemini resurrected Karras and committed the murders despite being confined to a cell. It's a question more suited to Houdini than Kinderman. But it does allow an examination of the persistence of evil and why unbelievers may be at a disadvantage when pursuing it.

Little of this heady philosophy was of any interest to the money behind *The Exorcist III*. It was variously titled *Legion*, *The Exorcist: 15 Years Later*, *The Exorcist 1980*, *The Exorcist III: Legion*, and finally *William Peter Blatty's The Exorcist III* (theatrical release) and *William Peter Blatty's Legion* (director's cut Blu-ray release).

Each version has its champions. Horror film scholar Tim Lucas prefers the theatrical version. "I found the reworked

version as much of a mess as *The Heretic*," he says. "In its theatrical form, it has some great moments and strong charac-
terizations, but there is something eccentric about Blatty's
direction. For me, it's what we used to call a sleeper: an okay
film studded with some unexpected, inspired moments, not
a masterpiece."

*Exorcist* devotee Mark Kermode got it right, reviewing the
film in *Time Out* magazine in 1990, observing that "Blatty's
sequel eschews the visceral effects of its predecessor to rely
on the chilling power of suggestion. The excessively wordy
dialogue is interrupted by intervals of brooding malevolence,
and by a couple of contrived but startlingly effective shocks.
The real terror, however, comes from Brad Dourif's straight-
to-camera serial killer monologues which breathe eerie life
into the script. With the exception of an unnecessarily spec-
tacular climax, this is a restrained, haunting chiller which
stimulates the adrenaline and intellect alike."[23]

Both *The Exorcist* and *Legion*, despite their supernatural trappings, are written as mysteries. Why? When Blatty
speaks of "the mystery of faith," he is being disingenuous; for
him, the mystery has already been solved in faith's favor. The
mystery, therefore, lies not in the solution but the quest.

The mystery form is an especially forgiving literary
genre. Although it has numerous subgenres (noir, ama-
teur, procedural, etc.), there are three that cover most of the
ground. In the first, often called a "whodunnit," the reader
follows a protagonist as he or she solves a crime by assem-
bling clues to reveal the guilty party. In the second, the
reader or viewer knows who the culprit is, and the tension
comes from watching the detective pursue and capture him
or her. In the third, there may not be a solution, but the
quest itself reveals compelling ideas. This is the form that
drives *Legion*. We know that Karras is dead. We know that

the Gemini Killer is dead. Then we learn that the Gemini Killer has somehow returned, yet we know that he is locked away. The mystery is how and why these three elements can coexist and how they contribute to five murders which, although nominally solved, can never be avenged. We have stepped away from the realm of reality. The overriding mystery becomes "How is this possible, and how can God allow it?" It's more a "whydunnit" than a "whodunnit."

Blatty places stones in the path by complicating Kinderman's character rather than the villain's. He makes him more eccentric than any of the people with whom he interacts. This is a cop who quotes Shakespeare, scripture, movies, talks about a carp swimming in his bathtub, and seems to be giving an ongoing performance for the benefit of someone who isn't in the room. He allows himself to show weakness, breaking down in tears over the death of his friend Dyer and almost fainting, so that a police colleague (Grand L. Bush) has to steady him. There is nothing particularly innovative about his investigative methodology; in fact, he just gets lucky. Unlike the ending of the novel, in which Kinderman reiterates Dyer's contention that it all works out in the end, in the film Kinderman may be more confused than ever. Clearly Blatty had more interest in the mystery of faith than he had faith in the mystery.

"The gist of *Legion*," Blatty said, "is that there is a God. I don't know how successful I was at delivering that, but I think the good guys win." They do, but considering that all the priests portrayed in the film are either murdered or ineffectual, and that the case is solved but not explained by a lapsed Jew (played by an actor who was an atheist), and we still don't know if "The Master" is going to find another body to resurrect the Gemini Killer, the question is, at best, as wide open as the mystery of faith itself.

SIDEBAR

# Synopsis of the Novel *Legion*

*In 1983, William Peter Blatty published his long-awaited successor to* The Exorcist. Legion *wasn't a sequel as much as a continuation of the themes he had explored in his novel* The Exorcist *and that he felt William Friedkin had minimized, or which had eluded viewers of its 1973 screen adaptation: that the existence of evil presumes the existence of good. Unusual for a novel (where such things are assumed), he ran a disclaimer that it was a work of fiction and that "characters, places, and incidents are either a product of the author's imagination or are used fictitiously."*

## Part One

Chapter 1:   Sunday, March 13.[1] Washington, D.C. police detective Lieutenant William Kinderman examines the mutilated body of a twelve-year-old boy, Thomas Kintry, who has been murdered near the Georgetown University crew boathouse. The wounds are similar to those inflicted by the infamous Gemini Killer, except the Gemini Killer was executed twelve years ago. A disoriented old woman is found near the crime scene and is brought to a shelter.

Chapter 2:   Kinderman and Father Joseph Kevin Dyer see a movie and have lunch. Both were friends of Father Karras, who sacrificed himself for Regan MacNeil on this day fifteen years ago, and each thinks he is helping the other get over Karras's death. Dyer believes in God and marvels at humankind;

Kinderman has no faith and explains life as a series of mechanical functions. As they finish, Atkins from the lab tells Kinderman that the fingerprints on the Kintry boy's body unaccountably match those of the frail old woman they found at the scene.

*Chapter 3:* Dr. Vincent Amfortas is haunted by memories of his dead wife, Ann. He is also becoming more depressed as he checks his patients in Georgetown Hospital, all of whom are doomed in one way or another. Even the bonhomie of his colleague Freeman Temple doesn't cheer him. He writes a letter to his supervisor asking to be relieved of his duties. Time is wearing on him.

*Chapter 4:* The coroner's report on Thomas Kintry shows negative for all drugs except for succinylcholine chloride.

*Chapter 5:* Kinderman and his colleagues are baffled that the long-dead Gemini Killer seems to have struck again. The substance used on the Kintry boy was a paralyzing drug that kept him fully conscious while the horrific injuries were inflicted. The old woman found at the scene is dazed and offers nothing. When he gets home, Kinderman's wife, Mary, sees his ennui. Their daughter Julie stops by. That night Kinderman dreams of angels. In the morning he wonders if God created man to be in pain. He is called away to the scene of another crime: A priest has been decapitated.

*Chapter 6:*  Monday, March 14. The deceased is identified as Father Kenneth Bermingham, once the president of Georgetown University, who was hearing confession when he was killed. His wounds match those created by the Gemini Killer. Witnesses awaiting confession saw a doddering old man in the confessional. Assessing the case, Kinderman muses to his crime team about evolution.[2]

*Chapter 7:*  Tuesday, March 15. Kinderman visits Father Dyer, who is in Georgetown Hospital for unspecified tests. He brings him hamburgers, which Dyer can eat even though it's Lent, because he's sick. The men discuss the problem of evil. Dr. Amfortas stops by and we learn that he still mourns the death of his wife. Dyer knows of the murder of Bermingham. Kinderman takes Amfortas aside to discuss the nature of pain, God's goodness, and why little children die. He also ascertains that anyone who knew to look for the painkilling drug succinylcholine chloride could have easily lifted it off a hospital med cart.

*Chapter 8:*  Mrs. Lazlo, the old woman found at the boathouse, is a patient in Georgetown Hospital's psychiatric ward. Somehow she had been signed out on the morning of the Kintry murder. Questioned by Kinderman, Dr. Temple and Nurse Allerton have no idea how that happened. Kinderman says hello to Father Dyer, who is still undergoing tests in the hospital. The Gemini file comes in. Mrs. Lazlo dies. At home that night, Kinderman dreams. Awakening, Kinderman examines the Gemini file; the killer's real name was James Vennamun and his activities were confined to San Francisco. He was an abused child very close to his brother. As soon as Kinderman finishes reading the file, his phone rings. Father Dyer has been murdered.

**Part Two**

Chapter 9:    Wednesday, March 16. Dr. Amfortas writes a long letter to Father Dyer (apparently not knowing he is dead). He encloses a tape and says he made spectrographic recordings after his wife died. He was trying to reach the spirit world, and he heard voices.[3] He places the letter in an envelope to Father Dyer with instructions to open it "in the event of my death."

Chapter 10:    Dr. Tench, hospital supervisor, goes ballistic at Kinderman's order to lock off the hospital and run IDs on everybody, including the patients. A pair of surgical shears is missing. They are strong enough to decapitate. Kinderman reveals that the killer must be Gemini and not a copycat because the current killer knew details of Gemini's murders that were never released to the public. He also went after people whose names began with K. Dyer's middle name is Kevin. Kinderman then sees something written on the wall of Dyer's room: "It's a Wonderful Life." The two "L"s were also a Gemini trait. And yet none of the prints harvested from any of the murder scenes match those of James Vennamun, the proven Gemini Killer, who is dead.

*Chapter 11:* Thursday, March 17. Kinderman visits Damien Karras's grave. He asks to see Father Riley, a priest who knew Father Karras. Kinderman and Riley discuss Karras's involvement in the MacNeil case and how the now-deceased Father Ken Bermingham had been the one who gave him permission to perform the ritual. A nurse tells Kinderman about Patient 12, who wandered into their ward years ago and has been catatonic until recently when he broke his silence and talked of a priest. Kinderman meets him and is shaken. Patient 12 looks like Damien Karras.[4]

*Chapter 12:* At a Washington, D.C., mission, Karl Vennamun, James Vennamun's father, considers returning to preaching.

*Chapter 13:* Friday, March 18. Kinderman and Father Riley exhume Karras's body. Only it isn't Karras. Kinderman enters the cell of Patient 12, the man known as "Tommy Sunlight." The man identifies himself as "Legion, for we are many." The man says he's the Gemini Killer and starts recounting in detail the murders he has committed. The two men engage in disturbing badinage, then Morning passes out. Afterward, Kinderman asks why Dr. Temple spends so much time with Morning. Kinderman suspects him of letting patients out. Kinderman investigates further the death of Karras and learns that, when Karras was autopsied, the medical examiner discovered that it wasn't Karras's body, but was that of another priest. What happened to Karras?

*Chapter 14:* Amfortas dies from a fall at home while talking to an imaginary double of himself and musing over his lost love, Ann.

*Chapter 15:* Saturday, March 19. At the hospital, Kinderman talks with an old man whose mind has gone, but who has written on a bathroom mirror: "Call me Legion, for we are many." Kinderman visits Sunlight, who acknowledges killing a nurse. Whenever Kinderman asks Sunlight how he gets out to kill, Sunlight changes the subject. In the ward, a boy named Vincent Korner is being checked in. Kinderman warns the nurses not to let the boy out of their sight. Later he finds the child all right but a nurse dead and stripped of her uniform. He complains to another nurse and sees that her name tag reads "Julie Fantozzi."[5] Kinderman realizes that someone is on the way to kill one of his family members. He races home to find one of the psychiatric residents dressed as a nurse poised to kill one of his kin with surgical dissecting instruments. Kinderman confronts Sunlight, who regresses into infancy and dies. Simultaneously, his father Karl dies of a stroke.

*Chapter 16:* Sunday, March 20. Father Riley commiserates with Lieutenant Kinderman for having, in effect, lost his friend Karras twice. They go off to get a drink.

## Epilogue:

Kinderman is still at a loss for who the murderer was. An autopsy reveals that Vincent Amfortas only had two weeks to live anyway because of an untreated lesion. In April, Temple had a stroke. No other murders took place. Atkins, Kinderman's police associate, tries to ground him. They go to White Castle for burgers and Kinderman explains his theory. Perhaps the "Big Bang" was the Fall from Heaven by Lucifer and that—using *The Brothers Karamazov* as an example—we may avoid evil by remembering the goodness of our childhood. First and above all, he says, be kind. "That is why God cannot interfere: evolution is this person growing back into himself."

SIDEBAR

# Synopsis of the Release Version of *The Exorcist III*

*The release version and the director's cut diverge in various ways, minor and major, as each progresses. See a separate sidebar comparison of the more notable differences.*

Georgetown, 1990. A church "awakens" as its statues and icons come alive. Its doors fly open and in blow trash and leaves. Prayer flyers go everywhere. The camera glides dreamily along Prospect Street toward the Hitchcock steps. A cassocked priest runs in the distance. A young Black boy, Thomas Kintry (James Burgess), offers a rose.

The next day, Father Joe Dyer (Ed Flanders) visits the long flight of steps down which his friend Father Damien Karras threw himself in 1975 to save a little girl, Regan

MacNeil.[1] A sheet of newspaper blows up the stairs as Dyer contemplates his loss.[2]

In his home in Washington, D.C., police detective Lieutenant William Kinderman (George C. Scott) also mourns Damien's death (which is shown in flashback).

While Father Dyer says Mass and includes Damien in his prayers for the dead, Lieutenant Kinderman is at a crime scene. The Kintry boy has been murdered and horribly mutilated near the Georgetown University boathouse.

At breakfast, Dyer tells the university president (Lee Richardson) that he and Kinderman are going to see a movie and have lunch to help Kinderman through the mourning for Karras.

Kinderman, making numerous literary allusions, tells his police colleagues that the murdered Kintry was killed in the manner of the Gemini Killer—except the Gemini Killer was tried, condemned, and executed fifteen years ago.

At home, Kinderman's job is weighing on him. His daughter, Julie (Sherrie Wills), is off to dance class, and Kinderman tells his wife, Mary (Zohra Lampert), and mother-in-law (Barbara Baxley) that he is off to meet Father Dyer to lift his spirits on the anniversary of Damien Karras's death.

Dyer and Kinderman attend a revival showing of *It's a Wonderful Life*. Over lunch, they talk of Father Karras (Jason Miller).[3] Kinderman asks why God creates death and Dyer counters that it will all work out at the end of time because everyone will be spirits.

Father Kanavan (Harry Carey, Jr.)[4] is murdered while hearing an old woman's confession. The old woman has been seen being walked by Nurse Allerton (Nancy Fish). At the crime scene, Kinderman notes the mark of the Gemini Killer on the priest's body. Later he learns that the priest was immobilized with the same drug that rendered the Kintry boy unable to move or scream while he was being butchered.

Kinderman visits Dyer, who is in the hospital for unspecified tests. As he leaves Dyer, he doesn't notice that a religious statue near the elevator has been decapitated. Later, he learns from his police team that the fingerprints around the murdered boy and the murdered confessional priest are from two different people.

Kinderman can't sleep. He dreams of angels and celebrities. The dream ends with an image of Father Dyer flopping up and down in his bed like the possessed Regan. Kinderman is awakened by a call summoning him to the hospital: Joe Dyer has been murdered. In shock, Kinderman investigates and sees the signs of the Gemini Killer. He questions arch Nurse Allerton and learns that a patient, Mrs. Clelia (Mary Jackson), was in the hallway at the time of Dyer's death. He questions Mrs. Clelia in the presence of Dr. Temple (Scott Wilson) and realizes that she is lost in catatonia and thus could not be a witness to Dyer's murder. Then the chain-smoking Temple brings Kinderman to the lockdown wing where Kinderman hears "Bill" being called to him from isolation cell eleven. The patient, straightjacketed and in shadows, recites John Donne's "Death Be Not Proud" in Damien Karras's voice but adds, at the end, in a different voice, "I was only twenty-one when I died."

Meanwhile, the hospital director complains about the police lockdown but backs off when Kinderman tells him that the Gemini Killer has returned using a modus operandi no copycat could have known. He says that the Gemini Killer doubled the letter "L" on the end of words and always killed people whose names began with "K." In the strain, he momentarily breaks down over Dyer's loss. He recovers and learns that a huge, heavy clipper suitable for decapitation has vanished from the hospital. He shares his questions with the university president who points out that Fathers Kanavan and Dyer were both involved with Father Karras in the Regan MacNeil exorcism; when he reveals this, the sound of Regan as the demon is heard, the office door creaks open, and lights flash. The men then offer exposition/recap of the MacNeil case, including a reference that links the Kintry boy's mother to Karras.[5]

Father Morning (Nicol Williamson) is disturbed in his dormitory room when a pet bird dies, a crucifix falls off the wall, a plastic Christ's wounds bleed, and room lights darken.

Kinderman is astonished when the Dyer crime scene fingerprints match the aged Mrs. Clelia.

In his office, Dr. Temple practices explaining to Kinderman that Patient X, the man in cell eleven, was found wandering along the C&O Canal fifteen years ago in a catatonic state but, over time, became violent. Kinderman thinks the man in cell eleven is Karras and visits him. He looks like Karras (Jason Miller), but he says he's the Gemini Killer, James Venamun,[6] and begins recounting his grisly crimes, all of them "K"-related, blaming them on his father, named Karl. He alludes to people on "the other side." When Kinderman says the Gemini Killer is dead, Venamun (Brad Dourif) suddenly appears instead of Jason Miller. The two figures (Dourif and Miller) switch back and forth, but Kinderman does not distinguish between them. Finally, hearing details of how he murdered Dyer, Kinderman slugs him.[7]

Nurse Allerton says that the man in cell eleven has gone in and out of catatonia for the past week. Kinderman connects his behavior with the schedule of the recent murders. In a church library he looks up a quote used by the man in cell eleven; it comes from the Ritual of Exorcism. As Kinderman familiarizes himself with the Ritual, so does Father Morning.

Late night at the hospital, someone murders Nurse Keating (Tracy Thorne) with the missing heavy-duty clippers. While Kinderman is investigating Keating, Nurse Allerton summons him to see that Dr. Temple has taken his own life. In his cell, Venamun takes credit for Keating. He explains to Kinderman why he looks like Karras: After he was executed, he was held in limbo and finally was given Karras's body, but it was so damaged after falling down the steps that it took a long time to heal.

While at the hospital, Kinderman finds the dead body of a nurse whose uniform has been taken. The person wearing the uniform is a dementia patient (Viveca Lindfors). Seeing Nurse Allerton's name tag with her first name Julie, Kinderman deduces that the missing patient is on her way to his home to kill his daughter Julie.[8] Racing there, Kinderman saves Julie from the nurse/patient, who reverts to her demented personality.

Father Morning arrives at the hospital and enters cell eleven to exorcise the unnamed patient. Kinderman arrives at the same cell and finds Morning flayed into a pulp. Karras/Venamun takes his wrath out on Kinderman, who admits under pressure that now he believes in the existence of evil. The room is blown to pieces. Father Morning springs back to life and, using a crucifix, tells Karras to throw off his possession and save Kinderman. He does, and becomes Karras long enough to tell Kinderman, "Kill me now," which Kinderman does.

Karras is buried in the priests' cemetery.[9]

# Synopsis of the Director's Cut
# of *The Exorcist III*

*Cobbled together from release prints and existing VHS copies of dailies, then issued on Blu-ray by Shout! Factory along with the theatrical version of the film, the director's cut is closer to the novel* Legion *in spirit. Comparing the two versions (see later sidebar) offers a unique lesson in what happens when ambition collides with pragmatism.*

*NOTE: People familiar with Jason Miller's memorable performance as Father Karras must keep in mind that Karras was played solely by Brad Dourif in Blatty's script as first filmed.*

Georgetown, 1975. A body tumbles down a seemingly endless flight of steps. A church "awakens" as its statues and icons seem to come alive, and its doors open and in blow trash and leaves. Prayer flyers go everywhere. The camera floats dream-like along Prospect Street toward the Hitchcock stairs,[1] seeing a cassocked priest running in the distance, then the young Black boy, Thomas Kintry (James Burgess), offering a rose. An as-yet-unidentified voice (Brad Dourif) is heard, and the camera tumbles down the steps.

Georgetown, 1990. Father Joseph Dyer (Ed Flanders) says a prayer for the dead, namely his friend Father Damien Karras, on the fifteenth anniversary of his sacrifice to save the soul of possessed Regan MacNeil. He tells an altar boy (Kevin Corrigan) that he is going to have lunch with Washington, D.C., police detective Lieutenant William Kinderman (George C. Scott), who was also a friend of Karras.

Kinderman is at the Georgetown University boathouse

investigating the mutilation murder of young Kintry. Father Dyer looks down the stairway where Karras tumbled and relives the moment. At lunch, he tells the university president[2] (Lee Richardson) that he and Kinderman are going to see a movie and have lunch to help Kinderman through his mourning for Karras.

Kinderman, making numerous literary allusions, tells his police colleagues that the murdered boy, Thomas Kintry, was killed in the manner of the Gemini Killer—except the Gemini Killer was tried, condemned, and executed fifteen years ago. When he gets home, the weight of his job is affecting Kinderman. His daughter, Julie (Sherrie Wills), is off to dance class, and Kinderman tells his wife, Mary (Zohra Lampert), and mother-in-law Shirley (Barbara Baxley) that he is off to meet Father Dyer to lift his spirits. Each man thinks he is helping the other.

Dyer and Kinderman see a revival showing of *It's a Wonderful Life*. Over lunch, they talk of Father Damien Karras (played by Brad Dourif), as they sit in a booth below a photo of him and his friends on the restaurant wall. Kinderman asks why God created death and Dyer counters that it will all work out in the end of time because everyone will be spirits.[3]

Father Kanavan (Harry Carey, Jr.)[4] is murdered while hearing an old woman's confession. The old woman is seen being walked by Nurse Allerton (Nancy Fish). At the crime scene, Kinderman notes the mark of the Gemini Killer on the priest's body. Later he learns that the priest was immobilized with the same drug that rendered the Kintry boy unable to move or scream while being butchered.

Kinderman visits Dyer, who is in the hospital for unspecified tests. As he leaves Dyer, Kinderman doesn't notice that a religious statue has been decapitated. Later, he learns from his police team that the fingerprints around the murdered boy and the priest are from two different people. At the hospital, the chain-smoking Temple brings Kinderman to the lockdown wing, where Kinderman hears "Bill" spoken to him from isolation cell eleven. The patient, whom they all call Patient X, in straightjacket and in shadows, recites John Donne's "Death Be Not Proud."

Meanwhile the hospital director complains about the police lockdown but backs off when Kinderman tells him that the Gemini Killer has returned using a modus operandi no copycat could have known. He says that the Gemini Killer doubled the letter "L" on the end of words and always killed people whose names began with "K." In the strain, he momentarily breaks down over losing Dyer and says that Father Dyer's middle name was Kevin. Patient X's voice says "Kevin." Kinderman also learns that a huge, heavy clipper suitable for decapitation has vanished from the hospital. He shares his questions with Father Riley, who points out that Fathers Kanavan and Dyer were both involved with Father Karras in the Regan MacNeil exorcism; when he does, the sound of Regan as the demon is heard, the office door creaks open, and lights flash. The men then offer exposition/recap of the MacNeil case, including a reference that links the Kintry boy's mother to Karras.[5]

Kinderman is astonished when the Dyer crime scene fingerprints match the aged Mrs. Clelia, a patient at the hospital who is near catatonic.

In his office, Dr. Temple practices explaining to Kinderman where the man in the isolation room came from fifteen years ago, wandering the C&O Canal. He says that the man was catatonic and has since become violent. Kinderman visits Patient X (Brad Dourif) and is shaken. He looks like Damien Karras.[6]

When Karras's coffin is unearthed from the priests' cemetery, the body inside is not that of Karras.

Kinderman confronts Patient X—Karras—in cell eleven. He insists he's James Venamun, the Gemini Killer, not Karras,[7] and describes in graphic detail how he murdered a little girl named Karen and then how he bled Father Dyer to death. Hearing that, Kinderman slugs him and leaves the cell.[8] Patching Kinderman's bruised hand, Nurse Allerton says that the man in cell eleven has gone in and out of catatonia for the past week. Kinderman connects his behavior with the schedule of the recent murders.[9]

From the university president, Kinderman learns that the body in Karras's coffin has been identified as Father Fain, who prepared Karras for burial but was never seen again. Kinderman says that an autopsy suggests that the priest died of fright.

At home that night, Kinderman reads up on the Ritual of Exorcism. His daughter, Julie, sleepily wanders into the kitchen for a snack and goes back to bed. At the hospital, Nurse Keating (Tracy Thorne) is killed and decapitated by someone wielding the missing heavy-duty clippers.

Dr. Temple is discovered dead from a suicidal drug overdose.

Kinderman returns to Patient X, who explains that when Venamun died, the "Master" put him into Karras's body as revenge for Karras's participation in the MacNeil exorcism. But it took a long time for Karras's body to heal, having been damaged from falling down the steps. Moreover, Karras's soul is in torment knowing what is being done using his body. He demands that Kinderman tell the press that the Gemini Killer is back, refuses to say how he gets out of his cell to murder, and offers to cure Kinderman's "un-belief." Then he repeats that he is not Karras, he just looks like him.[10]

While Kinderman is at the hospital, the dead body of a nurse is discovered naked. Her uniform has been taken. The person wearing the uniform is a dementia patient (Viveca Lindfors). Nurse Allerton monitors the sleeping Patient X, who, though now catatonic, has active brain-wave activity suggesting (to the viewer) that he has inhabited the body of Kinderman's daughter, Julie. Seeing Nurse Allerton's name tag with her first name Julie, Kinderman deduces that the missing patient is on her way to his home to kill his daughter.[11] Racing home, Kinderman saves Julie from the nurse/patient, who reverts to her demented state.

Returning to Patient X's cell, Kinderman says, "Pray for me, Damien. You're free," and shoots him dead.

SIDEBAR

## Differences between the Theatrical Cut and the Restored Director's Cut of *The Exorcist III*

Appreciating *Exorcist III* requires accepting that Brad Dourif is Damien Karras, except he isn't *always* Damien Karras; sometimes Jason Miller is. For this reason alone, the director's cut makes more sense because it allows the viewer to see only one Karras, even as Karras's body is inhabited by the Gemini Killer. Given that Jason Miller became iconic as Damien Karras in *The Exorcist*, recasting him with Brad Dourif was risky. The filmmakers ease viewers into this process by showing a photograph of Karras and his Jesuit friends on the wall of the restaurant where Kinderman and Dyer meet to comfort each other on the anniversary of their friend's death. This bit of footage was removed from the release version because, by then,

Karras was being played again by Jason Miller and the Gemini Killer by Brad Dourif—except when they weren't.

The most successful screenplays develop plot and character at the same time. The trick, as William Peter Blatty explained in numerous interviews, comes in hiding the function of "Morris the Explainer"—a character who delivers exposition. Writing a film's synopsis shows where Morris is hiding, and with *Exorcist III*, it uncovers assumptions in the novel's construction that Blatty had to clarify in his screenplay.

*Legion*, at 269 pages, is a detective story only in the sense that its main character is a detective. In point of fact, in *The Exorcist*, Detective Kinderman does not find Burke Dennings's murderer (although we are led believe he thinks it's Regan[1]), and in both *Legion* and *The Exorcist III*, the murderer, James Ven(n)amun, is already incarcerated and makes a willing confession. What mystery, then, is left to solve? Why, the existence of God.

A study of Blatty's script for *The Exorcist III* finds that he tries to rectify the structural flaws in *Legion*. But his true purpose in *Legion*, as it was in *The Exorcist* and in *Twinkle, Twinkle, "Killer" Kane* (aka *The Ninth Configuration*), is not the destination but the journey. All three books, and to some extent the films made from them, are best considered as life support systems for the author's message, which is transcendence—the presence of God, whose power surpasses that of the material universe and its physical laws. In each of these works, but chiefly *Legion*, he has a character who tries to reconcile the pain and evil in the world with the supposed existence of a benign Creator. Blatty's choice of Kinderman to express the skeptical side of the debate is daring: Kinderman is a lapsed Jew, well-read (though probably an autodidact), and filled with an inflated sense of his own charm.[2] In *The Exorcist*, Lee J. Cobb, a Jew, was a perfect Kinderman; George C. Scott, an atheist and a Gentile, was pushing it. Cobb was *hamish*; Scott only acts it.

The main differences affecting plot and meaning between the theatrical release of *Exorcist III* (*EIII*) and the director's cut (*DC*) are as follows:[3]

- *DC* opens in black-and-white showing Karras leaping from Regan's bedroom window and tumbling to his death down the Hitchcock steps. This is either newly shot footage or previously unused outtakes from *The Exorcist*. A title says, "Georgetown 1975." It then cuts to color footage of rowing skulls on the Potomac and the title "Georgetown 1990."

- Kinderman and Dyer see *It's a Wonderful Life* at a Washington, D.C., revival house. Their after-movie lunch conversation, during which neither of them eats, includes reminiscences about Karras, whose group photo is on the wall. *EIII* joins the scene after these moments and focuses on God and how all will be answered in the End Times.

- Kinderman visits Dyer in the hospital, where he has come for unspecified tests. In the *DC* they discuss Father Kanavan's murder and, through a nurse, note that drugs are readily available from an unguarded hospital cart. *EIII* does not contain this clue.

- Isolation cell eleven that contains Patient X has a brick background for *DC* and a padded background for *EIII*. Karras (Miller) gets the padded cell, Venamun (Dourif) gets the bricks, except for newly shot scenes with Dourif, which are against Miller's padded cell wall. The characters are essentially the same in each version even as the speaker changes.

It was on this street and in this house that the alleged 1949 possession began that led to *The Exorcist*. It's the former home of Ronald Hunkeler at 3807 40th Avenue in Cottage City, Maryland. The family moved away years ago. *Stan Levin*.

The former Hunkeler home in Cottage City, Maryland. It was in this house's second floor window that teenage Ronald was supposedly possessed. *Stan Levin*.

The town hall of Cottage City, Maryland, the sleepy Maryland community that awoke to a demonic possession that inspired *The Exorcist*. *Stan Levin.*

The Mesopotamian demon Pazuzu, who held dominion over the wind, also held dominion over Regan MacNeil. *British Museum/ Wikimedia Commons.*

The "Exorcist house" from across Prospect Street in NW Washington, D.C. For the movie, the owners of the private residence allowed the Warner Bros. construction crew to build an extension over the long stairwell for purposes of defenestration. *Stan Levin.*

The "Exorcist house" remains a private residence in the Georgetown section of Washington, D.C., but that hasn't stopped tourists and Exorcist fans from making a pilgrimage. They are invariably disappointed to see how different it looks fifty years on. *Stan Levin.*

The house used to shoot the exteriors of *The Exorcist* at 3600 Prospect Street, NW Washington, D.C. An extension was built to place Regan's bedroom over the steps on the left. *Stan Levin.*

On October 30th, 2015, a plaque was posted on the stairwell connecting Prospect and Canal Streets, Georgetown, commemorating them as the "Exorcist stairs." *Stan Levin.*

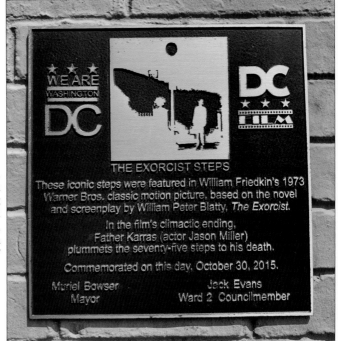

THE EXORCIST STEPS

These iconic steps were featured in William Friedkin's 1973 Warner Bros. classic motion picture, based on the novel and screenplay by William Peter Blatty, *The Exorcist.*

In the film's climactic ending, Father Karras (actor Jason Miller) plummets the seventy-five steps to his death.

Commemorated on this day, October 30, 2015.

Muriel Bowser
Mayor

Jack Evans
Ward 2 Councilmember

Looking down at the "Exorcist steps" beside 3600 Prospect Street in NW Washington, D.C. Formerly known as the "Hitchcock steps" after director Alfred Hitchcock's 1935 thriller *The 39 Steps*, they became known as the "Exorcist steps" after their important appearance in the 1973 movie *The Exorcist*. *Stan Levin.*

The "Exorcist stairs" looking up from Canal Road and the Whitehurst Freeway. Steps and stairs are used interchangeably. *Stan Levin.*

William Friedkin in a contemplative
moment during the making of
*The Exorcist*. Presskit photo
*N26825/Wikimedia Commons*

Georgetown University White Gravenor Hall.
Only William Peter Blatty's connections with the
University enabled Warner Bros. to use it as a movie location.
*Daderot/Wikimedia Commons.*

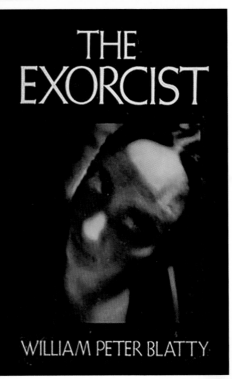

The cover for William Peter Blatty's novel, *The Exorcist*. Shirley MacLaine, on whom the character of Chris MacNeil is based, claimed that her friend Blatty took a photo of her daughter, distorted it, and used it as the haunting illustration.

Original teaser (advance) poster for *The Exorcist*. Note that it carries the wrong opening date. The film actually opened December 26th, 1973, not the day before.

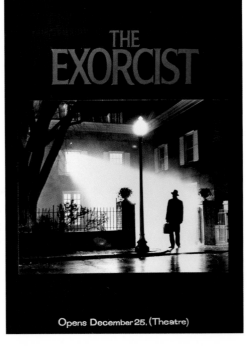

Father Pierre Tielhard de Chardin, whose writings on possession informed William Peter Blatty and inspired Max von Sydow, who even looked like him as Father Lankester Merrin. *Wikimedia Commons.*

Ellen Burstyn tries to comfort Linda Blair on her shaking bed in a publicity photo from *The Exorcist*. *Wikimedia Commons.*

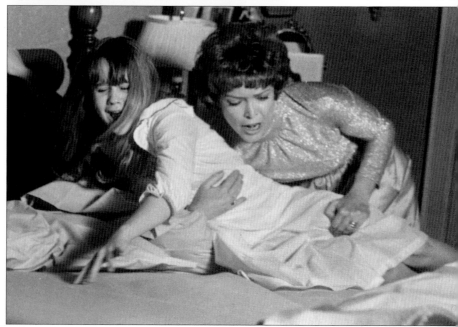

The mechanical Regan doll designed by Marcel Vercoutere and Dick Smith. It now lives at the Museum of the Moving Image. *Meg Gilbert/Wikimedia Commons.*

Linda Blair—happy and healthy— years after her *Exorcist* experience. *CelebHeights.com/Wikimedia Commons.*

*Exorcist II: The Heretic* poster.

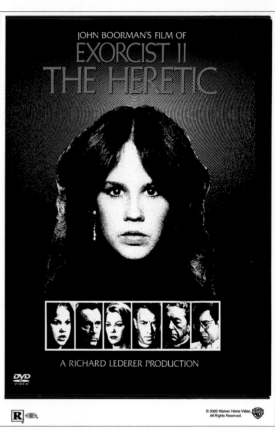

Director John Boorman,
the man behind
*Exorcist II: The Heretic.*
*Lionel Allorge/Wikimedia Commons.*

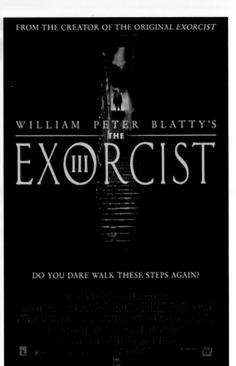

*The Exorcist III* poster.

William Peter Blatty stretches out,
enjoying his success.
*William Peter Blatty/Wikimedia Commons.*

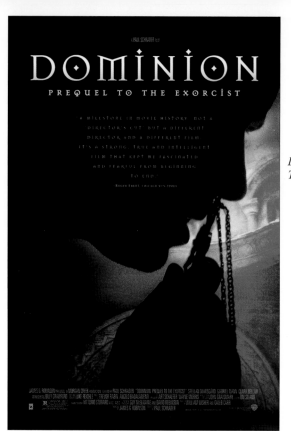

*Dominion: The Prequel to The Exorcist* poster.

Filmmaker Paul Schrader directed
*Dominion: Prequel to The Exorcist.*
*Frank Scramm Montclair Film/*
*Wikimedia Commons.*

*Exorcist: The Beginning* poster.

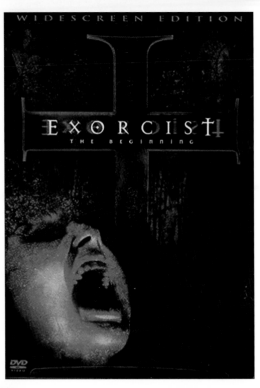

Filmmaker Renny Harlin reshot
Paul Schrader's *Dominion* and turned it
into *Exorcist: The Beginning*.
*Don Bigileone/Wikimedia Commons.*

William Friedkin at the 2012 Deauville American Film Festival. *Elen Nivrae/Wikimedia Commons.*

The author has been writing about both William Friedkin and *The Exorcist* since his 1990 biography of the Oscar-winning director, *Hurricane Billy: The Stormy Life and Films of William Friedkin.*

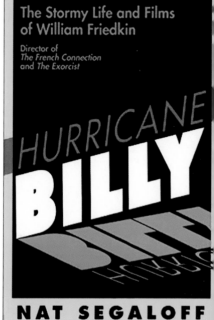

roducer Noel Marshall relaxes (?) with one
f the cats that he and his wife Tippi Hedren
ised on their California ranch. *Nancy Hardin.*

Writer-director David Gordon Green,
the filmmaker behind the new *Exorcist* trilogy,
at the 2018 San Diego Comic-Con.
*Gage Skidmore/Wikimedia Commons.*

riter-producer Jeremy Slater created and
as showrunner for *The Exorcist* TV series.
*Luigi Novi/Wikimedia Commons.*

Paperback edition book cover of *Legion* that William Peter Blatty hated.

Title page of *Legion* that Blatty signed to the author. He tore out the page before it.

- The Gemini Killer, whose father was named Karl, is not as random as he claims; his victims all have "K" somewhere in their names (Kintry, Kanavan, Keating, Nurse Bierce [?], and Father Joe Kevin Dyer). Of course, there's also Kinderman's daughter, Julie. *DC* and *EIII* use different takes of Miller and Dourif saying "Kevin."

- After Kinderman and the university president discuss the MacNeil exorcism of fifteen years earlier, *EIII* introduces Father Morning, none of whose scenes appear in *DC*.

- After Kinderman has an unfulfilling discussion with Dr. Temple in *EIII*, he exits cell eleven shaken. In *DC* we see that he is shaken because he recognized Damien Karras inside.

- The most significant differences between *DC* and *EIII* kick in when Kinderman learns from Patient X in cell eleven how he (the Gemini Killer) inhabited Karras's body, which took fifteen years to heal. Karras, though dead, escaped his coffin. Karras's coffin is exhumed in *DC*, and the body of an old priest, Father Fain, is discovered there. He likely died of a heart attack when the dead Karras rose up. No inference is made of the Resurrection.

- After his conversations with Patient X, Kinderman researches the Rite of Exorcism in *EIII* but not in *DC*. In *EIII* he also sees the Gemini Killer's file, which carries Dourif's photo.

- Scenes between Scott and Dourif that were reshot with Miller show them in the padded cell.

- In *DC*, Kinderman leaves Venamun's cell and phones university president Riley. In *EIII* the dialogue is dubbed so that he asks for Father Morning.

- While Nurse X is in Kinderman's house to kill Julie, Venamun, in *DC*, is passed out in his cell and shows brain-wave action. This is his way of controlling the mentally compromised patients to do his bidding. This is not in *EIII*.

- None of the long, bloody exorcism scene with Father Morning is in *DC*.

- As noted earlier, the final confrontations between Kinderman and the Gemini Killer differ. In *EIII*, Kinderman executes Venamun and asks Damien to pray for him. In *DC*, Damien begs to be killed, and Kinderman accedes.

It is to the credit of Morgan Creek and Shout! Factory that both versions of this film have been made available. Not only does it provide material for a debate about the different portrayals of good and evil, it allows inspection of the commercial filmmaking process. The satisfyingly detailed *Death Be Not Proud* special feature by Michael Felsher and Heather Buckley, in which many of the crew members who worked on *The Exorcist III* are interviewed, is refreshingly frank and tremendously helpful in untangling decades of rumors about this unusual and continually relevant film.

SIDEBAR

# Original Beginning and Ending of *The Exorcist III*

An additional opening was shot and edited but never used for the beginning of *Exorcist III*, showing Kinderman identifying the body of Father Damien Karras in the morgue with two technicians attending. Once Kinderman leaves, the men routinely use an ultraviolet light to check for any marks on the body that might indicate murder in addition to the defenestration. As they scan the body, the lights in the morgue flicker and a voltage meter shows slight movement. This reflects Blatty's interest in the Konstantin Raudive and Friedrich Jürgenson studies of patterns of sound heard in static noise, suggesting life after death.

The original ending in Blatty's script has Kinderman visiting Patient X in his cell after the attempt by Nurse X on the Kinderman family. Patient X quietly dies in front of him, but then lunges for Kinderman and begins choking him. While this is happening, Nurse Allerton enters the cell and makes no effort to save Kinderman. Suddenly Kinderman is no longer being choked—it was all in his imagination—and Allerton pronounces Venamun dead as of 12:10. Later Kinderman leans that Venamun's father also died at 12:10.

"The man who looks like Karras" is buried in the priests' cemetery. Afterward, Kinderman asks the university president why all this suffering is necessary.

"It could be there's no other way to make a man," the president responds, and says that, even under anesthesia in surgery, our unconscious feels the pain, yet when we wake up, it's gone. "So maybe when we go back to God, that's how it will be with all the pain in the world." This is a restatement of what Dyer told Kinderman over lunch.

SIDEBAR

## The Ninth Configuration

William Peter Blatty's fascination (obsession?) with the themes of sacrifice, God's existence, and transcendence did not start with *The Exorcist* in 1971. In 1966 he had written a novel called *Twinkle, Twinkle, "Killer" Kane* that placed his as-yet-unformed views in a darkly comedic setting. Reworked post-*Exorcist* in 1978 into *The Ninth Configuration*, the story concerns a Marine psychologist, Colonel Hudson Kane, who is sent to "Center 18," a secret military "rest camp" (aka asylum) for twenty-seven officers who have all succumbed to what appears to be mental illness. His mission is to determine whether they are faking it to shirk their military duties or if they truly are incapacitated.

Where such hijinks would understandably be an excuse to satirize the military during America's fervent antiwar era (e.g. *M\*A\*S\*H*), *The Ninth Configuration* is a meditation on God's gift of life and the act of sacrifice as a holy statement. But that isn't apparent going in. What Colonel Kane sees when he takes charge of Center 18 is a ragtag group of eccentrics, each of whom is, by permission of the Marines, indulging in his own path to a cure. With the consultation of his subordinate, Colonel Richard Fell, Kane is also seeking the reasons behind his disgraced brother Vincent's murderous war record. But his focus quickly becomes astronaut Billy Cutshaw, who aborted his mission on the launchpad because he didn't want to fly into the Godless void. Cutshaw and Kane engage in conversation about the existence of God and the notion of whether one person would actually give up his life to save another.

In the course of the story, it develops that Kane is also a patient, although he doesn't know it; in fact, Colonel Fell has been in charge all along. Hudson Kane is, in fact, the real "Killer" Kane whose wartime actions were so horrifying as to make him assume another identity. And yet he believes in redemption so strongly that he allows himself to die by slashing his own wrists to shock (persuade?) Cutshaw back to sanity.

Rather than use a murder mystery to convey his themes,

in *The Ninth Configuration* Blatty treads familiar territory: bizarre comedy. Not only are the characters' situations comedic in and of themselves, their flatly delivered lines underscore the peculiarity of their situation. The only humorless person in the piece is Kane, and whether this comes from his mental state or his religious convictions (Blatty walks a dangerously narrow line), he is the perfect foil for those around him.

*The Ninth Configuration* has a twisted history from novel to film. Budgeted at $4 million, the movie was contracted to be released by United Film Distribution, a company linked with United Artists Theatres (as distinct from the production company United Artists). UFD would only put up half the budget, so Blatty arranged with the Pepsi-Cola Company for the other half, not in cash, but as credit through the use of blocked funds that Pepsi had tied up in Hungary. This meant that the film had to be shot in Budapest, with script changes to explain why the US military had a secret asylum in a gothic castle.

A December 1979 release was planned, but at some point UFD fell out of love with the picture and Warner Bros. picked it up for a February 8, 1980, release. It fared so poorly that United Film Distribution reacquired it, retitled it *Twinkle, Twinkle, "Killer" Kane*, and relaunched it theatrically on August 8. One has to commend both companies for releasing a picture that defies genre categorization; alas, by neither title could the public be enticed to see it. Over the years the film has been released in no fewer than five different versions[1] between domestic, international, and home video. And yet, in whatever form, it consistently piques audience curiosity and has developed a following as quirky as its tone.

"*Twinkle, Twinkle, 'Killer' Kane* was published by Doubleday in 1966," Blatty said,[2] "and it was very short on construction and carpentry and it was more attuned to *Catch-22* than it is today. Over the years I kept deepening the meaning of the screenplay. *Twinkle, Twinkle, 'Killer' Kane* lacks the shock, the mystery, the thrills, and the depth of meaning that *The Ninth Configuration* has, in addition to the comedy. Well, that's not entirely true. In *Twinkle, Twinkle, 'Killer' Kane* I was having fun with language as Joe Heller did in *Catch-22*. It was stylistic humor rather than one-liners, and of course, when you take a serious approach to the novel, even when there's comedy in it, you just can't play those S. J. Perelman games with words." Perhaps the best description is one given by Jason Miller, who appears in the film version as a man interpreting the works of Shakespeare for dogs: "It's a Marx Brothers comedy as written by Saint Thomas Aquinas."

Even more than Father Karras's death in *The Exorcist*, the death of Hudson Kane in *The Ninth Configuration* argues for the sanctity of giving one's life for another. Blatty is adamant that *giving* one's life is different from *taking* one's own life—i.e., suicide.

How does giving one's life prove God's existence when that life is God's gift? "I worried about this while I was shooting it," Blatty reveals, "and I shot the film two ways. I had another ending, another possibility. However, you will note two things: Even in the film itself a careful distinction is made between two of the characters about suicide and giving up your life. Suicide is an act of despair, that's the essential difference. This is an act of love. I'll give you an example. You are on top of the Empire State Building in the tower with a lot of sightseers, lots of women, lots of children. A maniac breaks in with a Kalashnikov machine gun. He's never seen you before in his life, and he says, 'You! By the count of ten you jump out that window to your death or I'm gonna spray the room and kill everybody in it, all these women, all these children.' And assume that you jump out the window. Was this an act of despair or was it an act of love? And that's the distinction I make."[3]

Yet there are many kinds of sacrifice. Citing the case of Sir Thomas More, who suffered execution by King Henry VIII rather than endorse the king's separation from the Church of Rome (and wound up destroying Church influence in England), isn't the sacrifice of integrity far greater than the sacrifice of one's life?

"Of course it is," Blatty continued. "It is what I intended. The same point is made here. A loss of integrity? My God! A man gave his life for a stranger. He exemplified what he preached. It was a Christ-like action, and better to salvage his integrity than to preserve his life, surely. I'm seeing the good Lord looking down at Vincent Kane [Hudson Kane's real name] as he's taking his life and saying, 'Vincent, you didn't hafta do that, why did you do that, you shoulda left Cutshaw to me, right? But God love you for it, God love you for your intention and love.' That Kane has hope that Cutshaw will be cured by his act of sacrifice bears out his intentions."

Even though his film did not break commercial records, it has gone on over the years to inspire others by its message, which is not a treacly "God loves you" Hallmark card moral but a stimulating, intellectual challenge to consider the meaning *and obligations* of faith.

"I know that the film haunts people who have seen it," Blatty said, "even those who don't like it, for days if not weeks. I hadn't anticipated that; my only intention was to give hope, to oppose the problem of evil with a greater mystery: the mystery of goodness. Assuming there is no God, how do you explain the mysteries of goodness in man? It's a far greater mystery than assuming, 'How can there be a God when there is evil in the world and the suffering of the innocent?'"

*Twinkle, Twinkle, "Killer" Kane* and *The Ninth Configuration* are important tangents to the *Exorcist* canon—they encapsulate William Peter Blatty's ongoing efforts to create compelling stories that illustrate the moral tenets of religion and faith by providing concrete, relatable examples. They are less sermons than parables whose characters, while being complex enough to compel attention, are working out simplistic—or call them eloquent—themes. All this from a man who felt he could no longer get arrested writing comedy, so he decided to scare the hell *into* people.

## CHAPTER 11

# *Dominion: Prequel to The Exorcist* and *Exorcist: The Beginning*

In Hollywood's heyday, when each studio ground out fifty films a year, retakes and reshoots were part of the normal production process. At MGM, for example, it was said that films were not made, they were remade. Depending on how well or badly a sneak preview went—and sometimes while a picture was still being spun in the dream factory—production chief Irving Thalberg might order anywhere from one scene to a whole film back before the cameras to bring out the best of the script or to fix moments that didn't pay off.

Reshoots were feasible because everybody—actors, directors, writers, crew—was under contract and all it took was rearranging their schedules to call them back together. If a freelance director had moved on to another film across town, the studio would summon any available director from its stable to take over seamlessly. Charles Walters, for example, reshot part of *Gigi* (1958) when Vincente Minnelli's footage was deemed unusable; versatile MGM house director Richard Thorpe was often tapped to do reshoots; William Wellman quietly reshot parts of *Tarzan Escapes* (1936); and no fewer than six people shot and reshot and re-reshot David O. Selznick's 1946 *Duel in the Sun*—including Selznick himself—after King Vidor left in a huff (none of them got credit except Vidor). Twentieth Century-Fox studio chief Darryl F. Zanuck is said to have personally written and shot a new ending for *The Grapes of Wrath* (1940) with director John Ford's permission after Ford had moved on. These reports drive auteurists nuts, but they were standard operating procedure in Hollywood's heyday.

Now it's a different circus. Everybody is freelance, and so, after a film wraps, people scatter for other projects in other places, and reassembling them for reshoots is like herding cats. Yet this is what Morgan Creek Productions faced when they decided that Paul Schrader's version of *Dominion: Prequel to The Exorcist* (shot in 2002 but released on DVD on May 20, 2005) wasn't what they expected, so they shelved it and hired director Renny Harlin to create a 90 percent different film, *Exorcist: The Beginning*, released theatrically August 18, 2004.

Almost immediately William Peter Blatty sued Morgan Creek on grounds that he had not been paid for the non-release of *Dominion*. He wasn't objecting to the movies themselves. The suit revealed that he was to have been paid $930,000 for the first theatrically released film and $750,000 at the start of principal photography on the second (i.e., the reshoot).[1]

The money only underscores the bold decision for the independent company, remarkably because they had done the same thing fourteen years earlier with *Exorcist III* (after which, in 1996, they had settled with Blatty over unnamed issues). Only after Harlin's version was released did Morgan Creek give the go-ahead for Schrader to complete *Dominion*, albeit only on home video, to allow for a comparison.

Each work has much to commend it, but there is a significant difference between them: Paul Schrader made a *film* whereas Renny Harlin made a *movie*.

The chronology is noteworthy. Sometime in 1997[2] screenwriter William Wisher (*Terminator 2: Judgment Day*, *Judge Dredd*) got a call from his friend Bill Todman, Jr., then head of production at Morgan Creek Productions, with news that Morgan Creek had acquired the rights to *The Exorcist* and would Wisher want to pitch him a sequel? Reticent to even attempt following in the hoofprints of the original, Wisher had a better idea: a prequel. "It occurred to me," he realized while taking a shower before the Todman meeting, "there's one story left and, if you recall in both the first film and in Blatty's book, the reason they go get Father Merrin is that he'd performed an exorcism in Africa in the late forties. They don't say much more than that.[3] I said, okay, that's a big hole to fly a plane through. Then I thought, God, young Father Merrin, in Africa, post–World War II. And so I go out to dinner with Bill and said, 'Yeah, I gotta tell you something. I came up with an idea. I know I said no, but I think this might be a fun idea.' And he said, 'I love that.' I think that might actually be the time we did a deal memo on a cocktail napkin!" Wisher chuckles at the innocence with which his gambit began, then drops his voice to say, "This was one of the worst professional experiences I've had, and I've been doing this for about thirty-five years. It didn't start out that way but it turned into that."[4]

A subsequent meeting with Morgan Creek's James G. Robinson brought Wisher down to earth. "It's a horror film," Wisher recalls the executive insisting. "It has to be a horror film." Countered Wisher, "You know, Jim, *Exorcist* movies really aren't horror films. It's more disturbing than scary. It's really about, and Blatty's spoken about this quite a bit, the negative proof of the existence of God. In other words, if you can prove there's a devil then there has to be a God. It's really about how the priests, in the first film, and then the young Merrin that I wrote, how their faith is tested. How they lose their belief or their faith in God. And how the devil trying to destroy them ironically becomes the vessel to get their faith back."[5]

Robinson cut through the writer's song and dance, saying, "Just make sure it's scary."

Wisher turned in his first draft and Robinson pointed out the obvious: It wasn't scary enough. "So I made some changes, did a couple of drafts, and came up with some more disturbing stuff to throw in there like the two soldiers that are crucified upside down. Creepy stuff. It got better in his eyes but he had doubts on it." Wisher wrote two more drafts before stepping away.[6] William Peter Blatty reportedly read both versions and found them objectionable.[7]

Nevertheless, Morgan Creek gave Wisher's last draft to their chosen director, John Frankenheimer, in 2001.[8] Frankenheimer immediately brought in Caleb Carr to rewrite it.[9] He then hired Liam Neeson to play Merrin[10] and Billy Crawford as the possessed boy, Cheche.[11] For a time, Ryan Phillippe was considered for the role of Father Francis,[12] but the collar eventually went to Gabriel Mann.[13] There was even an unusual open call for an "African-American boy, ages 10–14" advertised in the *Hollywood Reporter.*[14]

On June 5, 2002, however, Frankenheimer announced that he was withdrawing from the project over "health concerns" and checked into Cedars-Sinai Hospital for surgery to relieve a chronic bad back.[15] While recovering, he announced that he was setting up a production company with Gary Sinese[16] Instead, on July 6, he suffered a massive post-operative stroke and died at the age of seventy-two.[17]

After Frankenheimer's departure, Paul Schrader was approached. It seemed a perfect fit. Schrader, whose ascetic Calvinist upbringing touched many of his projects with religious overtones (*The Last Temptation of Christ*, *Mishima*, *Taxi Driver*, *First Reformed*, etc.), found the subject matter challenging, if intimidating.

"I was raised in the bosom of the church and attended

church seminary on my way to becoming a priest," he told *Screen International*'s Jacob Neilendam. "Some of the issues in *The Exorcist* weighed heavy on me as a young man. No matter how fast you run, you don't outrun that. It is an area I still find interesting, so I believe I can bring something new to this dance."[18]

"The problem with the script as a horror film lay in the origins of its premise," Schrader later said in his DVD commentary. "The feeling, even before I became involved, was that you had to get away from the Friedkin *Exorcist* because it was such a classic. One of the ways to do that was to switch the possessed person from a girl to a boy but, even more importantly, to switch the very nature of the possession. So in this case the boy who is possessed is afflicted (Cheche, Billy Crawford). He's an outcast and, as the possession takes hold, he gets better and everyone else gets more and more insane."

The change was ingenuous (ignoring the fact that *The Exorcist* had switched an actual boy into a fictitious girl) but created another problem. Schrader: "When you have a young person getting better you have essentially taken the motor out of the horror vehicle because horror is based on an innocent tormented while the clock runs. Well, we didn't have an innocent tormented anymore, we had an innocent getting better, and try as you might through whatever gimmicks or sound effects or whatnot, that's not a very effective horror mechanism."[19]

By the time Schrader had regrouped the production and was set to roll, Liam Neeson was no longer available and so Stellan Skarsgård was engaged to play the young Lankester Merrin. By one of those coincidences that looks good in a press release, Skarsgård, like the previous Merrin, Max von Sydow, was Swedish. By then both Wisher and Carr were long gone. There is no indication how much of the shooting script Schrader, an acknowledged master, may himself have rewritten.

Forging ahead, the *Dominion* company shot exteriors for five weeks in late 2001 in Morocco, with sets and landscape built to represent, first, Kenya, then the Turkana area near the Ugandan border. As Christmas neared, Morgan Creek received word of unrest and pulled the company out of Morocco. By spring 2002 they were shooting interiors at the more hospitable Cinecittà studios in Rome.[20]

Schrader chose a formal visual approach, eschewing the sort of camera gyrations that had come to typify modern filmmaking, especially genre movies where, if the story doesn't move at every moment, the camera does. "The whole tradition of a well-crafted film has gone the way of other traditions," he said. "I wanted this to look like a forties film, yet hip enough not to feel stodgy." This would later become an issue.

Continuing William Peter Blatty's concept that *The Exorcist* is about the mystery of faith, Fathers Merrin and Francis have several conversations about lost faith, the nature of evil, and guilt. Scenes carry religious imagery, from an inverted crucifixion, a severed head (John the Baptist), and Father Francis being shot with arrows (St. Sebastian), to the artwork in the buried church reflecting not just the Fall but the torments of Hell. More challengingly, it is a highly subversive film in that Father Francis believes he has found a blessed child in Cheche, only to finally realize that he is about to pray to Satan's vessel. (How many televangelists walk that same path but keep going?)

In keeping with his feelings about tradition, Schrader used very little computer-generated imagery. There was some alteration of exteriors (e.g., prop people seen tossing Styrofoam rocks off the top of a crumbling building were removed digitally) and second unit shots of hyenas that were manipulated following several wasted hours discovering that real hyenas cannot be trained.

The design and the themes work well in unison, but the performances do not. Clara Bellar, playing Rachel Lesno, a fellow doctor, is simply not up to the task and gives Skarsgård little to play against, considering his textured performance later in the same role against Izabella Scorupco in *Beginning*.

*Dominion* is a contemplative film whose action is internal and psychological. By design, the manifestations of Satan are varied and subtle: the presence of hyenas, wind blowing, images of Captain Howdy (which unfortunately look like Jim Carrey in *The Mask*), creaking sounds, and so forth. But classicism, intellectualism, and biblical references do not a horror film make. *Dominion* was a disappointment for the Morgan Creek people when they saw Schrader's first cut, even though they were familiar with the script. What the film truly lacked, they felt, was the kind of Grand Guignol ending that audiences expect when they see the word *exorcist* in a film's title. The showdown between Merrin and Satan/Cheche becomes a two-hander in the cave beneath the church while, outside, northern lights illuminate a world gone insane. The final shot—after Merrin has exorcised Cheche and returned to the clinic and Dr. Lesno—shows Skarsgård walking out the door frame à la John Wayne at the end of *The Searchers*.

Morgan Creek stopped postproduction on *Dominion* before the musical score (by Angelo Badalamenti) and sound work were complete. They then made the unusual decision not to shelve and write off the production but to remove Schrader and practically start over from scratch.[21] To do this, they brought in a director more comfortable with action films, Renny Harlin, to conduct reshoots. Harlin looked at the footage, deemed it 90 percent unusable, and brought in

Alexi Hawley for a "production polish" of what Wisher and Carr had wrought.[22] An article in the *Village Voice* posited that it was Warner Bros., which was slated to release the film, rather than Morgan Creek, that "wrested it" from Schrader and handed it to Harlin.[23]

Harlin faced overwhelming odds when he accepted the challenge of reshooting Schrader's film. Schrader was a darling of the critics, an intellectual filmmaker whose credits as writer and/or director included *Taxi Driver*, *Hardcore*, and *Blue Collar*. Harlin was a highly accomplished action director, with *Cliffhanger*, *The Long Kiss Goodnight*, *Deep Blue Sea*, and *Die Hard 2* on his résumé. The two couldn't have been more different. It would be Harlin's job to make *Dominion* accessible to the public at large, and if that meant adding action and gore, that was his mandate. He was given six weeks for reshoots, but under hazy conditions: It was in Schrader's contract that only his name would appear as director, not Harlin's. "The DGA has a clear policy that there will be only one director assigned to a motion picture," said DGA spokesperson Morgan Rumpf.[24]

When the $40 million reshoot was released, Harlin had sole credit.

Schrader is unable to address certain matters because of a reported non-disparagement agreement with Morgan Creek.[25] Nevertheless, he told *The Times* (of London), "I always knew there would be blood on the floor, I just didn't know it would be all mine. But I never lost faith. What worried me about Renny's film is that it was going to be sort of good. In fact, I went to see it with William Blatty and the worse it got, the better I felt. He, conversely, just felt worse. By the end of the film he was cursing and yelling in the lobby. I was smiling, saying, 'Maybe the film has a chance after all.' The great battle now is to see if it can assume some sort of life."[26]

The release was not without incident. Linda Blair complained that footage of her from *The Exorcist* appeared in the trailer for *Beginning* and she wanted compensation. Warner Bros. responded with an offer of $279 ($93 times three, the SAG day player rate for reused footage). Morgan Creek's response was that her appearance in their film constituted "heritage."[27]

However gifted Harlin is as a filmmaker, it's impossible to ignore that he had Schrader's version as a guide in remaking *Dominion* into *Beginning*, even if only in the sense of knowing what *not* to do from Morgan Creek's point of view. Where Schrader and cinematographer Vittorio Storaro use basic eye-level camera setups through much of *Dominion*, Harlin, also collaborating with Storaro, employs a constantly moving camera and a wider color palette. Schrader, like Friedkin, lets the material sell itself with minimal cinematic interference; Harlin, on the other hand, employs so many camera moves to keep the viewer engaged that style quickly overwhelms substance. Where *The Exorcist* had perhaps one thousand cuts, Harlin points out in his DVD commentary that *Beginning* has three thousand, explaining that modern audiences have shorter attention spans and need to be kept visually engaged. His camera dive-bombs around the room like a housefly, constantly calling attention to itself. But that's how movies had changed in three decades. Bizarrely, it makes *Beginning* look more like a prequel to *The Heretic* than to *The Exorcist*.

"I went to a screening of it," Wisher, the original writer, recalled of the Harlin film, "and it was very strange. I didn't like it at all. It's way over the top. What the fuck are werewolves doing in it now? And I just thought I guess Renny was doing what he was told to do. He was a good soldier and he went off and made it. So they released it and it bombed."[28]

A year later, Wisher got a surprise call from Paul Schrader.

"He said, 'I think this is funny. We've made a movie together and we've never met.' He was unhappy that they shelved his movie and was able, with lawyers, to force Morgan Creek to release it on DVD. So it went from being *Exorcist: The Beginning*, which was my original title, to *Dominion*. I never heard of that happening before, where you shoot a movie, you shelve the movie, you rewrite the movie, you get a new director, same cast pretty much, and then reshoot the whole thing all over again. I think that might be a Trivial Pursuit question."[29]

An even larger question is: How many times can filmmakers go to the *Exorcist* well? It would be answered in subsequent years with a two-season television series and three feature films.

## Synopsis of *Dominion: Prequel to The Exorcist*

Nazi-occupied Holland in 1944 is the scene for a showdown in which an SS lieutenant orders the local priest, Father Lankester Merrin (Stellan Skarsgård), to either produce the name of the villager who has killed a German soldier or choose ten parishioners to be executed for the crime. Merrin, after offering himself as sacrifice, reluctantly names ten people in trade for the rest. The guilt makes him lose faith in a God who would allow such a thing to happen.

Three years later, Merrin, on sabbatical from the priesthood and now an archaeologist, is in Derati, a remote Turkana region in British-occupied Kenya, where an ancient church has been discovered buried in the sand. It was built and then buried years before Christianity arrived in this area. Young Father Francis (Gabriel Mann), a Maryknoll missionary, arrives there on a vague mission to witness the dig. Major Granville (Julian Wadham), the martinet British officer in charge; Chuma (Andrew French), a local translator; and Rachel Lesno (Clara Bellar), a doctor and Holocaust survivor, welcome him.

A tour of the excavated church reveals it to be in perfect condition, except it's not a church, it's a shrine to St. Michael and contains fabulous art chronicling the Fall of Satan. Merrin makes contact with a handicapped boy, Cheche (Billy Crawford), who has been outcast by the Turkana because of his physical afflictions.

Even after guards are posted on the sealed church site to prevent looting, two British soldiers enter and steal jewels. They are later discovered brutally executed inside its confines. Granville blames the locals, but the locals know that the guards were somehow compelled to kill each other. Then Jomo, a Turkana warrior, kills children who have come to Father Francis's school because he believes the Christianity they are being taught to be evil.

Cheche undergoes surgery to correct his twisted body and recovers so quickly that Father Francis believes he is blessed by God. In reality, Cheche is possessed by Satan. The stronger his possession takes hold, the more insane everyone around him becomes. Granville, overcome by guilt for his actions executing a local woman, takes his own life. Father Francis tries to baptize Cheche, but the latter is possessed and the next day Father Francis is found tied to a tree, pierced with arrows like St. Sebastian.

Moved by the death of Father Francis, Merrin suits up in his old priest's vestments and prepares to do battle with Cheche/Satan. He and Rachel go to a cavern beneath the church. Merrin dismisses Rachel and confronts Cheche/

Satan. Among his taunts, Cheche/Satan allows Merrin to go back in time to see if he could have stopped the SS officer from killing townspeople; this time Merrin shoots the Nazi but fails to change history.[1] Returning to the present, his guilt is resolved and he can bring his full faith to the exorcism.[2] Outside, bizarre Northern Lights illuminate the British and Turkan armies marching against each other. Rachel wanders, bleary-eyed, about to cut her own throat. The evil that the church buried has been unearthed.

Merrin exorcises Cheche, the boy returns to his original physical condition, Rachel regains her sanity, and so do the people in the surrounding land. The British soldiers leave Turkana, and Merrin heads to the Vatican.

SIDEBAR

## Synopsis of *Exorcist: The Beginning*

Fifteen hundred years ago in what will come to be called Kenya, an army has massacred itself. The sole survivor is a priest of the newly formed Catholic Church, who finds in the ruins a carved icon of a demon called Pazuzu.

In 1946, Father Lankester Merrin (Stellan Skarsgård), who has lost his faith as the result of having to make a Sophie's Choice in Holland during its Nazi occupation in World War II, is in Cairo, Egypt, on an archaeological dig. He is enticed by an antiquities dealer, Semelier (Ben Cross), to visit another dig in the Turkana region of Kenya to bring back a small demon statue (Pazuzu) before the occupying British forces discover and confiscate it. Merrin agrees and, on arrival, finds himself in the middle of intrigue between the British Major Granville (Julian Wadham), Vatican missionary Father Francis (James D'Arcy), the chief excavator Jeffries

(Alan Ford), and Dr. Sarah Novak (Izabella Scorupco), who is haunted by her wartime confinement in a concentration camp. His translator, Chuma (Andre French), is the only person who seems able to make sense out of anything.

The dig has uncovered a church that was built and buried fifteen hundred years before Christianity arrived in this region. Strangely, it is not so much a place for worship as a shrine to St. Michael, and yet it has somehow been desecrated. Moreover, local workers keep quitting the dig believing that the area around it is haunted.

Searching for answers, Merrin visits Monsieur Bession (Patrick O'Kane), the previous archaeologist who explored the church, who has been institutionalized. Rather than speak with Merrin, Bession slashes his own throat. Father Gionetti, who runs the asylum, opines that Bession has been "touched" by a demon and hands Merrin a copy of the Roman Ritual of exorcism.

Unusual events swirl around the dig when Merrin returns. A boy is torn apart by hyenas; his younger brother, Joseph (Remy Sweeney), falls into a trance-like state; and the tribal chief's wife gives birth to a maggot-covered stillborn fetus. Merrin discovers a passageway to a structure below the church that was used for human sacrifice. He confronts Father Francis, who reveals that he is not a missionary but was sent by the Vatican to investigate why a church this old was kept secret, why a team of priests and tribesmen who looked into it fifty years ago all died and were buried nearby, and why the matter has been covered up. When Merrin presses Francis, the young priest reveals that the Vatican believes that this valley was where Lucifer fell after the war in Heaven.

History begins repeating itself as the British contingent and the Turkana tribesmen gird for war against each other. Believing Joseph to be possessed, Father Francis takes him

to the temple under the church to exorcise him. Suddenly
Francis is killed by Sarah, who is the actual possessed person
(it turns out that she was married to Monsieur Bession and
entered the temple with him, thus becoming contaminated).
Now believing in the existence of a personified devil, and
realizing that if there is a devil there must be a God, Father
Merrin summons all his dormant faith to do battle with
Satan in the form of Sarah. After a struggle, he forces Satan
from Sarah's body, saving both her and Joseph. As Merrin
and Joseph emerge from the temple, they discover that the
soldiers and tribesmen have killed one another just as it happened fifteen hundred years ago.[1]

Merrin meets Semelier in Rome and lies that he could not
find the Pazuzu statue. He then dons his hat, takes his black
bag, and heads off for a job in the Vatican dressed as he will
look in twenty-five years when he shows up at the MacNeil
house in Washington, D.C.

## CHAPTER 12

# The TV Series

Network television development and demonic possession have a lot in common. Both involve dedicated antagonists, ancient rivalries, dogmatic beliefs, and long-established rituals, all in passionate conflict for the souls of viewers. The two-season, twenty-episode *Exorcist* series that ran on Fox between September 23, 2016, and December 15, 2017, is a perfect example of everybody being on the same page, except on different sides.

The *Exorcist* franchise had languished since the disappointing 2004 theatrical release of *Exorcist: The Beginning*. Morgan Creek and Fox Network's decision to resurrect it as a television series was a move to keep the flame burning, but it had the misfortune to come along at the exact moment when viewer habits were transitioning from weekly "must see" appointment TV to binge-watching on an emerging number of streaming services.

Jeremy Slater is the writer/show runner who unlocked the key to creating a story that both harkened back to and extended the Blatty original. Emerging as a writer with the screenplays for *The Lazarus Effect* and *The Fantastic Four* (both 2015), *Pet* (2016), and *Death Note* (2017), he also developed *The Umbrella Academy* (2019, about which more later). This focus on horror and superheroes made him a brand name in the genres that Hollywood deemed most commercial. And yet the series *The Exorcist* was not a slam dunk.

"It was a nightmare," says Slater, who had a general

development deal with Morgan Creek when they approached him to put together a series. They had just tried to develop a sequel (as they would do several years down the line) but, at the time, thought a series had a better chance. Slater was not impressed. "My take was a very strong, very emphatic 'You can't retell the same story. You're never gonna do it better, you're only gonna do it longer, and people are always gonna compare it to those original performances, the original set pieces. You're setting yourself up to fail.' I begged them, 'Let's not tell the same story in a kind of sanitized, drawn-out fashion. Let's continue the legacy of *The Exorcist*. Let's see what an exorcist looks like in modern-day America.' They were really excited about that."

Unfortunately, they were alone in their excitement. Slater and Morgan Creek took it everywhere in town, but only Fox shared their enthusiasm, and not necessarily because their viewers favored occult shows, but because corporate Fox wanted to increase their visibility on the cable spectrum. Buoyed by the network's commitment, Slater sought and received Blatty's blessing.[1]

The story broke on the trade news website *Deadline Hollywood Daily*, and that's when the monkey wrench arrived in the form of a call from Warner Bros. "They're saying Bill Blatty signed some kind of contract with them that gives them right of first refusal," Slater reports being told by Morgan Creek. "It was a contract that Blatty didn't remember signing because it was thirty years ago and it wasn't important to him at the time.[2] It was just some document, so he thought we were in the clear, he told Morgan Creek they were in the clear. It was one of those things where no one had double-checked to make sure that we actually had 100 percent of the rights. Warner Bros. came in and said, 'You can't do it at Fox, you can only do it with us.' I had one meeting with Warner Bros. where I pitched, 'Here's the show that Fox wants to buy and I'm fine doing it with you guys instead.' They were like, 'No, no, no, we have no interest in that show; we're going to develop our own thing; we're gonna do our own *Exorcist* TV show.'"

When Warner Bros. failed to develop their own iteration, they gave up the show but exacted unspecified royalties for every episode that was produced. It took so long to settle that by the time Slater got the green light, pilot season had passed and he had to race to get his series on the air. "There were big benefits but huge drawbacks at the same time because it was so rushed," Slater says. "That's why we didn't have a clear-cut view of our two main priests. What are their ages? What are their ethnicities? What are their backstories? We were laying down tracks in front of the speeding railroad as fast as we could and hoping we wouldn't hit a bridge or a ravine."

The first season was a stealth sequel to *The Exorcist*, stealth in that what appears to be the routine possession of a teenage girl in a nice upscale suburban family is actually a case of demonic revenge. Angela Rance (Geena Davis) has an almost perfect life in her Chicago suburb. Although her husband (Alan Ruck) suffered a traumatic head injury some time ago, her two daughters, Casey (Hannah Kasulka) and Kat (Brianna Howley), are normal teens. This changes when Casey becomes possessed and Angela, surprisingly aware of the symptoms, heads to her priest, the dynamic young Father Tomas Ortega (Alfonso Herrera), seeking an exorcism. Tomas recognizes the symptoms but is refused Church permission to perform one. When an experienced but flawed exorcist, Father Marcus Keane (Ben Daniels), shows up, the ritual begins, set against a parallel story of the demonic infiltration of the Vatican by a cabal of high-placed clergy and conservative business interests. At mid-point it is revealed that Angela Rance is the now-grown

Regan MacNeil, who was possessed when she was twelve years old and sees her daughter's possession as the demon's revenge. The stakes are raised when Chris MacNeil (Sharon Gless) arrives to apologize to Angela/Regan for exploiting her possession in order to boost her acting career.

"One of my big things going in was that I knew the Geena Davis twist all along; that she was going to be presented as Angela Rance and then, midway through the season, oh, my God, this is Regan MacNeil. But I never told anyone that except for Rolin Jones, who was my partner and our show runner for the first season, obviously, and we told Geena when I talked to her. It was a secret I even kept from Fox until they got the script just because I wasn't 100 percent sure creatively that it would work. We knew we had to keep the studio and the network out of the loop because the second we dropped that bread crumb in front of them, it would've gotten bumped up, it would've been shoved into the pilot episode. They wouldn't have wanted to wait for it."

There was some fudging when the writers avoided explaining why Angela knew so quickly that the scratchings in the Rance walls were signs of ensuing possession, and why she fought so valiantly to skip the part where Casey visits a succession of shrinks, to go straight for the Roman Ritual. She knows from personal experience but she can't tell anyone.

These plot enhancements allowed the writers (fifteen of them including Slater, David Grimm, Alyssa Clark, and Yasemin Yilmaz) to expand the original two-hour movie into ten forty-two-minute episodes per season. But the series also forced them to adhere to traditional television formatting. This played havoc with the overall dramatic needs.

"The season was designed to be a slow burn," Slater explains. "We needed time to get all the pieces in place. I think if we had been a Netflix show nobody would have batted an eye, but I think the fact that we were buried on a Friday night on Fox, people just forgot to keep tuning in, so once Fox saw the numbers drop off, the tune changed from 'Let's go make a movie' to 'Well, maybe this needs to be a little more of a TV show.' As a result, tricks such as a rumbling musical bed were added under softly spoken dialogue scenes to generate unease, eerie music cues telegraphed an approaching shock, and moments of violence almost always occurred before a commercial. You saw a focus on 'We gotta have big cliffhangers' and 'We gotta have shocking moments' to keep you coming back," Slater says. "Part of it was Fox pushing for that and part of it was [that] this was my first time doing anything in television so I hit the ground running and had a thousand things to learn and a thousand mistakes to make. One of the things it took me a couple weeks to realize is that horror themes only work if you can build that tension and that fear in the preceding scenes. If you can get the audience in a state of anxiousness or get their nerves jangling, and then hit them with a scary scene, it's so much more effective than having a scary scene come out of nowhere."

The network was uneasy with long-form storytelling. "Look, this isn't the network TV version of *The Exorcist* where you have a pair of sexy priests drive around the country in a Camaro and do the possession of the week," Slater told Fox. "It isn't like 'Oh, we're gonna roll into a carnival town and have an exorcism here, and next week we'll go to a Louisiana creepy gothic mansion and have an exorcism there. It just didn't work. Between the premiere and third episode, viewership dropped off by 80 percent."

Form was one issue, but the producers had both hooves tied behind their back when it came to language. The kind of soul-searing vulgarity that Friedkin had Blatty put in their demon's mouth was fine for premium cable and streaming, but it was prohibited by FCC rules guiding American broadcast content.[3] Denied the freedom to cauterize the audience with words, the producers fell back on television's traditional vocabulary—violence. Says Slater, "We had to sit there and say, 'Can we still make something that's disturbing and psychologically gripping without the crutch of profanity,' which is one of the most effective tools in Blatty and Friedkin's tool kit? The stuff that comes out of that kid's mouth is horrifying. The way I ultimately justified it to myself was saying, 'Look, every demon can have a different personality or manifest itself in slightly different ways. Swearing was a bigger deal back in the sixties and seventies when you couldn't even say *damn* or *hell* on network TV, and if you look at what's permissible or allowed now, swearing has become much more commonplace and it doesn't have quite the same statement. It was one of those compromises we knew we'd have to make from the beginning. We're losing a valuable piece of *The Exorcist* by not being able to do the R-rated, explicit version. Is that something we can live with? And ultimately the choice came down to do it at Fox or don't do it at all, and we chose to do it at Fox. But every second of that show was an ongoing battle of, How explicit can we get? What can we imply? What can we show? There were a lot of battles that we won and a lot of battles that we lost. The show aired during the death rattle of network TV; I think if you look now, there's nothing airing on network TV that has any kind of cultural cache or anything like that. Everything is on Netflix or HBO Max or Disney+. So we had bad timing; I think if the show had come out a few years later there would have been a dozen different streaming homes for it and all the content warnings would have evaporated. It was maybe two or three years ahead of the curve, which ultimately kind of doomed us."

Season One ended so poorly that its cancelation seemed

a forgone conclusion, yet Fox held off making a renewal decision. Slater, hearing nothing, sold *The Umbrella Academy* to Netflix and began running that show. But then every one of the pilots that Fox green-lighted failed to sell and they called Slater with an order for Season Two. With a short time to lasso writers and other creatives into place to get another ten episodes together, Slater reluctantly turned over *The Umbrella Academy* to others and concentrated on *The Exorcist*.

"It was frustrating," he says, "having to give up a dream job where they were going to give you $100 million to go make ten episodes of TV knowing it was going to be big and crazy and seen by a lot of people, and go back to a network where, 'Oh yeah, your marketing budget for season two is zero dollars.' We knew we were being set up to fail, so we figured, Why not take some risks? Why not change the formula? There is no way we're going to limp to a third season, so let's find a way to do something we find interesting and we find compelling. At the same time, Fox's mentality was the exact opposite of that. Their idea was that season one didn't work because it wasn't 'network' enough, so let's make Season Two network and maybe it will run for ten years. I'm really proud of what we did, but I really think the second season is compromised in a way the first season wasn't."

Season Two introduced a wider range of characters and advanced the subplot of Vatican infiltration. The concept of "integration" was introduced; that is, an irreversible possession where the soul of the victim is indissolubly merged with that of a demon. Adding integration to the canon was akin to Anne Rice or Stephenie Meyer expanding Bram Stoker's original rules of vampirism. In Season Two, a foster father (John Cho) and his social worker friend (Li Jun Li) must fend off a demonic threat to their home full of foster children. Priests Father Tomas and by-now-excommunicated Father Marcus deal with Cho's possession on an island off Seattle, Washington, that has a history of unreported possessions. The series ends with Tomas and Marcus splitting up after a snit just in case Fox wanted to get them back together by triggering a third season. It didn't happen.[4]

"When we were canceled at the end of Season Two I kind of breathed a sigh of relief," Slater says. "I was sad for my friends, and I was sad for Ben and Alfonso, but there was a sense that I was beaten and defeated. It was my first Hail Mary to keep my friends from losing their jobs."

What critics and audiences failed to notice in their eagerness to find flaws in the *Exorcist* lore was that the series was exquisitely produced, well cast, and well acted, with an admirable consistency of tone and seriousness (given that the whole premise demanded a leap of faith, so to speak). A television demimonde caught between the death of network and the birth of streaming, it was sent into the arena with everybody pulling for it, but in different directions.

## Synopsis of the TV Series

*NOTE: A detailed synopsis of a fourteen-hour story would be confusing, but condensed to the broad strokes, the series is about a worldwide scheme by the demon Pazuzu to subvert the Catholic Church and make every human his servant.*

### Season One

Father Tomas Ortega (Alfonso Herrera), an up-and-coming priest in the Chicago archdiocese of the Catholic Church, is haunted by dreams in which he sees another priest, Father

Marcus Keane (Ben Daniels), failing to exorcise a young boy in the slums of Mexico City. At the same time, one of Tomas's parishioners, Angela Rance (Geena Davis), tells him that there are strange sounds coming from the walls of her town house and she suspects a demon. Her younger daughter, Casey (Hannah Katsulka), hears them, too, while her older daughter, Katherine (Brianne Howey), is merely a recluse in her bedroom following what we later learn was a vehicular homicide. Henry Rance, the father (Alan Ruck), an architect, lives debilitated with a brain injury he suffered when scaffolding collapsed on a job.

Tomas's skepticism is erased when he visits the Rance home and has an otherworldly encounter with young Casey in the darkened attic. Henry leads Tomas to Father Marcus, who warns him that he is already in over his head, but follows him to Chicago. Tomas may be a comer, but he is not without sin; he has a lingering relationship with a pre-vow woman friend, Jessica (Mouzam Makkar), that temps his celibacy.

Casey's possession increases as she is befriended by a mysterious "salesman" (Robert Emmet Lunney), who accords her the power to hurt others. As her condition worsens, Angela takes her to a succession of doctors, until Casey's assault on a subway letch causes her to be involuntarily hospitalized for observation. During this ordeal, Tomas and Angela grow closer and he becomes convinced that Casey needs an exorcism. Marcus agrees but warns Tomas that he is not an experienced co-exorcist.

The Church, however, forbids an exorcism, and soon Father Bennett (Kurt Egyiawan), who is responsible for security during an upcoming visit by Pope Sebastian, delivers news to Marcus of his excommunication. Meanwhile, a group of church and business leaders, led by philanthropist

Maria Walters (Kirsten Fitzgerald), make Pope visit plans. Maria also gives Tomas's church a $100,000 donation.

Freeing Casey from the hospital, Marcus and Tomas begin her exorcism. Casey persuades Kathleen that she is being abused rather than cured, and Kathleen calls the police, who take the girl away. En route to custody, Casey causes the emergency ambulance to crash and contort, killing its two EMTs. At the height of the Rance family dysfunction, a woman shows up at the door. She is Chris MacNeil. Moreover, Angela is her grown-up daughter, Regan, who long ago changed her name to escape the publicity of her childhood exorcism.

It emerges that the Pope's welcoming committee are actually devil worshipers bent on assassinating the pontiff and bringing about the return of the earth to demons. Their goal is "integration," that is, a possession that is so complete an absorption of the soul by a demon that exorcism is impossible. (Integration was invented for the series.)

Chris tries to make rapprochement with Angela/Regan, who detests her for a lifetime of lies. The Rance family begins to dissolve under the pressure and public scrutiny brought by Chris's presence.

Father Marcus enlists the aid of a convent of nuns whose Mother Bernadette (Deanna Dunagan) uses forgiveness rather than the Roman Ritual to exorcise people. This is becoming more necessary as a series of ritual murders in Chicago involving the harvesting of organs point toward an apocalypse.

Marcus and Tomas bring Casey to the convent to continue Casey's exorcism. It looks hopeless, and Mother Bernadette suggests poisoning the girl to save her soul. The Salesman, visible only to Casey, begins to take her soul.

Angela, recognizing the agony, grasps her daughter and tells the demon to take her instead, which he does.

Angela/Regan, now repossessed and claiming to be Pazuzu, kills Chris, Mother Bernadette, several other nuns, and insinuates herself on the cabal preparing to kill the Pope. Fathers Bennett and Marcus, now held prisoner, are offered a choice of integration or death. Before they need decide, the group exits to meet the Pope, leaving Maria behind.

In short order Tomas exorcises Angela, Marcus foils the Pope's murder, Casey is saved and re-bonds with Katherine, and most of the integrated Satanists, including the cardinal, survive.

## Season Two

Season Two is able to free itself from obeisance to Blatty's story even as his seminal work is noted as having inspired it. As a result, it is more sure-footed and complex, laying down moments designed to blossom in subsequent seasons. Richer characters are introduced, a far more diverse cast appears, there is a greater range of effects, and the thesis of a world-wide possession conspiracy is advanced involving the Vatican. There are four intertwined stories, three of which merge by the season's end:

1. Andrew Kim (John Cho) runs a foster home for challenged young people on an island in Washington State that has known the presence of a demon for years. Kim becomes gradually possessed. Social worker Rose Cooper (Li Jun Li) monitors the kids, who include Caleb (Hunter Dillon), Truck (Cyrus Arnold), Verity (Brianna Hildebrand), Grace (Amélie Eva), and Shelby (Alex Barima).

2.  In Seattle, the exorcists visit a mother, Lorraine Graham (Rochelle Greenwood), whose daughter, Harper (Beatrice Kitsos), is possessed.

3.  A mysterious woman (later mouse [Zuleikha Robinson]) kills Cardinal Guilott (Torrey Hanson) and his fellow integrated friends, waging a personal campaign against demons that began years ago when she was close—perhaps too close—to Father Marcus (Ben Daniels).

4.  A fourth plotline has Father Tomas (Alfonso Herrera) and ex-Father Marcus in Montana trying to flush the demon from Cindy (Elizabeth Allen), a young mother who has lost her baby, while the townspeople (villagers?) beat them and "rescue" her. Tomas has already had a dream in which Cindy cradles her "miracle" baby while other children smash a piñata which leaks oil. He also, while exorcising Cindy, allows the demon to see inside his mind. This plotline practically disappears until the very end of Episode 10 of the season, but even that isn't assured.

As with Season One, there are tangents about previous island murders caused by the demon, some clever throwbacks to *The Exorcist III*, a blink of homosexuality, an ongoing theme of children placed in jeopardy, and reminders about a demonic conspiracy that has reached inside the Vatican.

The spine of the series is the gradual possession of Andy Kim, a caring man whose wife, Nikki (Alicia Witt), drowned herself years earlier and left him emotionally vulnerable. Not only is his foster child, the innocent-looking Grace, a figment of his mind (she is his Captain Howdy), she changes to dead Nikki when it comes time to kill his children. Marcus and Tomas spend a great deal of effort trying to exorcise the demon from Andy, who struggles to keep hold of his soul yet drifts off into flashbacks throughout the ritual.

In the end, Marcus forsakes being an exorcist to join a fishing boat, but it is clear that Tomas will return to fetch him and link with the first episode.

## CHAPTER 13

# The New Trilogy

Given that his trepidation about agreeing to *Exorcist II: The Heretic* was soothed by what he called "a dizzying amount of money," it's fair to ask what William Peter Blatty, if he were alive, might think not only of the *Exorcist* TV series but a trilogy whose first entry was poised for release to mark the original film's fiftieth anniversary.

On July 26, 2021, it was announced that Universal Pictures and NBCUniversal's streaming service, Peacock, in partnership with Morgan Creek and Blumhouse, would spend $400 million on a new *Exorcist* franchise. To be directed by David Gordon Green, the films would feature Ellen Burstyn recreating her role as Chris MacNeil opposite Leslie Odom, Jr., as a father who solicits her help to rid his child of a demon. Green would direct from a story by Scott Teems and a screenplay by Peter Sattler. Danny McBride (who also wrote) would executive produce, as would Green, Blumhouse's Jason Blum, Morgan Creek's David and James G. Robinson, Couper Samuelson, and Christopher H. Warner. Ryan Turek is listed as producer. All of the production executives have a rich history in horror films.[1]

But Blatty had already written a trilogy, says his friend and collaborator Mark Kermode. "He and I had always talked about the Trilogy of Faith being *Exorcist*, *Ninth Configuration*, and *Legion*," reports Kermode, who cautiously adds, "But as you know, Bill could change his mind from one day to the next, like anybody else, and that was his right." Blatty always considered *The Heretic* and the TV series as business decisions (mindful that he had planned his own earlier TV series).

Such choices became moot when the rights were sold to Morgan Creek, a decision which led to *The Exorcist III*, *Dominion*, *Beginning*, and the TV series.

*The Exorcist* planned to hit theaters on October 13, 2023 (a Friday), and would thereafter be streamed, as would its two sequels, on Peacock.

The moment the film was announced, a cloak of secrecy descended on the enterprise. Nothing beyond an enthusiastic press release gave insight into the filmmakers' plans:

> "There's no better time to be joining forces with the team at Peacock, reuniting with the great team at Universal and finally getting to work with my friends at Blumhouse, than on this classic franchise," Morgan Creek president David Robinson said in a statement Monday. "David Gordon Green, Danny McBride, Scott Teems and Peter Sattler have put together a compelling continuation of this iconic tale and I can't wait to bring this to fans around the world."

> "Blumhouse has always experienced incredible partnership from the team at Universal, and I'm grateful to Donna Langley and Jimmy Horowitz for believing in the vision of David's film and having the foresight to be flexible with distribution, so the team feels top notch support through the lifeline of the film. They're committed to theatrical exhibition and will also serve streaming viewers well by bringing an exciting franchise like *The Exorcist* to Peacock too," Blumhouse founder and CEO Jason Blum said. "I'm grateful to be working with David Robinson and the great team at Morgan Creek on this iconic franchise."

Even Ellen Burstyn, whose participation legitimized the remake, was cautiously spare with details. "I have shot one and I have not committed to the other two," she said after the first one wrapped, "because I want to see what kind of event this becomes. When Warner Bros. made *Exorcist II* they offered me a whole lot of money to do it and I said no, I'm not going to do a ripoff of *The Exorcist*. So all of the various iterations of that I've said no to. When this one came up, again, I was offered a whole bunch of money. I met the director-producer, David Gordon Green, and I liked him very much, I liked what he said, and he was very accommodating and so forth. I said I'm not inclined to want to do that. He said, 'Let me write something and I'll see if you like it.' I read it and I said no. It was more money that I ever would have earned on any movie in my lifetime. And I said no. And they surprised me and doubled the offer."

But Burstyn, who is co-president of the Actors Studio with Al Pacino and Alec Baldwin, had something else in mind. "I said, Okay, I need to think about this. It's too much money to say no that fast. So I hung up the phone and I just sat where I was and the first thought that came to my mind was 'I feel the devil is asking me my price.' And the second thought that came was 'My price is a scholarship program to the Actors Studio Master's Degree Program at Pace University.'"

Founded in 1947 by Elia Kazan, Cheryl Crawford, and Robert Lewis, the Actors Studio was designed as a safe place where theater artists could gather and explore new and deeper connections to the work. Entry is tough, but membership is for life, as is the emotional support provided by the fellow actors. It is not an overstatement to say that the people who emerged from the Actors Studio changed American acting. They included Marlon Brando, Paul Newman, Julie Harris, Geraldine Page, Lee J. Cobb, Bradley Cooper, and Marilyn

Monroe among many others, including those who did not become stars but always remained actors.

"It's something I had always wanted," Burstyn continues. "We have a wonderful program but we don't have a scholarship fund. Yale does, and a lot of other schools do. It's something I wanted, and when that came up as the second thought, I said okay. And I was back in. Then we played the up-the-ante game for a while until I finally got lots and lots and lots of benefits.

"So I shot that and I am Chris MacNeil and that's all I'm at liberty to say. I have not agreed to the other two and wouldn't negotiate for them, wouldn't say I would do them. I will do this one and then we'll see. I'm gonna wait till it's out before I know whether or not I want to continue in this way."

Filmmaker David Gordon Green had a lot on his shoulders and soul as he began work on the new trilogy. Celebrated for his canny reboot of the *Halloween* franchise, he had already produced and/or directed dozens of genre TV episodes and films before setting his sights (and his nerve) on *The Exorcist*.

Because he was still in production when this interview was conducted by correspondence in late April 2022 he, like Ellen Burstyn, was chary with information. This is being written more than a year before the film appears, but this early interview offers a highly personal insight into a man who has put his career and his soul on the line. To ensure accuracy, Green's remarks are being presented in a Q&A format exactly as he provided them.

**DAVID GORDON GREEN:** Any hesitation I have about interviews at this point is because we've only shot a small portion of the film and each production process I have always assumes a significant evolution in the characters and narrative as we rehearse and find locations and discover new ideas.

I'd hate to be presumptuous about the outcome of the film at such an early stage.

*How did you become involved in this project? Did Morgan Creek and Blumhouse come to you? Was it always a trilogy? Did they send around word that they were open to pitches? Or did you bring them the idea of a new trilogy out of the blue?*

I'd been working with Blumhouse on projects for several years and they had been discussing the *Exorcist* property with Morgan Creek. I live in Charleston, South Carolina, and David Robinson from Morgan Creek moved to town, and we became friendly and started discussing possibilities of what could be done in respect to the original film in a similar fashion to what I had done with the *Halloween* franchise reboot. It was three groups of creatives with a similar passion and vision for the material. It seemed like a great fit.

*How much of the existing* Exorcist *canon do you feel obligated to reference?*

I watched the first two episodes of the TV series. I spoke with Rupert Wyatt[2] to ask him about his mindset of following in the footsteps of a masterpiece. He had a good sense of humor about it. I'm approaching our film as an offshoot of the original film and don't feel any creative obligation to any of the others. That being said, I've seen the other features and I don't think that there's anything we're planning to do that betrays any of their content. On the *Halloween* series, I made a conscious decision to clean house of the mythology after the first film, and we're not doing that with this title.

*How do you meet or exceed the expectations of audiences who have seen other* Exorcist *films over the last fifty years while putting your own talents and touches onto tis trilogy?*

It's a very daunting endeavor. That bar is obviously high. My ambition is not to replicate the fingerprint that Friedkin brilliantly established. I have a different process. But my writing partner and I have done a tremendous amount of research in efforts to make a film that captures the drama of these events and I've assembled a creative team. I'm excited about exploring these ideas on camera.

*The original film had no CGI and it was the apparent reality of the effects that enhanced the viewing experience. Today's audiences expect CGI. How do you plan to overcome this cynicism?*

So far we don't have any significant set pieces that rely on CGI. That being said, according to Ellen, the original film shot for over two hundred days and we'll probably do ours in about fifty days, so I'm sure economics and efficiency will be considered.

*What was your first encounter with the original* Exorcist *in that you were negative two years old when it came out?*

The first time I saw the film was as a freshman at the University of Texas. I watched it on VHS cassette in a library: I was in a small cubicle, wearing headphones. In some ways the compromised presentation proved the power of the film to me.

*I'd love to know how you worked with Ellen Burstyn. How did you persuade her to recreate her original role?*

I approached Ellen before we started writing the script. She was intrigued by the concept. I would reach out to her for thoughts and inspiration over the year or so that it took to write the screenplay. We would recommend books to one another. I'd tell her she should read *The Infinite View* by Ellen Tadd and she'd tell me to read *Karloona* by Gontran de Poncins. Eventually we developed a friendship and creative trust of each other. We also make each other laugh and challenge one another. It's what I look for in a performance partnership. Sometimes we'll have intense discussions about what happened to Chris MacNeil after the events in Georgetown, and other times we'll just drink tea and observe the baby pigeons as they nest on her balcony in New York City.

*Some people call* The Exorcist *a horror film. Billy Friedkin and Bill Blatty always called it a film about the mystery of faith. What do you call it? What do you call yours?*

I've always thought of *The Exorcist* as an incredible drama. The mystery of faith is what draws us in and lets the audience ask questions of themselves. I'm not sure exactly what our film will be yet, but I'm hoping to explore the story of families that are struggling with events of the unknown. We're constructing our approach outside of the horror genre. But I do think some valuable techniques of horror films help make these films unnerving and entertaining.

*Do the pitfalls and successes of any of the previous* Exorcist *films and their recuts inform your creation of these three?*

I'm trying more and more to not be disparaging about other filmmakers and their ambitions. We all face so many obstacles on a daily basis. And if you consider budgetary constraints and often creative intervention, sometimes the noble intentions can get confused or lost entirely. I think that *Exorcist II* and *III* have some incredible moments of filmmaking that would probably be appreciated more if they were exhibited outside of this particular franchise.

*Do you believe in religion? Possession? Demons?*

I am very open to all of these concepts. I operate spiritually outside of organized religion, but take great meaning from many of them.

*Please tell me about Scott Teems and Peter Sattler. How did you choose to work with them, and what did they bring to the project?*

Scott Teems and Pete Sattler and Danny McBride have been close friends and collaborators of mine for many years. And as fans of the original film and writer/directors in our own right, we all broke the story together. I knew that we all have different religious backgrounds and beliefs and ideas about parenthood. Yet we have great respect for each other and an intense work ethic. (Alongside our *Exorcist* efforts, Danny and I work on an HBO comedy series that has strong religious themes, so it's a fun parallel exploration.) After we had an outline I was excited about, Pete and I dug in to do the research and write the script.

## CHAPTER 14

# Billy Goes to Hell:
## *The Devil and Father Amorth*

In 2017, William Friedkin returned to his documentary roots with *The Devil and Father Amorth*. He was eighty-two. After directing the theatrical film *Killer Joe* to acclaim in 2011, he had ceased to be interested in Hollywood (or perhaps it was the other way around) and moved into directing grand opera. Despite admitting he knew little of the art form, in 2015 he staged *Aida* in Turin and *Rigoletto* in Florence with success before discerning Italian audiences. He also directed opera in Germany and Los Angeles to similar praise.

In April 2016, he had gone to Italy to receive the Puccini Prize when, through a friend, he arranged a visit with a man of whom he had heard, and who had also heard of him: Father Gabriele Amorth. Just about to turn ninety-one, Amorth was known as the Vatican exorcist. Born in Modena, Italy, in 1925, ordained in 1954, and appointed to his post in 1986, the Paulist priest was a fan of *The Exorcist*. "The special effects were a little over the top," Friedkin said, quoting Amorth's letter to him, "but it helped people to understand his work." In return, Friedkin wrote to Amorth asking if he could meet him. The priest immediately agreed.

It was the capping of a long emotional and spiritual journey for Friedkin, who wrote, in an article about his experiences with Amorth, "I am an agnostic. I believe the power of God and the human soul are unknowable."[1] And yet the more he read about and spoke with Gabrielle Amorth, the more he

248

became interested in seeing, for real, what he had imagined so graphically on film in 1973. While in Italy, through the graces of translator/assistant Francesco Zippel, he was at last introduced to the elderly priest.

"Father," Friedkin said, "you write of dialogues you've had with Satan. Have you ever seen him?"

Responded Amorth, "Satan is pure spirit. He often appears as something else, to mislead. An exorcist requires specific training and must be thought to have a personal sanctity. His prayers often cause a violent response as he attempts to shine a beam of light into the darkness."[2] Amorth revealed that he receives a constant stream of letters begging for his services but said that perhaps one or two in a hundred meet the threshold. Before considering any, he ensures that all psychological and physical avenues have been explored. Interviewing him for *Vanity Fair* in April 2016, Friedkin, his filmmaker's instincts piqued, naturally asked Amorth's permission to shoot an exorcism.

"Permission is never granted," Friedkin reported Amorth telling him, "and rightly so. So I decided to push my luck and said, 'Would you let *me* film it, Father?' He came back two days later and said, 'You can film it, but alone, no crew and no lights.'"[3]

The case he was permitted to record involved a thirty-year-old woman he called "Rosa" in the article but reveals as Christina in the film he subsequently directed. She was convinced that her brother's girlfriend had put a curse on her and said that both her brother and the girlfriend were Satanists. Was this truly possession? In eight previous exorcisms by Amorth, Christina had writhed, nodded her head, roared in a bestial voice, rolled her eyes back, and otherwise appeared to lose control of her faculties. After each session, she pronounced herself rested and clean and went on with her life—until she had to return for another exorcism, for which she arrived calm and unaffected. Unlike Regan MacNeil's, Christina's exorcism (at least on video) appears as casual as somebody checking in at the hairdresser, and less an ancient ritual invoking the power of Christ against Satan. In interviews for the documentary she is composed and lucid.

On May 1, 2016, Friedkin, holding a small camera, entered Amorth's room to meet Christina, her brother, mother, father, and her greatly extended family. As expected, once the ritual began, a different personality emerged, one that struggled against those holding her, roared like an animal, and swooned as Amorth prayed over her. At the conclusion of this ninth exorcism, she relaxed and appeared cured. But when Amorth then blessed her father and mother sitting nearby, Christina, hearing the prayers, began writhing again. Not only had the ninth exorcism failed, this time she seemed worse. Friedkin captured it all on video.

Although there is an inescapable tinge of voyeurism, Friedkin (who hosts the documentary) is rigorous in exploring medical alternatives to exorcism. Showing the Christina footage to doctors back in America, he gleaned a range of medical opinions, none of which supported possession, but none of which ruled it out, either. Said Michael B. First, professor of clinical psychiatry at Columbia University, "It fits recognized psychiatric syndromes that have been defined. It's classic. I would say she fits into the pattern that we call Dissociative Trance and Possession Disorder. There is no obvious known psychopathology. Exorcism as a therapeutic technique could work."[4] When Friedkin asked a room full of medical doctors at Columbia University, "Do you think this is unconscious fraud?" they all responded, "No," and explained the woman's actions in psychiatric rather than religious terms.

Itzhak Fried, MD, professor of neurosurgery at Tel Aviv

Medical Center, was more theoretical. "You have to believe in it in order to go through it," he said. "People are very much context-dependent," meaning that somebody with a religious background would accept it while others might not. "So you ask me do I believe in exorcism? I only look at it as a behavioral phenomenon. If I were a Catholic priest or a Jewish rabbi I would have a different [explanation]." In other words, quoting the clinic director in *The Exorcist*, "The victim's belief in possession helped cause it; and in just the same way this belief in the power of exorcism can make it disappear."

As he concluded his Italian filming visit, Friedkin sought a follow-up interview with Christina. She agreed to meet him at an acropolis in the village of Alatri. When he and his producer arrived, however, Christina was a no-show. He called her cell phone to ask where she was. She became angry and told him to meet her in a church down in the village. Friedkin reports that, when he arrived in the church (without his camera), Christina's brother threatened his life if he did not give him the memory chips carrying the exorcism. Christina interceded, Friedkin says, saying that she wanted the world to see the video. Friedkin and his producer left the church and Alatri in silence.

Gabrielle Amorth never performed another exorcism. He died five months later, on September 16, 2016.

Friedkin's footage in hand, his life spared, and his documentarist's creative fire rekindled, he engaged *Exorcist* scholar and BBC presenter Mark Kermode to cowrite the narration of what would become a 69-minute video, released in 2017, titled *The Devil and Father Amorth*. It is as personal a film as Friedkin has ever made, and as revealing about himself as he has ever been. He even delivered his introduction to the video standing in front of the actual house in Cottage City—the first time he publicly identified it—although he withheld the number and street name. After forty-five years he was closing the circle.

At the end, standing at the base of the "*Exorcist* stairs" in Georgetown, he concludes, "Like the doctors, I cannot tell you exactly what's wrong with Christina. My own belief is that there is a far deeper dimension to the universe. We know there is evil. There is also good. And if there are demons, there must be angels."[5]

The outstanding question is: Did William Friedkin, his generation's leading cinema provocateur, believe what he was saying? Mark Kermode, who had known Friedkin since he interviewed him for the film *The Guardian* (1990), was surprised to be asked by the director to help him write the final script for *Amorth*.

"He sent me an early rough cut and I wrote him an email and said what's fascinating is that it's not a film about possession, it's a film about doubt. It's absolutely a film about doubt. And the thing that he said was that his whole take on it was, you know [quoting *Hamlet*], 'There's more in heaven and earth than is in your philosophy.' His whole approach to it was 'I actually don't know about any of this.' Obviously, I think that the [1949] stuff is pretty debunked now. I mean, we all know that it wasn't what it looked like. It doesn't matter, incidentally. What matters is that when Bill Blatty read that story in the *Washington Post* it struck a chord with him. That's what's so lovely about it. *The Exorcist* is a film about faith and *The Devil and Father Amorth* is about doubt."

## CHAPTER 15

# A Possession Primer

Just as Stephenie Meyer's *Twilight* book series upended the rules of vampirism that Bram Stoker invented in *Dracula*, so does William Peter Blatty's *The Exorcist* rewrite the checklist for demonic possession. According to Church doctrine, the more of these symptoms a person displays, the more chance that he or she is possessed:

- Changes in physical appearance
- Coldness in the room
- Speaking in language hitherto unknown
- Intense hatred of the Church, Scripture, and/or clerics
- Change in speaking voice
- Knowledge of events the victim could not logically have known
- Supernatural physical strength
- Subjecting others to verbal or physical attack
- Moving of objects (telekinesis)

One of these indices include head-spinning, projectile vomiting, crotch-grabbing, levitation, and other histrionics that the public now associates with possession. Depending upon the era in which such symptoms were observed and the level of what that society understood about medicine and psychiatry, the less people were bound by superstition. Knowledge has a way of doing that.

The *Roman Ritual* of exorcism (*Rituale Romanum*, 1855, produced under Pope Pius V) is not to be considered lightly. It is a complex, highly structured ceremony—an ordeal, actually—that takes many hours to perform and is exhausting to all parties, not only the priest who is responsible for it but others who may join him in prayers and, in some cases, in restraining the possessed.

Once the officiating priest has obtained evidence of possession and received permission from his bishop, which may take time and require a consulting examination by a psychiatrist, he begins the exorcism. He remains constantly alert for lies, insults, and devious devices by the inhabiting demon. It is not unusual for the demon to appear to flee the possessed person but actually go into hiding, emerging later to both injure and demoralize those present.

After devout preparation, the rite of exorcism begins with Psalm 53, "God by your name save me and by your might defend my cause." (The entire ritual will not be presented here but is widely available on the internet or from the Vatican; see below.) This is followed by a lesson from John 1:1–14 recalling the power of God, followed by Mark 16:15–18 in which Jesus told his apostles to "Go into the whole world and preach the Gospel to all creatures." Lessons from Luke (10:17–20 and 11:14–22) reporting how Jesus drove out the demon are followed by the familiar rite which begins, "I cast you out, unclean spirit," which is reiterated with scriptural references for some thousand words. Then comes a responsive reading, "Canticle of the Magnificent" (Luke 1:46–55), "Canticle of Zachary" (Luke 1:68–79), the *te deum*, and the Athanasian Creed. Presuming that the afflicted has been delivered, there are general prayers exhorting God to keep the victim safe from further torment.

For informal exorcisms there is a shorter ritual involving prayers to Saint Michael, Psalm 67 ("God arrives; his enemies are scattered, and those who hate Him flee before Him"). In both rituals there is genuflection and sprinkling of holy water.

In 2014, the Vatican officially recognized the International Association of Exorcists, 250 priests in thirty countries who liberate demons from the faithful. Rev. Francesco Bamonte, who heads the group, told *L'Osservatore Romano*, "Exorcism is a form of charity that benefits those who suffer." Pope Francis himself was known to have forced four demons from a possessed man in 2013 by laying hands on the victim's forehead.[1]

It is not known whether the rite of exorcism was arrived at all at once or if it evolved through gruesome trial and unfortunate error. What is known, however, is that possession and exorcism are not limited to Christianity.

Michael Scott, the bestselling Irish folklorist whose prolific bibliography includes the *Secrets of the Immortal Nicholas Flamel* series, specializes in long-held myths that persist generation unto generation.

"Demons exist in every mythology, in every race, in every culture," Scott explains. "Every single culture has a demon. If you have light you have dark. There is an argument that Adam and Eve is your first demonic possession story because Eve is possessed, not physically by the devil or by the serpent, but by the spirit of the serpent. Prior to Eve of course, we have Lilith, [Adam's] first wife. She goes out of the Garden of Eden and consorts with demons outside the walls, and out of this she bears all of the demons in the world, including all the vampires. She's considered the mother of all vampires and is your first proto-demon.[2]

"Every culture has demons," he continues, "every culture has gods, and every culture has possessions. But not every culture deems possession to be evil. It's really only the Christians who view possession to be evil, and we can lay that on the church."

Just as the Church made money by perpetuating the myth of celibacy in the 1100s and by selling indulgences in the mid-1400s, so it entrenched its power by creating an exorcism industry. "At the end of the day," Scott says, "every Catholic parish has an exorcist. The church still trains exorcists. On the Vatican website, the exorcist book, *De Exorcismis et Supplicatrionibus Quibusdam*, which is translated as 'Exorcisms and Certain Supplications,' is on sale. But you can only buy it if you have a letter from the archbishop, which you must include with your order to get the book. So the argument then is that the Catholic faith, which now has 100 million adherents, firmly believes that it works. The Pope, not just this Pope, the previous Pope, and the previous Pope have all conducted exorcisms themselves. There's a school of exorcism in the Vatican. Catholics believe it works and therefore, if you believe it works, it works. Right now, even as we are speaking, there's a Catholic priest somewhere doing an exorcism, and some of these exorcisms end badly."

One of the dramatic points in *The Exorcist* is Regan's possessing demon declaring that he is the devil himself. Scott puts this in perspective: "In most cases [of possession] it's not the devil. There is a hierarchy in Hell, and once you go down this rabbit hole, you will find the devil at the top of the chain and under him is a whole range of sub-demons: the lords of hell, the marshals of hell, the demons, the sub-demons, the imps. The devil is too important to go out. It's usually one of the minor demons." He also adds, and not as a joke, that there is nothing that says a possessed person, once exorcised, cannot be immediately re-possessed.

Who was Satan? According to Rabbi Stan Levin, who has made a detailed study of Hebraic Scripture, "The noun *Ha'satan* means 'the adversary.' In Numbers 22, the angel is not Satan, but somebody (some*thing*?) that functions as an adversary. This is the chapter that deals with Balaam, a Moabite prophet, who has been hired by King Balak to curse the Hebrews. As he rides to see King Balak, his she-ass sees an angel in the road, although Balaam does not. In Numbers 22:22, the Torah says, 'And G-d's anger flared because he [Balaam] went [to see the King], and the angel of Ha'Shem set himself in the way to be an adversary [l'Satan] to him; and he was riding on his she-ass and two lads were with him.' The only personification of Satan that I could find is in 1 Chronicles 21:1. The person who wrote Chronicles tended to be a historical revisionist, often euphemizing events that occur in the Tanakh."[3] Given that the Ten Commandments prohibit idol worship, the argument is strong against a personified devil.[4]

The motivation for Blatty's trilogy of faith is establishing proof of God by showing the existence of the devil. Scott acknowledges Blatty's claim but dismisses it. "You're applying logic," he says, and offers an alternate theory: that the devil is proof of an impotent God. "We have the story of Lucifer, the shining one, the favorite of God, who rebelled against God because he wasn't happy with the way that God was treating humans. And 'my God is an old and angry God,' that great phrase. God creates the Earth and goes, 'I'm not happy with that'—flood, plague, turning Lot's wife into a pillar of salt. Not a particularly nice God. And Lucifer says, 'I'm not happy with the way you're treating humans.' There's the rebellion in Heaven in which the archangel Michael versus Lucifer, the angels split. We have the big fight and the angels fall to earth.

As part of that deal, the earth is given over to Lucifer to rule. So the earth is not under the rule of Heaven. The earth is under the rule of the devil, which is hell. When Christ went out and did his forty days and forty nights in the desert, the devil can take him up to the mountain and say, 'I'll offer you all of this.' He was in a position to offer the world because the argument is God didn't rule the world. The world is the devil's domain. We are all In hell.

"Look," he concludes, "it doesn't matter. Stories come out of the tiniest of spots. [Blatty] took a tiny story and he added all the bits to make it wonderful and bizarre: the rotating head and all that good stuff, and the vomiting green, and it made an impression and that impression [comes from] the power of the cinema, which I think is really important so it wasn't a single priest on a pulpit preaching to an audience of twelve people saying this girl was possessed. It was this image that went all around the world and suddenly it spikes and comes back to Father Amorth, for example, who didn't want people reading *Twilight* or *Harry Potter* because it was a gateway drug—you know you begin to read that and suddenly two minutes in, you're a Satanist."

## CHAPTER 16

# The Mystery of Faith

In the beginning, God may have created the heavens and the earth, but it took religion to create Satan. The Hebrews didn't pose him as a red-hided, horned, pointy-tailed being that committed evil by himself but as a force that lured humans into doing it for him. He appears in Job and Zechariah, although *appears* is imprecise as the Jewish religion does not consider him corporeal. That was left to the Christians in the Books of Numbers, Kings, and Samuel, who posed him as an evil force in and of himself. Not until Matthew, Mark, and Luke in the New Testament was Satan specifically identified, when he tempted Christ.

As one of the original angels, Satan predates the Creation, and the date of his falling out with God—literally, the Fall—is never specified. The inference is that he was the serpent that tempted Eve but, like so much else in Scripture, it is kept purposely vague. It took John Milton in *Paradise Lost* to dramatize the whole event in a manner which most people believe is drawn from the Bible; i.e., Satan abdicated his position as God's favorite angel by saying it was better to reign in Hell than serve in Heaven. As for his physical attributes, artists from Gustave Doré onward have designed him as the creature everybody thinks they know, whether he goes by the name Satan, Lucifer, Mr. Scratch, the Devil, Beelzebub, or Number 44.

"Adam's fall is not Jewish," explains Rabbi Stan Levin. "However, it could be derived from Genesis 8. After the flood,

Noah made an animal sacrifice. In Genesis 8:21, the Torah says, 'And Ha'Shem smelled the sweet aroma, and Ha'Shem said to His heart [meaning to Himself], "I will no longer curse the ground any more for the sake of the human, for the inclination of the heart of the human is bad from his youth, and I will no longer smite any more any life that I have made."[1] Levin further explodes tradition by proposing that the serpent's temptation of Eve was not spiritual but sexual. The snake in Eden is not satanic in the Christian sense. "The adjective describing the snake is *Arum*, Hebrew for *subtle* (which happens to be the same word as *naked*, which is used in Genesis 2:25, 'And they were both of them naked [*Arumim*], the human and his woman, and they were not ashamed.'). In Genesis 3:1, the Torah says, 'And the snake was more subtle than any wild animal in the field that Lord G-d made; and he [the snake] said to the woman: "Surely that G-d said do not eat from any tree in the garden."' Eve explains that they can eat from any tree except from the tree of the knowledge of Good and Evil. But the snake is never described as 'ha'satan.'" Some interpretations may even say that the snake is Adam's penis that gives Eve knowledge of sex.

Given the imprecision of Satan in the Old Testament, his definition in *The Exorcist* is also a discussion point. Although the demon tells Karras, through Regan, "And I'm the devil," Karras almost immediately expresses doubt by telling Chris, "If you've seen as many psychotics as I have, you'd know it's like saying you're Napoleon Bonaparte." In fact, it develops that the entity possessing Regan is not Satan but Pazuzu, a minor demon of Assyrian and Babylonian mythology who controls the winds. His likeness is seen at the dig in Nineveh and as a vision in Regan's bedroom at the film's climax.

But Satan is as crucial to William Peter Blatty as he has been to all the Abrahamic religions. He is a key element in

Blatty's oeuvre which, to one degree or another, addresses this weighty and insoluble philosophy of transcendence and the yin and yang of good and evil. Blatty's proof of the existence of God is not the traditional romantic idea of the marvels of life but the pragmatic, almost mathematical reason that if there is a personified devil, there must thus be a God. Indeed the question "If we say the devil is responsible for all the evil in the world, how do we account for all the good in the world?" is frequently asked or implied in his writings, from *The Exorcist* to *Legion* to *The Ninth Configuration*. It is a flawed equivalency, mired, as it is, in religious dogma. It's backwards. There is no reason that the existence of demons would dictate the existence of angels any more than the existence of apples would prove the existence of oranges. This goes directly to the logic of the philosopher Epicurus (341–270 BC), who said:

> Is God willing to prevent evil, but not able? Then he is not omnipotent. Is he able, but not willing? Then he is malevolent. Is he both able and willing? Then whence cometh evil? Is he neither able nor willing? Then why call him God?

Scottish philosopher David Hume (1711–1776) in *Dialogues Concerning Natural Religion* (1779) expanded on Epicurus:

> If God is omniscient, then He must know about all the suffering, so why doesn't He help? If God is omnipresent then He must see all the suffering, so why doesn't He want to help people? If God is omnipotent, then He must be powerful enough to stop the suffering, so why does He continue to let it happen? If God is omnibenevolent, He must love everyone

enough to stop all the suffering, surely a loving God wouldn't want to see people suffering?[2]

Obviating such logic was a formidable challenge to those who invented religion. The maxim "God works in strange and mysterious ways" hardly mollified plague sufferers, people grieving a family loss, or victims of other catastrophic events labeled "acts of God." A disinterested God is as demoralizing as an impotent one. Perhaps this explains the convenience of a personified devil: Like Tom Sawyer, God always means to do good, but sometimes Satan gets in the way.[3]

Blatty compellingly, if glibly, deflects such a test in his 1978 novel and 1980 film *The Ninth Configuration*, in which a Marine psychiatrist,[4] Colonel Vincent Kane (Stacy Keach in the movie), debates a reluctant astronaut, Captain Billy Cutshaw (Scott Wilson), on the nature of good and evil:

KANE:    Maybe God can't interfere in our affairs.

CUTSHAW: So I've noticed.

KANE:    Maybe He can't because to do so would spoil
         His plan for the future—some evolution of man
         and the world so unthinkably beautiful that it's
         worth all the pain of every suffering thing that
         ever lived.

CUTSHAW: I say it's spinach and to hell with it.[5]

KANE:    You're convinced that God is dead because
         there's evil in the world.[6]

CUTSHAW: Correct.

KANE:    Then why don't you think He's alive because of
         the goodness in the world?

In fact, good and evil are moral relatives. If, for example, an evil man has a heart attack and dies, it may be a bad thing for those who love him but a good thing for the rest of the world. A forest fire that destroys a housing tract may be a bad thing for those whose homes are lost, but if it clears land for the resurgence of the forest that was mowed down to build the houses, it's a good thing—depending on whether one is a real estate developer or the ecosystem.

In the end, Blatty (through Kane) bases his belief in God on convenience rather than analysis, bending the precision of science to justify the ineffable:

> In order for life to have appeared spontaneously on earth, there first had to be hundreds of millions of protein molecules of the ninth configuration. But given the size of the planet Earth, do you know how long it would have taken for just one of these protein molecules to appear entirely by chance? Roughly ten to the two hundred and forty-third power billions of years. And I find that far, far more fantastic than simply believing in God.

In choosing pragmatism over curiosity, Blatty compromises the academic discipline of his Jesuit training and dismisses any challenge to his logic with what he explains as "the mystery of faith." Except, to him, faith is no mystery because he has it. Such expediency is reminiscent of what is known as "Pascal's Wager." Propounded in the unfinished *Pensées* by French mathematician, physicist, and theologian Blaise Pascal (1623–1662), it states that one might as well live one's life as if God exists because, if He doesn't, one has only forsaken a few pleasures whereas, if He does, one will be able to ascend to Heaven in glory. The cynicism is overwhelming; critics have noted that Pascal does not prove God's existence, possibly the result of a conflict between his disciplines as both theologian and physicist. As the *Pensées* were published in 1670, two years after Pascal died, he alone would know who won his wager.

Blatty's characters wrestle with such contradictions, but their world is practical, not theoretical. In *Legion* he toys with bringing Kinderman into the fold but, in the end, has him watch helplessly while the Gemini Killer, or whoever he is, simply dies. The movie adaptations are more dramatic. In the release version of *Exorcist III*, Karras is able to force Venamun's spirit out of his body long enough to have Karras tell Kinderman, "Kill me now." As in *The Exorcist*, this permits Karras to once more give his life in sacrifice (although it's unclear whom he is giving his life to save). In the director's cut, however, it is Kinderman who initiates the execution, saying, "Pray for me, Damien. You're free," as he kills him. Taking the statement at face value, it exposes Kinderman to a charge of murder (albeit a mercy killing) and asks whether his sacrifice is the same as if he gave his life as did Karras in *The Exorcist* and Kane in *The Ninth Configuration*. As stated earlier, his use of "Pray for me" suggests he now acknowledges God. Kinderman's act makes the ending of *Legion* as morally complex as the ending of *The Exorcist*.

"Okay," sighs Mark Kermode, "let me lay this out for you, because Bill [Blatty] and I have had this conversation. In the book, it's not until the Gemini's father dies that it's over. He's dead, and then Patient X dies. That's how the book ends. [Bill] felt that the problem with this is that this isn't cinematic enough. You can't just die spontaneously. 'I need a film ending,' [he said]. But the film ending that Blatty came up with was that Kinderman basically does what Karras does, but Kinderman sacrifices himself by killing the Gemini.

Kinderman knows that he's going to face summary imprisonment. That's the end of his job, that's the end of his life. It's a direct callback to the end of *The Exorcist*. Bill's version was that Kinderman sacrifices himself. He's gonna go to prison. Because it's an act of mercy. Then when they get into the studio version in which there's all this other stuff going on, all that gets lost. There's Father Morning stuck to the ceiling and George C. Scott says that the producers wouldn't have been happy unless Madonna came out and sang a song. And then the idea of the shooting gets twisted, 'Now Bill [Kinderman], shoot me now, kill me now.' Bang! [Blatty] absolutely had it in mind that what Kinderman does in *Legion*, like what Karras does in *The Exorcist*, is an act of *sacrifice*."

The ultimate question is whether Blatty achieved his goal of telling a supernatural detective story that argues for the existence of God. In posing God as the antithesis of Satan, he is far more ambitious than other filmmakers who inspire belief in God by showing sunsets and playing Bach. Blatty goes into the ring slugging. Yet, going back to where it all began, many people continue to regard *The Exorcist* as a horror film.

"Though the movie may indeed have a nobler purpose," Tim Lucas avers, "it *is* a giant shock machine with lots of frightening images and jolting multi-directional sound effects. It's definitely a horror film, and one of the best."[7]

"It's a spiritual film," says director Alexandre O. Philippe, whose *Leap of Faith: William Fredkin on The Exorcist* (2019) examines the themes behind the film rather than its special effects. "If you had to assign a genre to it, you'd be hardpressed not to call it a horror film. What makes it great is the fact that it is about fundamental, essential, powerful human emotions that we can all relate to. At its core is the idea that we have this mother who is losing her child to a thing that she does not understand. In this case it's demonic possession, but the idea of losing a loved one to something we don't understand is something we can all relate to on some level. It's emotional filmmaking, and I think that's why *The Exorcist* resonates so much."

While *The Exorcist* was still in production, Friedkin played both sides of the street, telling Peter Travers and Stephanie Reiff, "In editing *The Exorcist* every attempt has been made to underplay the metaphysics and play up the horror."[8] But over the years he declined to call it a horror film, preferring to stress its philosophical subtext, most recently in a 2016 *Vanity Fair* article: "I made the film believing in the reality of exorcism and never, to this day, thought of it as a horror film."[9] What this reflects is not uncertainty but his creative process to see where the material takes him and use the journey as a means of enlightenment.

Yet it's almost as if there's something disgraceful about making a horror movie. On one level, they did make one, though what makes the film truly frightening is not what it shows but what it says. This is something its legions of imitators have been unwilling or unable to comprehend. Its power comes not merely from shocks (it is nearly half an hour before anything truly scary occurs) but from the overwhelming sense of believability that suffuses the entire work. With traditional horror figures like Frankenstein, Dracula, the Mummy, the Wolfman, and even newcomers like Freddy Krueger, Michael Myers, and Jason Voorhees, the public knows they're fictitious. With Satan, two thousand years of publicity have established him as real to hundreds of millions of believers. Dracula can't follow you home from the movie theater. But Satan may be waiting for you when you open the door.

Blatty and Friedkin tapped into a vein of cultural fear

that those who came after them also tried mining. But where Blatty and Friedkin found gold, the others came away with pyrite. Despite the pyrotechnics, noises, makeup, and CGI, and regardless of what people have come to expect from a movie with the word *exorcist* in the title, what truly scares them is something they brought with them into the theater: uncertainty. Christian or Atheist, Muslim or Buddhist, Taoist or Pagan, people feel fear when their strongly held beliefs are assaulted. More than those films that followed it, and more than any other "horror movie" ever made, *The Exorcist* has been taking on all comers and besting them for fifty years and counting.

# Mark Kermode

The *Exorcist* steps in Georgetown were first called "the Hitchcock steps" in reference to Hitchcock's 1935 British thriller *The 39 Steps*. That esoteric homage changed in 1973 with the release of *The Exorcist*. On October 30, 2015—the day before Halloween—the District of Columbia formally named the seventy-five foot-worn stairs after *The Exorcist*, and they have been an official tourist destination ever since. And not just tourists, as Mark Kermode—Britain's chief film critic and certainly the film's number one fan—relates with a smile:

"I'll tell you a lovely story. I'm in the East Coast at some point and I've got a day that I'm not shooting and I said to Bill Blatty, who was in Bethesda, Maryland, 'I've got a day free, I can come up and I'll see you,' and he went, 'Okay, that would be nice, you know, hang out. Where d'you wanna go?' I said, 'Bill, sit where you are, how about we go to Georgetown and I walk you around Georgetown and we swap stories,' and he went, 'Really?' And I went, 'Bill, come on, we can eat in the Tombs [the campus tavern].' He went, 'If it's the Tombs is gonna be burgers,' and I went, 'Yeah, but it's the Tombs, you know.' 'Look, I don't want to eat burgers in the Tombs, but let's do the thing, we'll walk around.' I took a tape recorder and I recorded Bill doing all this stuff.

"So we're at the top of the *Exorcist* steps and, of course, there's all these tourists. A lot of Japanese tourists, as it happens, and they're all taking photographs and I'm standing there with Bill looking down and this person looks at Bill and they come up to Bill and they go, 'Could you take a picture?' And Bill goes, 'Yeah.' And they give Bill the camera and these two people, they stand at the top of the stairs and Bill takes a picture and I go, 'Should I tell them it's Bill?' And he says quietly, 'No!'

"Somewhere out there in the world there is somebody who made a pilgrimage to the *Exorcist* steps who has a photograph of themselves and their partner standing on the *Exorcist* steps who doesn't know that that photo was taken by William Peter Blatty."

# Colloquy with William Peter Blatty

*While I was researching my 1990 biography of William Friedkin, William Peter Blatty proved elusive. He wasn't avoiding me (we already knew each other), he just kept moving: Los Angeles, North Hollywood, Aspen, Washington, D.C., and—when we finally connected—Greenwich, Connecticut. I was living in Cambridge, Massachusetts, so it was easy to hop into a car and drive as fast as traffic would allow before he could relocate. As always, he was warm, quotable, intense, and self-deprecating. But he was also frank, perhaps too frank for Hollywood, so, when we finished, he asked to take certain portions of our interview off the record, explaining, "Nat, I've got enough trouble!" We kept in touch informally after that (not on the record), but, by now, enough time and funerals have passed that I have restored, here and throughout this book, applicable contents of our discussion, some of them restored from where they were excerpted in the text, edited only for clarity.*

**NAT SEGALOFF:** *The Exorcist* was so far and away above anything that Hollywood has seen before that I get the impression Paul Monash really didn't understand the property.

**WILLIAM PETER BLATTY:** No, he didn't, and in fact, I say, "Thank heaven for Mr. Monash" because the manuscript had already made the rounds of every studio, mini-major, major-major, fly-by-night independent from here to Panama and nobody wanted it. I never got anything more than a mimeographed form rejection slip. It was the usual "This doesn't fit into our production schedule," which shows what happens with story departments. Monash, at his level, was very hot then, of course—*Butch Cassidy and the Sundance Kid*, the *Peyton Place* TV series—he went right to the top [of Warner Bros.], and the top echelon read it. John Calley was one of those men, and he told me afterwards that he was certain it was a hit because he became so frightened that he tried to get his German shepherd up on the bed with him while he was reading it and the German Shepherd had been forbidden to get on that bed, ever; it would be punished. And there ensued a titanic struggle between John Calley and this dog, whining and digging with his claws, trying to prevent being dragged up!

**SEGALOFF:** I thought, at that point in your career, you were beyond having your stuff shopped around.

**BLATTY:** Oh, no, I had some reputation as a comedy writer and frequently was able to sell the scripts I had written on spec. But this was not a comedy and there was, I suppose, an "Are you *kidding*?" attitude when the material floated in to whomever was supposed to read it. "Blatty? Comedy? Something called *The Exorcist*?" I'd been through it; I couldn't get arrested whenever I was proposed by the agent for a non-comedy writing assignment. But, at any rate, I did find that letter [from Paul Monash] and it did have that point of view. One will never know what would have happened if those suggestions had been carried out, just as one would never know what would have happened if my first draft had been shot.

**SEGALOFF:** Were you really barred from the editing room?

**BLATTY:** This is *Rashomon*. I'm not sure I know the true story. There came a certain point where I was barred from the postproduction by Warner Bros. after the first cut. I viewed the first cut, Billy showed me the first cut. It was a masterwork. Really, a classic film. Which I don't think the version we've all seen is.[1]

**SEGALOFF:** Those were the deletions?

**BLATTY:** There was a certain deletion of scenes which made the construction extremely jarring; in fact, illogical. For example, as I recall, there was a shot of Regan walking around the party at Chris MacNeil's house. She was smiling radiantly and up to this point that's the only way we've ever seen her. Suddenly she urinates at that party on the rug and the next thing you know we're in the bathroom and her mother is telling her, "It's all right, honey, just keep taking the pills that the doctor said." What doctor? Why pills? How did this happen, but more, why was she so healthy and normal down at the party? It was extremely jarring for me.[2] There were little leaps in construction which resulted because, as Billy once told me, and he'll tell you, he didn't know he had a hit. And so he cut it, but much more serious is the excision of the moral center from the film. And that was all contained in a single, brief moment. It's the heart of the novel. When Merrin and Karras are resting between performances of the ritual of exorcism, they have a conversation in which Karras, in substance, is asking why she's possessed. What's the point? Doesn't Lucifer have better things to do, or worse things to do, than that? And Merrin explains to him in words you find in the novel that "the target is not the little girl, it has never been; it was the observers, especially you, Damien. The point was to make us despair of our own humanity, and to feel so bestial and vile that, if there were a God, He could not possibly love us." And what that did, and what that does in terms of the game, which is self-explanatory, but what it also does in terms of audience appreciation and relaxation and realization of the work is that it would have allowed them not to hate themselves for liking the repellent moments in the film: the shock and the vomit and the obscenity—because then you would have the answer to the question "Why?" and that's why you're sick as you are being subjected to those scenes. And that, I think, is what removes it from possibly the level of a truly masterful film to what is a superb thriller.

**SEGALOFF:** Billy has said, "I'm not making a commercial for the Catholic Church."

**BLATTY:** Yes. He said that; that is a true citation.

**SEGALOFF:** Bill O'Malley said, "He said, what should I do, see angels leaping out of his throat?" and what of the line, "If we credit Lucifer for all the evil in the world, then how do we account for all the good in the world?"

**BLATTY:** Let's stay with the other dialogue that was so crucial to the theme, namely Ellen talking about evil in the world and Father Dyer replying, "If all the evil in the world prompts you to believe in the devil, how do you account for all the good?" She has no answer, but obviously she starts thinking; it's a good question. Billy called me in the Marriott Hotel one night when we were filming in Washington to "Come down, I want you to hear this." And they're in a room with Ellen and Father O'Malley who played Father Dyer, and we talked. They were rehearsing that scene. Ellen and Bill O'Malley did the scene. It was abominable. They did it again. And [Billy] said, "Now, Mr. Smart Script Writer, what about it?" And I said, "If that's the way it's going to be on the screen, I recommend you take it out." And that's how we lost that scene.

**SEGALOFF:** Is there any sense of satisfaction to you, having won the Oscar and Friedkin didn't, that *the Exorcist* was considered a better job of writing than it was of directing?

**BLATTY:** I was, and I have the scars to prove it, deeply disturbed by the failure of Billy and some others to win the award. And roundly disliked by the Academy, who I don't think have ever forgotten it, for my giving out an interview in which I took them to task for their failure to award Billy Friedkin an Oscar as opposed to *The Sting*, which is not in the same category. I don't know why I won. I had confidence that the picture would do well and I was very surprised when they chose me. Shirley MacLaine said it was a backlash; every time you opened the trades there was another ad for *The Exorcist*, and it got to be nauseous [*sic*] after a while.

**SEGALOFF:** When I was publicizing the film we were loaned a lengthy pamphlet which was an eyewitness account of a Roman Ritual. It was graphic and terribly disturbing.

**BLATTY:** That's the only other American case I could ever get any solid information on. The case in Earling, Iowa, in 1928. In the other wild phenomena, all the participants are dead, when I began to write *The Exorcist*. And furthermore the only written account of it that I could find in the Library of Congress was the sort of thing one might find written by an overly credulous, pious person. I didn't put much stock in it. However, when I finally spoke with the exorcist—a man who, without a shadow of the doubt, was not an overly credulous man—he was an extremely reticent man, he would have nothing to do with giving me any information that might serve to compromise the identity of the victim. All he told me was, in his first letter to me, "I can assure you of one thing: this was the real thing. I had no doubt about it then, I have no doubt about it now." And that gave me the energy to write the novel because, in all my research, it always reduces down to the same thing—very consistent—though you might read a thousand cases—and the end of each individual case you ask, 'Who are these people? Are they telling the truth? Are they deluding themselves?' I had all of those doubts, but in this case, here was not only a living participant in the case, a contemporary case in the Western civilization, in a computerized society—here was the exorcist himself! And so I guess the point I'm getting around to is that it has been written and said, alleged, and it is absolutely untrue that I based *The Exorcist* on that 1949 case. Absolutely not. But that case pointed me in the direction of possession and finally inspired me with sufficient conviction to write about it.[3]

**SEGALOFF:** The effect of the film was so great that it led to people inventing stories about it, didn't it? I remember rumors that Linda Blair had become possessed, which, of course, were idiotic.

**BLATTY:** Oh, I'd heard that people were saying that underneath the house where I used to live, I had a subterranean room that was all black—black statues—where I would conduct a black mass. Where do these things begin? There was a friend of my former wife who got a rumor from another girl that the reason I decided to move out of Los Angeles was that my child was born possessed and had no eyes.

**SEGALOFF:** How does the author of *The Exorcist* regard the born-again preachers who've made religion into a cult?

**BLATTY:** Well, you cannot stop the religious impulse. I believe in transcendence; that every cell in our body knows where we come from and who we are and reflects it in this yearning for religious expression. We forget, we keep burying it, and then we keep digging it up again. The only thing that surprises me is, Why are there atheists? That's what requires explanation. I think *The Exorcist* poses the question, like Rabbi Kirschner,

"Why do bad things happen to good people?" And *The Exorcist* asked the question but never answered it.[4]

**SEGALOFF:** I'm not sure that religion has a whole lot to do with God anymore.

**BLATTY:** Well, think about such things. You'll appreciate it.

As I left the house, Blatty presented me with the newly issued paperback edition of *Legion* (pictured). You will notice a triangle-shaped hole in the cover. This is intentional; the publisher designed it so the killer's face, pictured on the frontispiece, would peep through at the reader.

"I hate it," Blatty said emphatically. "They never asked me about it, they just did it. It's cheap. I was in Washington when I got a call from a friend that it was out in paperback, so I went to the bookstore. I had trouble finding it. When I did, I saw that the cover was so disgustingly lurid that I skulked out of the store lest I be recognized."

With that, he ripped the offending page out of my copy, signed what was left, and handed to me with a conspiratorial smile. The inscription reads, "Nat, may all your blessings be . . ." and the title completes the sentence: "*Legion.*"

As I packed my tape recorder and notebook preparing to drive back to Boston, where I then lived, he said, "By the way, have you eaten?"

"No," I said, "as soon as you called and said you'd talk, I got right in the car and drove down before you could change your mind."

"Then you'd better take this," he said. He went to the refrigerator, pulled out a ham, and carved me a thick slice which he put between two pieces of rye bread. Wrapping it in a paper napkin, he handed it to me and said, "Have a safe trip."

His mother would have been proud.

# Acknowledgments

I first wrote about *The Exorcist* in *Hurricane Billy: The Stormy Life and Films of William Friedkin* (New York: William Morrow and Co., 1990). A lot has changed over the years. Back then the film was merely a hit; since then it has become a classic. The challenge in writing this book has been to find as many original sources as possible (sadly, many have left us) and write the film's history without the benefit of hindsight.

Many people, then as now, extended courtesy to me with information, connections, and material. Those whom I interviewed are quoted within, and they have my deep thanks. Those who extended varied kindnesses to me then and now begin with Mark Kermode. Mark admits to having seen *The Exorcist* over two hundred times and finds new things with each encounter. His 1997 deconstruction of the film for the British Film Institute (and its several subsequent updates for Bloomsbury) is an invaluable and highly accessible resource. The co-dedication of this book isn't enough; his scholarship, generosity, talent, and, most of all, friendship over thirty years cannot be overstated.

Lee Sobel, whose Lee Sobel Literary Agency landed an immediate sale with Kensington Publishing, has my thanks and affection. I also thank Kensington publisher Steven Zacharius and my editor James Abbate for their counsel and support.

Howard Prouty, acquisitions archivist for the Margaret Herrick Library of the Academy Foundation of the Academy of Motion Picture Arts and Sciences, rendered extraordinary help, as did the Herrick's director Matt Severson, supervising archivist/research Louise Hilton, and the dedicated staff. The Herrick is an essential resource for film scholars, as are the people who work there preserving the minutiae of Hollywood's history. Anyone who thinks that Oscars are the Academy's sole function needs to visit their archives. Genevieve Maxwell and Elizabeth Youle of the National Film Information Service came to my rescue when the archives were closed to the public for COVID.

Hollywood is a town controlled by executives but run by assistants, many of whom connected me with their agencies' clients. I also enjoyed the consultation over the years of numerous experts, friends, and colleagues, such as (alphabetically) Michelle Bega, Yoram Ben-Ami, Michael Blatty, Robyn Blumner, Gilles Boulenger, Sierra Byrons, Sammy Cahn, Tita Cahn, Michael Chiaverini, Donald H. Cragin, Mary Cross, Adele Joseph Curcuruto, Richard Dawkins, Derek (Photofest), Anthony DiSalvo, Patrick Donegan, Dwayne Epstein, Karl Fasick, Gary Fleder, Michael Gianino, Theo Gluck, Edgar Gross, Robert Hofler, David Kittredge, Barry Krost, Jim Landis, Pamela A. Liflander, Toni St. Clair Lily, Howard Mandelbaum (Photofest), Jennifer Nairn-Smith, James Robert Parish, Pamela A. Perry, Sean Redlitz, Helen Rees, Melanie Ruth Rose, Deac Rossell, Joel Searls, Isabel Seife, Todd (Photofest), and Laurent Vachaud.

My greatest thanks, of course, go to Billy Friedkin, who not only let me write his biography years ago but encouraged me to do so with his full permission, cooperation, and no demand for oversight. It's easy to admire him as a director, but it is a privilege to respect him as a man.

# Bibliography

Citations for individual articles and interviews are given in the footnotes. Otherwise, the following sources were helpful in researching this book.

Ben-Ami, Yoram, with Nat Segaloff. *Guiding Royalty: My Adventure with Elizabeth Taylor and Richard Burton*. Florida: BearManor Media, 2018.

Blatty, William Peter. *The Exorcist*. New York: Harper & Row, 1971.

———. *The Exorcist: Fortieth Anniversary Edition*. New York: Harper, 2011.

———. *The Exorcist* and *Legion*, Classic Screenplays. Introduction by Mark Kermode. UK: Faber and Faber, Ltd., 1998.

———. *I'll Tell Them I Remember You*. New York: Norton & Company, 1973.

———. *Legion*. New York: Simon & Schuster, 1983.

———. *The Ninth Configuration*. New York: Tom Doherty Associates Books (reprint), 1978.

———. *William Peter Blatty on The Exorcist: From Novel to Screen*. New York: Bantam Books, 1974.

Friedkin, William. *The Friedkin Connection*. New York: Harper Collins, 2013.

———. William Friedkin Papers, Margaret Herrick Library, Academy Foundation of the Academy of Motion Picture Arts and Sciences.

Kermode, Mark. *The Exorcist*. UK: The British Film Institute, Bloomsbury Publishing, 1997, 1998, 2003, 2020.

———. "The Mysteries of Faith: Misinformation and Missing Scenes in *The Exorcist.*" *Video Watchdog*, no. 6 (July/August 1991).

Key, Wilson Bryan. *Media Sexploitation*. New York: New American Library, 1976.

King, Stephen. *Stephen King's Danse Macabre*. New York: Berkeley Books, 1981.

Lucas, Tim, and Mark Kermode. "*The Exorcist*: From the Subliminal to the Ridiculous." *Video Watchdog*, no. 6 (July/August 1991)

Newman, Howard. *The Exorcist: The Strange Story Behind the Film*. New York: Pinnacle Books, 1974.

Pallenberg, Barbara. *The Making of Exorcist II: The Heretic*. New York: Warner Books, 1977.

Segaloff, Nat. *Hurricane Billy: The Stormy Life and Films of William Friedkin*. New York: William Morrow & Co., 1990.

Skal, David J. *The Monster Show: A Cultural History of Horror*. New York: Farrar, Straus and Giroux, 2001.

Travers, Peter, and Stephanie Reiff, *The Story Behind The Exorcist*. New York: Crown Publishers, Inc., 1974.

# Photo Captions and Credits

p. 1-A  It was on this street and in this house that the alleged 1949 possession began that led to *The Exorcist*. It's the former home of Ronald Hunkeler at 3807 40th Avenue in Cottage City, Maryland. The family moved away years ago. Stan Levin.

p. 1-B  The former Hunkeler home in Cottage City, Maryland. It was on the other side of this house's second-floor window that teenage Ronald was supposedly possessed. Stan Levin.

p. 2-A  The town hall of Cottage City, Maryland, the sleepy community that awoke to a demonic possession that inspired *The Exorcist*. Stan Levin.

p. 2-B  The Mesopotamian demon Pazuzu, who held dominion over the wind, also held dominion over Regan MacNeil. British Museum/Wikimedia Commons.

p. 3-A  The "*Exorcist* house" from across Prospect Street in NW Washington, D.C. For the movie, the owners of the private residence allowed the Warner Bros. construction crew to build an extension over the long staircase for purposes of defenestration. Stan Levin.

p. 3-B  The "*Exorcist* house" remains a private residence in the Georgetown section of Washington, D.C., but that hasn't stopped tourists and *Exorcist* fans from making a pilgrimage. They are invariably disappointed to see how different it looks fifty years on. Stan Levin.

p. 4-A  The house used to shoot the exteriors of *The Exorcist*, at 3600 Prospect Street, NW Washington, D.C. An extension was built to place Regan's bedroom over the steps on the left. Stan Levin.

p. 4-B   On October 30, 2015, a plaque was posted on the staircase connecting Prospect and Canal Streets, Georgetown, commemorating them as the "*Exorcist* stairs." Stan Levin.

p. 5-A   Looking down at the "*Exorcist* steps" beside 3600 Prospect Street in NW Washington, D.C. Formerly known as the "Hitchcock steps" after director Alfred Hitchcock's 1935 thriller *The 39 Steps*, they became known as the "*Exorcist* steps" after their important appearance in the 1973 movie *The Exorcist*. Stan Levin.

p. 5-B   The "*Exorcist* stairs" looking up from Canal Road and the Whitehurst Freeway. *Steps* and *stairs* are used interchangeably. Stan Levin.

p. 6-A   William Friedkin in a contemplative moment during the making of *The Exorcist*. Press kit photo. N26825/Wikimedia Commons. https://creativecommons.org/licenses/by-sa/3.0/.

p. 6-B   Georgetown University White-Gravenor Hall. Only William Peter Blatty's connections with the university enabled Warner Bros. to use it as a movie location. Daderot/ Wikimedia Commons.

p. 7-A   The cover for William Peter Blatty's novel, *The Exorcist*. Shirley MacLaine, on whom the character of Chris MacNeil is based, claimed that her friend Blatty took a photo of her daughter, distorted it, and used it as the haunting illustration.

p. 7-B   Original teaser (advance) poster for *The Exorcist*. Note that it carries the wrong opening date. The film actually opened December 26, 1973, not the day before.

p. 8-A   Father Pierre Teilhard de Chardin, whose writings on possession informed William Peter Blatty and inspired Max von Sydow, who even looked like him as Father Lankester Merrin. Wikimedia Commons.

p. 8-B   Ellen Burstyn tries to comfort Linda Blair on her shaking bed in a publicity photo from *The Exorcist*. Wikimedia Commons.

p. 9-A   The mechanical Regan doll designed by Marcel Vercoutere and Dick Smith. It now lives at the Museum of the Moving Image in Queens, New York. Meg Gilbert/Wikimedia Commons. https://commons.wikimedia.org/wiki/File:Exorcist_model,_The_Museum_of_Moving_Image_(49400609567).jpg.

p. 9-B   Linda Blair—happy and healthy—years after her *Exorcist* experience. CelebHeights.com/Wikimedia Commons. https://commons.wikimedia.org/wiki/File:Linda_Blair.jpg.

p. 10-A  *Exorcist II: The Heretic* poster.

p. 10-B  Director John Boorman, the man behind *Exorcist II: The Heretic*. Lionel Allorge/Wikimedia Commons. https://commons.wikimedia.org/wiki/File:Master_Class_John_Boorman_Paris_novembre_2014_-_25.jpg.

p. 11-A  *The Exorcist III* poster.

p. 11-B  William Peter Blatty stretches out, enjoying his success. William Peter Blatty/Wikimedia Commons.

p. 12-A  *Dominion: Prequel to The Exorcist* poster.

p. 12-B  Filmmaker Paul Schrader directed *Dominion: Prequel to The Exorcist*. Frank Scramm Montclair Film/Wikimedia Commons. https://creativecommons.org/licenses/by/2.0/deed.en.

p. 13-A  *Exorcist: The Beginning* poster.

p. 13-B  Filmmaker Renny Harlin reshot Paul Schrader's *Dominion* and turned it into *Exorcist: The Beginning*. Don Bigileone/Wikimedia Commons. https://creativecommons.org/licenses/by/2.0/deed.en.

p. 14-A William Friedkin at the 2012 Deauville American Film Festival. Elen Nivrae/Wikimedia Commons. https://creativecommons.org/licenses/by/2.0/deed.en.

p. 14-B The author has been writing about both William Friedkin and *The Exorcist* since his 1990 biography of the Oscar-winning director, *Hurricane Billy: The Stormy Life and Films of William Friedkin.*

p. 15-A Producer Noel Marshall relaxes (?) with one of the cats that he and his wife Tippi Hedren raised on their California ranch. Nancy Hardin.

p. 15-B Writer-producer Jeremy Slater created and was showrunner for *The Exorcist* TV series. ©Luigi Novi/Wikimedia Commons. https://creativecommons.org/licenses/by/4.0/deed.en.

p. 15-C Writer-director David Gordon Green, the filmmaker behind the new *Exorcist* trilogy, at the 2018 San Diego Comic-Con. Gage Skidmore/Wikimedia Commons.

p. 16-A Paperback edition book cover of *Legion* that William Peter Blatty hated.

p. 16-B Title page of *Legion* that Blatty signed to the author. He tore out the page before it.

# Endnotes

## Preface

1. "Something almost beyond comprehension is happening to a little girl on this street, in this house, and a man has been sent for as a last resort. This man is the exorcist."

2. Several films based their ad campaigns on making audiences sick; Hallmark Releasing's *Mark of the Devil* (*Hexen bis aufs Blut gequält*, 1970) famously gave barf bags (which are now collectibles) to ticket buyers, but *The Exorcist* got there accidentally. Says Tim Lucas, publisher of the authoritative *Video Watchdog*, "There were other movies that used vomit bags as a promotional device. Even Mario Bava's *A Bay of Bloo*d (1971; then called *Carnage* or *Twitch of the Death Nerve*) had that enviable distinction.

3. Kauyheck adds that, to this day, he has never seen the film, explaining, "I'm not a film buff." Interviewed March 19, 2022.

4. Universal Pictures, who produced *The Sting*, complained that the *Exorcist* crowds choked off ticket sales for their picture. They would have the last laugh come Oscar time.

## Chapter 1

1. William Peter Blatty, quoted in Peter Travers and Stephanie Reiff, *The Story Behind The Exorcist* (New York: Crown Publishers, 1974).

2. Stephen King, *Danse Macabre* (New York: Berkely Books, 1981).

3. David J. Skal, *The Monster Show: A Cultural History of Horror* (New York: Farrar, Straus and Giroux, 2001).

4. Responding to the Women's Movement, Hollywood produced roles for actresses to rival the days of Davis, Crawford, Russell, and Dunne. The 1970s saw major central starring performances by Barbra Streisand, Diane Keaton, Jane Fonda, Liv Ullmann[spelling as per imdb.com], Faye Dunaway, Meryl Streep, Sally Field, Jill Clayburgh, Sissy Spacek, and, of course, Ellen Burstyn.

5. Information from Friedkin's birth certificate. Friedkin is not, as was reported for years, the youngest person to win the directing Oscar (for *The French Connection* in 1972 at age thirty-two). He was, in fact, thirty-six. The youngest is Norman Taurog, age thirty-two, for *Skippy* in 1931.

6. Friedkin later made a donation in his mother's name to the Jules Stein Eye Institute in Los Angeles.

7. Nat Segaloff, *Hurricane Billy: The Stormy Life and Films of William Friedkin* (New York: William Morrow, 1990). All quotes from Mr. Friedkin not otherwise attributed are from expansive interviews originally conducted by the author, only some of which were used in that book.

8. Segaloff, *Hurricane Billy*.

9. Segaloff, *Hurricane Billy*.

10. William Friedkin, *The Friedkin Connection: A Memoir* (New York: HarperCollins, 2013).

11. Author interview with Blatty, April 10, 1988.

12. These and other Blatty quotes not otherwise attributed are from William Peter Blatty, *I'll Tell Them I Remember You* (New York: W. W. Norton & Co., 1973).

13. *William Peter Blatty on The Exorcist: From Novel to Screen* (New York: Bantam Books, 1974).

14. Author interview with Blatty, April 10, 1988.

15. Author interview with Blatty, April 10, 1998.

**Chapter 2**

1. By coincidence, the author was raised in Silver Spring, Maryland, during that same period.

2. Town of Cottage City website, https://www.cottagecitymd.gov/about.

3. Bill Brinkley, "Priest Frees Mt. Rainier Boy Reported Held in Devil's Grip—Ritual of Exorcism Repeated," *Washington Post*, August 20, 1949. To be fair, headlines are written by the editor and not the reporter. Brinkley's writing itself is less sensationalized.

4. Although Brinkley is remembered as the author of the article that inspired *The Exorcist*, his major credits are as a successful novelist, beginning the year before his exorcism piece appeared. His books include *Don't Go Near the Water*, *The Fun House*, and *Peeper*. Suffering from depression, he died by his own hand on November 22, 1993.

5. Mark Opsasnick, *The Real Story Behind the Exorcist: A Study of the Haunted Boy and Other True-Life Horror Legends from Around the Nation's Capital* (Bloomington, IN: Xlibris, 2006). Also Kyle T. Cobb, Jr., "The Exorcism of Ronald Hunkeler," http://www.lastgasps.com/page71.html, and author's interview with Opsasnick, June 10, 2021.

6. The Catholic Church uses two kinds of exorcisms: the private and the solemn. Only the latter requires permission from the archbishop, and it was this that was performed on Hunkeler.

7. Although William Peter Blatty was careful never to say so, this is in all likelihood the material that informed *The Exorcist*.

8. Diary references. (Sources: the *Sun*/UK; Wikipedia/William Bowdern; Geek Slop, "The Real-Life Exorcism of Ronald Hunkeler—the Terrifying True Story That Inspired The Exorcist," http://altereddimensions.net/2016/ronald-hunkeler-exorcism-inspired-the-exorcist.)

## Chapter 3

1. He totally flummoxed Groucho, who took pride in being able to spot frauds. When announcer/sidekick George Fenneman chided Groucho for missing a fake, Groucho replied, "That is incorrect, because I've had Fenneman in my employ now for fourteen years."

2. At the time, Marshall was married to actress Tippi Hedren.

3. *William Peter Blatty on The Exorcist*.

4. *William Peter Blatty on The Exorcist*.

5. *William Peter Blatty on The Exorcist*. Copies of this pamphlet were quietly circulated among those doing publicity for the film on its initial release, but they were confiscated afterward. In the years since, the brochure has become public: https://nonpareilonline.com/news/earling-site-of-last-sanctioned-exorcism/article_f943f041-ba99-528c-bdce-7ec7f88a0d29.html.

6. Blatty's dates are inconsistent. In his book *I'll Tell Them I Remember You* he sets his start date as July 1969. In a note for the fortieth anniversary edition of *The Exorcist* novel he doesn't give a date but says that his mother died while he was writing it, and Mary Blatty died in 1967.

7. *William Peter Blatty on The Exorcist*.

8. *William Peter Blatty on The Exorcist*.

9. William Friedkin, *The Friedkin Connection*. Friedkin is compressing the narrative; the book had not yet been sold to a studio.

10. Mark Kermode, *The Exorcist* (UK: The British Film Institute, Bloomsbury Publishing, 1997, 1998, 2003, 2020).

11. Author interview with Monash at the Film School in the Orson Welles Complex, Cambridge, MA, September 1972.

12. Author interview with Monash. *Bridget Loves Bernie* [as per imdb.com]was a 1972–73 TV series about a mixed ethnic marriage.

13. Kermode, *The Exorcist*. After forcing Monash off, Blatty would receive 31.7 percent of the profits and $600,000 of Monash's fee.

14. *William Peter Blatty on The Exorcist*. Blatty does not name Rydell and calls the director of the film he saw "Edmund de Vere."

**Sidebar: Synopsis of the Book *The Exorcist***

1. The book makes no mention of Merrin needing to take nitroglycerine pills to ameliorate a heart condition; the amulet is not found at the dig, nor is it near a St. Joseph medal. These textures were added for the film. "I asked, 'Billy, what is a St. Joseph medal doing in a four-thousand-year-old dig in Nineveh?' And Billy just said, 'resonance.' That was the only answer I ever got out of him." Author interview with Blatty, March 3, 1980.

2. Like most movie stars when they film on location, Chris rented a comfortable private home. The house is not hers, as shown when she and Regan leave D.C. for LA at the end.

3. The film's Washington sequence begins in the autumn, just before Halloween. The year is not specified in *The Exorcist*, but in *Exorcist III* it is revealed as 1975.

4. The astronaut is not named in the novel or film, and it's tempting to think that he is Billy Cutshaw, the astronaut in *The Ninth Configuration* who flipped out on the launchpad when he remembered Regan's curse. But no. The timelines don't match.

5. In the film Mrs. Karras's death is mentioned to Chris. Karras, when passed out, dreams flash memories of his mother descending into a subway, the St. Joseph medal, and other images related to Merrin that he could not have witnessed. These precognitive images were added during editing to create "resonance."

6. This is a scene that Blatty later wished he could have added to the movie. The young priest would have been part of Karras's dream.

7. The medical doctors' skepticism of psychiatry is more pronounced in the film.

8. This ninety-seven-step staircase, which is now called the "*Exorcist* steps," was first called the "Hitchcock steps," not because they were scary but in honor of Hitchcock's 1935 film *The 39 Steps*. Fun fact: The house itself, at 36th and Prospect Streets, NW, Washington, D.C., was owned by Florence Mahoney, who was persuaded by MPAA president Jack Valenti to lend it to the company. At the time, the house was leased by Senator Lloyd Bentsen (D-Texas; 1921-2006) who was not in residence during the filming.

9. Logicians point out that any mother whose daughter behaved like this would instantly ditch the doctors and seek an exorcist. Over the years, the filmmakers have insisted that the sequence was excised because the stunt did not work. Both would seem to apply.

10. The book's timeline is tighter than the film's. In the book less than a month has passed since the story started. In the film, we learn that Mrs. Karras had been hospitalized for four months for her leg to heal before returning home and dying.

11. In the film she chops between her legs with the relic instead of performing the expected erotic form of masturbation. The filmmakers insisted on calling it "mutilation" to avoid the issue of sexual gratification. "I personally thought it would be shot much more by suggestion," Blatty told Kermode for his British Film Institute book. "I wanted to see nothing below the girl's chest. I wanted to see the crucifix go below the frame, out of the shot, and to come back with blood on it, and let the mind tell us where it has been without showing the thighs or whatever." The final script bears out Blatty's claims.

12. This minimal allusion becomes crucial to *Exorcist II: The Heretic*, *Dominion*, and *Exorcist: The Beginning*.

13. The book goes to great lengths to eliminate all plausible medical and psychological reasons for Regan's behavior, something each reader has already done by virtue of buying the book. This was a major issue in structuring the screenplay.

14. The implication is that Elvira is offered drug rehab, thereby showing that good can come from evil. The subplot was excised from the film as a matter of narrative efficiency. It was Karl who, despite his denial, placed a crucifix beneath Regan's pillow in an attempt to protect her.

15. Chris's and Sharon's ministering to Regan were cut in order to speed the exorcism scenes for the film.

16. The twelve-week shooting schedule for Chris's film (April to June) has presumably concluded, although it is never discussed who took over from Burke Dennings or how Chris managed to both act and be with Regan.

17. This is odd in that Kinderman and Dyer have had no contact throughout the entire book, yet a *Casablanca*-style friendship is presumed to exist between them. This will be essential to *Legion* and *Exorcist III*.

## Chapter 4

1. *William Peter Blatty on The Exorcist.*

2. Tim Lucas and Mark Kermode, "*The Exorcist*: From the Subliminal to the Ridiculous," *Video Watchdog* No. 6 (July/August 1991).

3. Interviewed in the BBC documentary *The Fear of God: 25 Years of "The Exorcist"* (1998).

4. Interviewed by Jeff Kisselhoff on May 15, 1996, for the Archive of American Television, https://www.emmytvlegends.org. Additionally, such pressure befell Smith that he was compelled to have his doctor, Lawrence Edwin, write a note asking Friedkin to give him some time off. February 15, 1973, letter, William Friedkin Papers, AMPAS.

5. Interviewed by Stephen J. Abramson on February 24, 2003, for the Archive of American Television, https://interviews.televisionacademy.com/interviews/rick-baker

6. Author interview with Smith, July 15, 2006.

7. Interviewed in *The Fear of God*.

8. 1972 correspondence from Sgarro to Friedkin, William Friedkin Papers, AMPAS. No other date is given.

9. Leondopoulos did not respond to an interview request.

10. William Friedkin Papers, AMPAS.

11. William Friedkin Papers, AMPAS.

12. William Friedkin Papers, AMPAS. Bateson was an actual radiographer playing one in the fateful arteriogram scene. But Bateson had another life: In 1979 he was convicted of the murder of journalist Addison Verrill and was sentenced to a minimum of twenty years in prison. Later attempts were made to link him with the slayings of several other gay men. The case inspired Friedkin to write and direct the sordid *Cruising* (1980, loosely adapted from Gerald Walker's novel) about a series of unsolved murders of gay men in New York's S&M community. Bateson died in 2012 after being released on parole.

13. Interviewed in *The Fear of God*.

14. Stacy Keach would later play the lead in Blatty's film *The Ninth Configuration*.

15. *Empire of Light* by René Magritte. The photo that referenced this painting[Au: Not quite clear to me what this was. A photo of the painting?], and which became one of the most famous images in movie history, was taken by Josh Weiner. CAN'T ADD SIDE COMMENTS TO FOOTNOTES. KEEP MINE,.

16. Comments at the New York Film Academy, posted April 19, 2016, https://www.youtube.com/watch?v=pLCvMA4KM1I.

17. S. Ansky's 1916 play about a woman possessed by an ancient spirit known as a *dybbuk*. Written in Russian and translated into Yiddish by Ansky himself, it was first produced in 1918.

18. Remarks at AMPAS, October 22, 2018.

19. Travers and Reiff, *The Story Behind The Exorcist*.

20. Interviewed in *The Fear of God*.

21. Kermode, *The Exorcist*.

22. "The Curse of The Exorcist," *E! True Hollywood Story*, August 15, 2004.

23. Friedkin, *The Friedkin Connection*.

24. Travers and Reiff, *The Story Behind The Exorcist*.

25. Interviewed in *The Fear of God*.

26. Interviewed in *The Fear of God*.

27. Burstyn adds, "I loved that girl. I was very concerned about what effect this would have on her and I feel like she got through the movie without it hurting her. It was everything that happened afterward that was so difficult." Out of respect, she declined to elaborate. Author interview with Burstyn, Feb 1, 2022.

28. In 2000 Burstyn was made codirector of the Actors Studio, if any further credentials are needed.

29. Travers and Reiff, *The Story Behind The Exorcist*.

30. William Friedkin Papers, AMPAS.

31. Howard Newman, *The Exorcist: The Strange Story Behind the Film* (New York: Pinnacle Books, 1974).

32. Author interview with Hardin, March 26, 2022.

33. February 16, 1973, correspondence, William Friedkin Papers, AMPAS. There is a forty-page document of unknown authorship in the files. On November 2, 1973, Friedkin had advised Franklin Heller, his literary representative, that he would not be able to complete a manuscript. The next day Heller told Friedkin that veteran writer Bob Thomas wanted to do a "making of" book but that he would deflect Thomas's inquiry "in a way that would not arouse his journalist's interest." William Friedkin Papers, AMPAS.

34. The competing book was *The Story Behind The Exorcist* by Peter Travers and Stephanie Reiff. Friedkin would hold off on writing his memoirs until *The Friedkin Connection* (New York: HarperCollins, 2013).

35. The couple maintained a home in Sherman Oaks, California, and would bring the animals there for photo shoots (see photo section).

## Sidebar: Synopsis of the Film *The Exorcist*

1. Pazuzu is never named in the movie *The Exorcist*. The filmmakers were aware of how silly the name sounds.

2. Presumably this ends the party.

3. This refers to a first examination scene that was cut from the original film but was restored for its home video reissues and the theatrical release of *The Version You've Never Seen*.

4. This is where, in the extended versions, Merrin and Karras discuss the demon's intent.

5. Although Regan has never met Dyer, his priest's collar trips a memory. Originally, as in the book, Dyer was to have met Kinderman as he left the house, and the two men were to strike up the same kind of friendship that Kinderman and Karras had enjoyed. That scene was shot but not edited into the release version of the film.

## Chapter 5

1. Author interview with Donnelly, August 2, 2021.

2. Bud Smith editor's log, William Friedkin Papers, AMPAS.

3. Friedkin and Blair grew close during shooting. An avid horsewoman, on October 16, 1973, she wrote asking him for help financing entry into a horse show. At the time, Friedkin was deeply involved with actress-dancer Jennifer Nairn-Smith (the couple would have a child, Cedric), and Blair wrote that she knew he was "afraid" of taking a chance on marriage, "but what about horses?" His decision is not recorded. William Friedkin Papers, AMPAS.

4. Blatty had been quoted by Marvin Jones in the *Hollywood Reporter* saying that Blair has been undergoing psychotherapy. The rumor was repeated by an actress on a talk show. Friedkin demanded retractions until the periodical's lawyer Robert Yale Libott persuaded Ed Gross that there was nothing actionable in the item. William Friedkin Papers, AMPAS.

5. At the time of the film's release, the author had access to full-frame 16mm footage clearly showing the ceiling rig.

6. Incidentally Dennings was to have been played by Thompson himself, but he changed his mind prior to production.

7. *William Peter Blatty on The Exorcist.* A cutaway is inserted mid-rotation. By contrast, in the pilot episode of the television series *The Exorcist* (2016), a possessed boy dies when the demon lifts him from the bed and twists his head 180 degrees (via CGI).

8. Author interview with Blatty, April 10, 1988.

9. *William Peter Blatty on The Exorcist.*

10. From the *New York Times*, December 16, 1971: "The concluding [Felt Forum] act was by Richiardi, who is billed as the Master Illusionist, a title he fills persuasively. . . . Richiardi calls his *piece de resistance* the Perfect Illusion. A woman is sawed in half by an electric buzzsaw, complete with spurting blood and severed entrails. The audience is forewarned that this bit is not for the squeamish, but Tuesday night's audience appeared to be made of stern stuff because almost everyone accepted Richiardi's invitation to come on stage and view his handiwork."

11. A time-saving trick of filming during the day while adding filters to darken the image to look like night. It never really works, but it keeps you from having to shift the crew to overnight hours. In *The Friedkin Connection*, Friedkin pins the exchange as taking place at Warner Bros., with head of production Charles Greenlaw and his assistant Ed Morey.

12. Author interview with Blatty, August 10, 1988.

13. Ellen Burstyn remembers only one instance when her director fired a gun on the set.

14. Newman, *The Exorcist*.
15. Author interview with Donnelly, August 2, 2021.
16. Author interview with Burstyn, February 1, 2022.
17. Billy Williams interviewed on *Web of Stories: Life Stories of Remarkable People*, https://www.youtube.com/playlist?list=PLVV0r6CmEsFxBGKQuGhZS7KbsYR8vWyP5.
18. Friedkin wrote a remarkable, exquisitely detailed twenty-thousand-word memoir of his Iraq experience, the unpublished manuscript of which resides in his papers at the motion picture academy library.
19. Williams, *Web of Stories*.

### Sidebar: The Curse of *The Exorcist*

1. Newman, *The Exorcist*.
2. Author interview with MacLaine, October 1988.

### Chapter 6

1. Nicola went to great lengths to legitimize possession in a 112-page treatise titled *Diabolical Possession and Exorcism*. Nicola cites "excessive faith" as the explanation for many apparent possessions of people who see everything that happens as God's doing. He broke possessions into five categories: fraud, natural causes, parapsychology, diabolical influences, and miracles. Nicola confirms that "Mr. Blatty's novel is about eighty percent accurate to the actual case which motivated it. Another fifteen percent can be documented from one or another historical case, leaving only a small portion of the novel which is purely imaginative." William Friedkin Papers, AMPAS.
2. Author interview with Blatty, March 3, 1980.
3. Chris MacNeil was designed to have a potty mouth to make her seem less confined by convention. Regan was not, so when the demon says, "Your mother sucks cocks in hell," it became "Your mother still rots in hell" for the TV broadcast. Additionally, anyone who has heard Linda Blair's actual voice on the raw production tracks (YouTube) will understand why Mercedes McCambridge's voice was substituted for Blair's.
4. Author interview with Nordine, 1988.
5. Speculation at this late date is that it was provided by Blatty who obtained it surreptitiously from one of his religious consultants.
6. Author interview with McKay, July 26, 2021.
7. This is only about five miles as the crow flies, but if the crow had to drive in Los Angeles traffic in the seventies, it could have taken half an hour.
8. *Independent* (UK), August 27, 1962, https://www.independent.co.uk.

9. Lucas and Kermode, "*The Exorcist*." The authors credit Dennis Daniel, Sam Stetson, and Bret Wood for research assistance.

10. Wilson Bryan Key, "The Exorcist Massage Parlor," in *Media Sexploitation* (New York: Penguin Publishing Group, 1977).

11. From 1985 to 2016 Tim and his wife Donna published 184 issues of *Video Watchdog*, which gave attention to, and serious analysis of, countless horror films, from indies to studio releases, and from current to classic.

12. Correspondence with the author, July 16, 2021.

13. Correspondence with the author, July 16, 2021.

14. The medal, which pictures Joseph's wife, Mary, cradling baby Jesus, was introduced in the 1500s by Pope Pius V to commemorate the birth of Christ.

15. At this stage in postproduction the two-hour film would have been on six 2,000-foot reels of cut work print and another six 2,000-foot reels of magnetic film containing a perfunctory "slop" mix that would be projected in sync.

16. Author interview with Donnelly, August 2, 2021.

17. William Friedkin Papers, AMPAS.

18. Will Tusher, "Gross to File," *Hollywood Reporter*, November 5, 1973; November 6, 1973; November 20, 1973; November 23, 1973; January 7, 1974.

19. Friedkin interviewed in *A Decade Under the Influence* (IFC Films, 2003).

**Sidebar: A Word About Authenticity**

1. Friedkin interviewed in *A Decade Under the Influence*.

2. Except, as noted, the vomit hurl.

3. "The Curse of The Exorcist."

4. The Academy of Motion Picture Arts and Sciences, custodian of technical standards.

5. Sources differ on this. The possession scenes were certainly "looped," or dubbed after the fact, because of extraneous mechanical noises. One dialogue scene that was post-synced, however, as mentioned in Ellen Burstyn's comments earlier, was Karras meeting Chris on the bridge when she requests an exorcism. Friedkin wanted absolute silence in the background and for the actors to practically whisper to each other—unrealistic for the outdoor setting, but emotionally valid.

6. Over the years Friedkin has often chosen to have his actors redo and re-shade their lines in the informality of a recording studio rather than on a noisy high-pressure working set. "Looping," or, as it is more commonly known, ADR (automated dialogue replacement), restores and sometimes repairs an actor's performance. Other sources say that the only dialogue that was looped in *The Exorcist* was the meeting between Karras and Chris on the bridge where she asks him about getting an exorcism. The absolutely silent background created intense intimacy.

## Sidebar: Karras's Death

1. William Peter Blatty, *The Exorcist* (1998).
2. Author interview with Blatty, March 3, 1980.
3. Author interview with Blatty, March 3, 1980.
4. *Leap of Faith: William Friedkin on The Exorcist* (Exhibit A Pictures, 2019). Extended quote used by permission of the filmmaker.
5. Author interview with Kermode, April 27, 2022.

## Chapter 7

1. Warners may have had prescience; many of the film's first-run engagements were "four-walled," meaning that the distributor rented the theater at a flat rate and kept all the proceeds, leaving exhibitors only the concession sales, access to which was often choked off by the massive crowds.
2. Author interview with Blatty, April 10, 1988.
3. Author interview with Finlan, March 19, 2022.
4. Edgar Gross note to file, March 11, 1974, William Friedkin Papers, AMPAS.
5. It actually works out to 28¼ seconds. A breakdown of footage and frames prepared by Bud Smith is in the photo section. William Friedkin Papers, AMPAS.
6. Eileen Dietz Elber's mention of her first petition to SAG executive national secretary Chester L. Migden on February 1, 1974, is referenced in Elber's March 4, 1974 letter to MigdenWilliam Friedkin Papers, AMPAS.
7. February 3, 1974, press release, Warner Bros. Press Department.
8. Letter from Lipsky to Friedkin, March 1, 1974; Edgar Gross note to file, March 4, 1974. William Friedkin Papers, AMPAS.
9. Edgar Gross note to file, April 8, 1974, William Friedkin Papers, AMPAS.
10. Thomas Hobbs, "'We argued over the crucifix scene': What It Was Like Being the Demon in *The Exorcist*" *New Statesman's Network*, February 5, 2020, https://www.newstatesman.com/culture/film/2020/02/we-argued-over-crucifix-scene-what-it-was-being-Demon-exorcist.
11. Author interview with Blatty, April 10, 1988.0

## Sidebar: The X-orcist

1. *Ohio v. Jacobellis*, 1964.
2. Filmmaker Stanley Kubrick later made cuts to allow the second film to be re-rated R. As for *The Devils*, at this writing Warner Bros. refuses to allow director Ken Russell's original cut to be released on home video.
3. See the next sidebar, "Mrs. Warren's Profession."

4. He also helped secure an R rating for William Friedkin's highly controversial 1980 film *Cruising*. Stern died April 13, 2021, at age ninety-six.

### Sidebar: Mrs. Warren's Profession

1. Disclosure: The author was publicity director for Sack Theatres at the time and, as such, was among those indicted.

### Chapter 8

1. Author interview with Donnelly, August 2, 2021.
2. William Friedkin Papers, AMPAS.
3. Commentary tracks had been provided with some films on LaserDisc, but with DVDs they took off. Surprisingly, according to some industry sources reporting anecdotally, many people who buy DVDs seldom bother with the extras.
4. Author interview with Altman, 1993.
5. Author interview with Martin Scorsese, June 24, 1993.
6. Distinction is drawn with "restored versions" such as *Lawrence of Arabia*, *The Wild Bunch*, or *It's a Mad, Mad, Mad, Mad World*, where footage cut by the distributor against the director's wishes is simply put back.
7. Remarks included in DVD special features, 2000.
8. John Calley (1930–2011) was one of the most respected studio executives during the mid-1970s, a period regarded as the last great era in American filmmaking. Among the films he green-lighted were *All the President's Men*, *A Clockwork Orange*, *Blazing Saddles*, *Dog Day Afternoon*, *Mean Streets*, *McCabe and Mrs. Miller*, *Superman*, *Deliverance*, *Chariots of Fire*, and *The Exorcist*. He received the Academy's Irving G. Thalberg Award in 2000.
9. The messy "working" copy of a film being used for editing, marred by splices, grease pencil markings, torn frames, and basic, unmixed soundtrack.
10. Comments on DVD special features.
11. This has no connection with the 2016–2017 TV series, which Blatty denounced as having no connection with his work, or the announced 2023 trilogy, but it might be related to a 2009 announcement that both Blatty and Friedkin were considering a full remake (source: Jason Stringer, *Cemetery Dance Magazine*, November 11, 2009).
12. Correspondence with author, November 22, 1998, and author interview with Kermode, October 8, 2021 interview.

13. Readers wishing a more detailed description of the differences and the collaborative (and sometimes not) process by which they were decided are commended to Mark Kermode's authoritative BFI Film Classics book *The Exorcist*.

14. Blatty also said this in *The Fear of God* from 1998, when Kermode interviewed them together and used it as an epilogue to his BFI book, *The Exorcist*, as "Late Night Double Bill."

15. Comments in DVD special feature interview.

16. Correspondence with author, July 16, 2021.

17. Special features, 2000 release.

18. Remarks at AMPAS, October 22, 2018.

19. Author interview with Philippe, April 1, 2022.

20. It's impossible to give this notion full consideration inasmuch as all twenty works were supposedly destroyed following the filming, not to mention the unanswered question of whether they were to have been viewed from Picasso's side or, reversed, from the camera's.

21. In 2001 Friedkin and Blatty became upset when the Turner network scheduled a presentation of *The Exorcist*, which as a Warner Bros. company Turner owned, at the same time a theatrical release of the expanded film was planned. Charging a sweetheart deal among CBS, Warners, and Turner, the filmmakers rejected a $25,000 settlement as too low. Bert Fields letter, May 16, 2001, William Friedkin Papers, AMPAS.

22. Friedkin and Blatty interviewed by Mark Kermode in *The Exorcist*.

23. Warner Bros. DVD special feature.

## Chapter 9

1. "It's the worst piece of shit I've ever seen. It's a fucking disgrace," said William Friedkin. *The Movies That Made Me* podcast, Season 2, Episode 1.

2. Callum Russell, "The Unusual Horror Sequel Martin Scorsese Preferred to the Original," *Far Out* magazine (undated), https://faroutmagazine.co.uk/horror-martin-scorsese-favourite-original-the-exorcist/.

3. BoxOfficeMojo.com. Generally a film returns to the studio half as much as it grosses in theaters. This figure excludes ancillary income.

4. It was *Rocky III* (1982) that broke the mold. Even the immediate sequels to *The Godfather* and *Star Wars* didn't outgross their progenitors.

5. "Hoya" was the name of a Georgetown University sports mascot.

6. *New York*, December 23, 1974.

7. Comments to Michael Felsher for the *Exorcist III* Blu-ray.

8. Addison Verrill wrote a comprehensive interview article on Lederer in *Variety* (September 9, 1976) that barely quoted him.

9.  Barbara Pallenberg, *The Making of Exorcist II: The Heretic* (New York: Warner Books, 1977).

10. *Generation* (1965), about the parent-child generation gap, was filmed in 1969.

11. Boorman Blu-ray commentary.

12. Author interview with Fletcher, April 23, 2022.

13. *Daily Variety*, November 11, 1975.

14. *Daily Variety*, November 15, 1975.

15. *Hollywood Reporter*, February 5, 1976.

16. *Daily Variety*, September 8, 1976.

17. There are no reliable budget figures for *The Exorcist*, although $12 million is routinely cited. The studio originally thought it could make the film for $5.4 million. No one knows the final amount, but in the words (and hindsight) of Samuel Goldwyn, "Nothing is as cheap to produce as a hit."

18. *L.A. Herald-Examiner*, August 26, 1975.

19. *Daily Variety*, January 30, 1976.

20. *Hollywood Reporter*, February 2,1976. Voight was a notable graduate of the visionary Father Gilbert V. Hartke's drama program at Washington, D.C.'s Catholic University of America. At the time, an April start date was expected.

21. Army Archerd, *Daily Variety*, April 8, 1976.

22. Pallenberg, *The Making of Exorcist II*.

23. *Daily Variety*, April 21, 1976.

24. This strange adventure was told in Yoram Ben-Ami with Nat Segaloff, *Guiding Royalty: My Adventure with Elizabeth Taylor and Richard Burton* (Albany, Georgia: BearManor Media, 2018).

25. *Daily Variety*, November 11, 1975.

26. *Variety*, April 28, 1975.

27. Author interview with Blatty, August 10, 1988. In point of fact, the few real locusts were suspended on wires in front of a blue screen for optical printing, but the countless other locusts were Styrofoam packing peanuts painted brown (Pallenberg, *The Making of Exorcist II*).

28. Special features interview, *Exorcist II* Blu-ray.

29. Pallenberg, *The Making of Exorcist II*.

30. *Los Angeles Herald-Examiner*, September 19, 1976.

31. Pallenberg, *The Making of Exorcist II*.

32. AFI catalogue listing; IMDb opening date listing.

33. Michael Felsher interview on the *Exorcist III* Blu-ray.

34. Gerry Levin, *Hollywood Reporter*, May 21, 1976, and Gregg Kilday, *Los Angeles Times*, May 22, 1976.

35. Pallenberg, *The Making of Exorcist II*.

36. *Hollywood Reporter*, June 20, 1977.

37. *Hollywood Reporter*, June 20, 1977.

38. Author interview with Blatty, April 10, 1988.

39. April 14, 2013, https://www.youtube.com/watch?v=2D4cPXpvHjI.

40. March 4, 2012, http://www.money-into-light.com/search/label/Review%3A%20EXORCIST%20II%20-%20THE%20HERETIC

41. *Variety*, June 22, 1977.

42. *Wall Street Journal*, June 30, 1977.

43. *Daily Variety*. July 1, 1977,

44. Remarks from Boorman's commentary on the Blu-ray edition.

45. Author interview with Blatty, April 10, 1988. Boorman, according to his IMDb biography, attended Catholic schools but was raised Protestant. This alone was unusual in Ireland, given that it was during The Troubles.

46. Mark Kermode, "Alien Ancestry," *Kermode Uncut*, March 19, 2017.

47. The audience wasn't immune. The *Village Voice* (June 13, 1977) reported that two young women at an LA screening of the film "were actually hypnotized by the scene in *Exorcist II*. A Warner Bros. executive claims that [the studio] would not be liable for medical problems when *The Heretic* is released. The same company did, however, undertake medical costs for victims of the original *Exorcist*." Whether this was a publicity plant to inspire mass reactions such as those that greeted the first film is not known.

48. Of TheDigitalCinema website.

49. Film historian Mike White of the *Projection Booth* blog provides an equally compelling commentary to the truncated version in the Blu-ray set.

50. Interviewed in a Professional Films/Robbins Nest promotional featurette, 1977.

51. It may actually be a look-alike for legal reasons. The film mocks the controversial Geller by having Regan show Sharon a spoon she has bent. Sharon is fascinated until Regan opens her hand to reveal that it was a trick using two spoons.

52. Professional Films/Robbins Nest featurette.

53. Blu-ray special features.

54. Blu-ray commentary.

55. Box Office Mojo/IMDb.

56. "Spook Pix Cycle Over?," *Variety*, August 16, 1977.

57. *Variety*, June 28, 1977.

58. Blu-ray commentary. Boorman had been trying to make *Excalibur* (which was then titled *Merlin*) before *The Heretic* came along.

59. Author interview with von Sydow, December 11, 1980.

### Sidebar: Synops is of *Exorcist II: The Heretic*

1. One of the lingering continuity questions is why the Georgetown house remains abandoned. When the MacNeils lived there, it was a rental for the duration of the production of *Crash Course*. No mention is ever made of the actual homeowners, who seem to have vanished.

### Sidebar: The Two *Heretics*

1. Joseph McBride, *Variety*, July 11, 1977.

2. Shout! Factory deluxe Blu-ray edition. According to *Variety* (June 19, 1977) people in Hollywood were already calling Boorman's cut film *Exorcist III*.

### Chapter 10

1. Stephen Klain, *Daily Variety*, July 24, 1980.

2. *Hollywood Reporter*, January 8, 1985.

3. *Hollywood Reporter*, March 31, 1981. Founded in 1969 by Irwin Molasky, Merv Adelson, and Lee Rich, the company's name was a blend of Adelson's then-wife, *Lori*, with the name of San Diego's McClellan-Palo*mar* Airport. The company's history is colorful but is too complex to go into here.

4. At the time, Friedkin was making TV movies (*The C.A.T. Squad*) and low-budget thrillers (*Rampage, The Guardian*), so an offer to direct the official sequel to his most famous film should have been attractive both financially and professionally. It was also during this period that the author was writing Friedkin's biography, *Hurricane Billy*, and was in constant touch with the filmmaker, who made no mention of such a lucrative offer.

5. Here and elsewhere in this chapter, unless otherwise noted, Blatty's comments are to Michael Felsher in an interview accompanying the Shout! Factory Blu-ray release of the director's cut of *The Exorcist III*. In 1979, Friedkin had written and directed *Cruising*, a controversial murder story set in New York's gay leather community, in which the killer uses a knife on his victims.

6. Author interview with Blatty, April 10, 1988. The conversation with Friedkin had occurred the night before we spoke.

7. *Los Angeles Times*, February 5, 1974.

8. Blatty, *Hollywood Reporter*, February 17, 1981.

9. *Daily Variety*, April 17, 1989.

10. Blatty, *Los Angeles Times*, February 26, 1989. That pronouncement would return to haunt Blatty.

11. Blatty reported that Marlon Brando was interested but would only work for three weeks.

12. Interview with Brad Dourif, Blu-ray special features, *The Exorcist III*.

13. Blatty knew of Dourif from his performance as Billy Bibbit in *One Flew Over the Cuckoo's Nest*, for which he had written an early screenplay, which its then director, Kirk Douglas, did not use.

14. Interviewed in *Death Be Not Proud: The Making of The Exorcist III*, Blu-ray special feature.

15. *Variety*, July 12, 1989.

16. Sidney left to film *The Witching of Ben Wagner* for the Disney Channel. When her scenes had to be reshot, the *Exorcist III* producers contested paying Sidney her full fee. Marilyn Beck, *Long Beach Press-Telegram*, October 19, 1989. Subsequently, Beck reported that it was Sidney's now-former agent who told her she was "in the clear" to do both films. *Long Beach Press-Telegram*, October 21, 1989.

17. *USA Today*, August 21, 1990.

18. *Los Angeles Times*, April 2, 1989

19. Miller would make a handful of additional screen appearances before passing in 2001 at age sixty-two.

20. Comments to Michael Felsher for the *Exorcist III* Blu-ray.

21. "Possession" is questionable inasmuch as the Gemini Killer is never presented as a demon, although his access to Karras's body is by grace of "The Master" (presumably Satan).

22. Box Office Mojo, www.boxofficemojo.com.

23. *Time Out*, November 1990.

**Sidebar: Synopsis of the Novel *Legion***

1. The date becomes a passing reference in the pilot episode of the *Exorcist* TV series (2016).

2. This connects with an observation by Blatty in *Twinkle, Twinkle, "Killer" Kane* (1966) that explains its alternate title in its 1978 rewrite, *The Ninth Configuration*.

3. Blatty is referencing the work of Dr. Konstantin Raudive and Friedrich Jürgenson, who, in separate studies, searched for evidence of life after death.

4. By way of clarification, Patient 12 in the book becomes Patient X in the movie.

5. Tony Fantozzi was William Friedkin's first agent at the William Morris office. Also, in both novel and film, it is unclear how Kinderman connects seeing Nurse Julie in the hospital with his daughter Julie being in jeopardy.

## Sidebar: Synopsis of the Release Version of *The Exorcist III*

1. In the novel *The Exorcist*, Karras dies on May 16, 1971. In the movie he dies on October 9, 1975. (Source: Exorcist Wiki, https://exorcist.fandom. com/wiki/Damien_Karras.) In the novel *Legion*, the anniversary of his death is March 13. There is no attempt to reconcile these dates.

2. This is a motif throughout the film for the ineffable presence of a spirit or a soul, whether it's a sheet of newspaper or a piece of litter blowing across an otherwise trash-free street. Indeed, all the way back to *The Exorcist*, Karras is always shown ascending. Further to this motif, several shots in *Exorcist III* show a piece of paper (twice on the Hitchcock steps) blowing upward or across, never downward. (See also Blatty's description of his unfilmed epilogue to *The Exorcist*.)

3. In the original director's cut of the film, Karras was played entirely by Brad Dourif. In the re-edited version he is played by both Dourif and Jason Miller.

4. In the novel, Father Kanavan is called Father Bermingham. The real Rev. Thomas Bermingham played himself in *The Exorcist* as the administrator who authorizes the MacNeil exorcism. Presumably Blatty changed the name for the film to continue the letter "K" M.O.

5. Karras recorded Regan speaking a language she had never studied. It turned out that it was English backwards, as a male audio technician easily explained to Karras in *The Exorcist*. In *Exorcist III* the person who explained the tape was changed retroactively to Kintry's mother, apparently for consistency with the "K" theme.

6. Spelled *Vennamun* in the novel *Legion*.

7. It's unclear from the intercutting between Miller and Dourif whether Kinderman is supposed to notice at this point, although several scenes later he sees a photo of James Venamun and a music cue makes the connection between the two men.

8. This connection is not explained in the movie any better than it is in the novel.

9. Some of these shots were used in the director's cut when Kinderman has Karras's body exhumed.

### Sidebar: Synopsis of the Director's Cut of *The Exorcist III*

1. Carefully shot to hide the fact that the actual house used as the MacNeil residence no longer has the bedroom extension that was constructed for *The Exorcist* in 1972. The opening titles still carry a credit for Nicol Williamson, whose character does not appear in this cut.

2. Some versions indicate the president's name as Father Riley.

3. Further to this motif, as mentioned, several shots in *Exorcist III* show a piece of paper (twice on the Hitchcock steps) blowing upward or across, never downward. Additional footage shows both men reminiscing about their friendship.

4. In the novel, Father Kanavan is called Father Bermingham. Rev. Thomas Bermingham, SJ, played himself in *The Exorcist* as the administrator who authorizes the MacNeil exorcism. Presumably Blatty changed the name for the film to continue the letter "K" contrivance.

5. Karras recorded Regan speaking a language she had never studied. It turned out that it was English backwards, as a male audio technician easily explained to Karras. In *Exorcist III*, the person who explained the tape was changed retroactively to Kintry's mother, also for the "K" theme.

6. In other words, he looks like Damien Karras recast with Brad Dourif.

7. Viewers who see the release version of *Exorcist III* may have trouble realizing that Dourif plays Karras.

8. Because there is no intercutting between Dourif and Miller, the scene plays with a rising intensity.

9. The original script contains a flashback scene explaining how James Venamun snapped and became the Gemini Killer when his brother, Tommy, who was afraid of the dark, had his room lights turned off. If the flashback was shot, it either never made it into either cut or was lost.

10. Dourif's sustained monologue, even at VHS quality, is remarkably textured and compelling.

11. This connection is not explained.

### Sidebar: Differences Between the Theatrical Cut and the Restored Director's Cut of *The Exorcist III*

1. Blatty's script is more precise: At the point when Karras discovers Merrin's body upstairs, Kinderman arrives downstairs to further question Regan.

2. Blatty always insisted that he had not seen Peter Falk's Colombo when he created Kinderman.

3. For a more detailed listing, refer to the "Alternate Versions" category on the film's IMDb page: https://www.imdb.com/title/tt0099528/alternateversions?ref_=tt_ql_trv_5.

## Sidebar: *The Ninth Configuration*

1. They range from 99 to 140 minutes, but the 118-minute cut that originally ran theatrically in America is the only one that Blatty approved.

2. Author interview with Blatty, March 3, 1980. This is the first time this material has been published.

3. Of course, this presumes that one trusts a man brandishing a Kalashnikov to keep his word. By reference, a similar scene appears to great effect in *Dominion* and *Exorcist: The Beginning*.

## Chapter 11

1. Catherine Billey, *New York Times*, June 8, 2005.

2. Wisher was signed by the time Josh Chetwynd wrote it in the *Hollywood Reporter*, July 14, 1997.

3. The sole reference in the film is "The exorcism lasted for months. I hear it damn near killed him."

4. Author interview with Wisher, July 30, 2021.

5. Author interview with Wisher, July 30, 2021.

6. It will be remembered that the same situation existed on *Exorcist III*, where Morgan Creek okayed William Peter Blatty's script and then rejected the film he made that adhered to it.

8. *Los Angeles Times*, August 14, 2001. Of interest is that Frankenheimer directed *The French Connection II*, the sequel to Friedkin's *The French Connection*, and later dropped out of directing *The Brink's Job* (1978), which Friedkin wound up taking over. *Sic semper Hollywood.*

9. *Hollywood Reporter*, November 9, 2000.

10. *Hollywood Reporter*, October 30, 2001.

11. *Hollywood Reporter*, January 11, 2002.

12. Zorianna Kit, *Hollywood Reporter*, January 23, 2002.

13. *Hollywood Reporter*, March 22, 2002.

14. *Hollywood Reporter*, January 30, 2001.

15. Army Archerd, *Variety*, May 21, 2002, and *Los Angeles Times*, June 5, 2002.

16. Retrospective in *TV Guide*, August 10, 2002.

17. There were later reports that doctors, during the spinal operation, found heavily metastasized cancer.

18. Jacob Neilendam, *Screen International*, November 1, 2002.

19. DVD commentary track, recorded February 7, 2005.

20. *Variety* (summary article), October 23, 2002.

21. *Daily Variety*, September 18, 2003.

22. Chris Gardner, *Hollywood Reporter*, November 19, 2003.

23. *Village Voice*, August 25, 2004.

24. Dave McNary, *Variety*, November 3, 2003.

25. *Variety*, May 2004.

26. James Christopher, *The Times* [of London], March 25, 2005. By this time Schrader had already finished editing his version for DVD.

27. Army Archerd, *Variety*, August 17, 2004.

28. Box Office Mojo reports the worldwide gross of *Beginning* as $78,110,021 and *Dominion* as $251,495.

29. Author interview with Wisher.

### Sidebar: Synopsis of *Dominion: Prequel to The Exorcist*

1. In the flashback, Merrin kills the Nazi himself, prompting a massacre. If Merrin truly went back in time, he would have committed an unforgiveable sin, so it's hard to see how he could have had his guilt resolved. If it was a fantasy, same thing.

2. In *The Exorcist*, Father Bermingham says that Father Merrin has experience with exorcisms: "Ten, twelve years ago in Africa. The exorcism lasted for months. I hear it damn near killed him." What is missing is a reference to the demon's challenge to Merrin from *The Exorcist*, "This time you're going to lose." Given the 1975 date of the events in *The Exorcist*, this would place Merrin's African experience in 1962 or 1963, not 1947. It is also out of sync with the African exorcism in *The Heretic*.

### Sidebar: Synopsis of *Exorcist: The Beginning*

1. It's never clear what happens to Sarah.

### Chapter 12

1. The two had an encouraging telephone conversation but did not have the chance to meet in person before Blatty died. It will also be recalled that Blatty had, at one point, threatened to write his own three-hour adaptation of *The Exorcist* for television, though that never materialized.

2. It's speculation whether the rights that Blatty granted to Warner Bros. to make *The Heretic* ended with that sequel, and that the subsequent deal with Morgan Creek to make *Legion* (*Exorcist III*) were for that separate intellectual property which Morgan Creek later exploited with *Dominion* and *Beginning*. Thus it is understandable that Warner Bros. considered the TV series' use of characters from *The Exorcist*, which they retained, to be an infringement.

3. It would have been easy to double-shoot the series for eventual unrated release, but for some reason this was not done.

4. Cognoscenti will note that the scene in which Tomas and Marcus agree to separate is set in a motel in room number 237. Let's just leave that here.

## Chapter 13

1. These credits should be considered provisional as of this writing.
2. Executive producer of ten episodes of the *Exorcist* TV series.

## Chapter 14

1. William Friedkin, "The Devil and Father Amorth: Witnessing 'the Vatican Exorcist' at Work," *Vanity Fair*, October 31, 2016.
2. Friedkin, "The Devil and Father Amorth."
3. Interviewed by Raymond Arroyo on the video show *World Over*, August 9, 2018, https://www.youtube.com/watch?v=RB9du1L2QDM&t=142s.
4. Friedkin, "The Devil and Father Amorth."
5. *The Devil and Father Amorth* is available from Amazon: https://www.amazon.com/Devil-Father-Amorth-William-Friedkin/dp/B07B94XWQG/ref=sr_1_2?dchild=1&keywords=the+devil+and+father+amorth&qid=1628391307&s=movies-tv&sr=1-2.

## Chapter 15

1. *Guardian*, July 2, 2014.
2. Lilith does not appear in the Bible; she is a creation of rabbinical commentary in an attempt to reconcile the creation of the woman in Genesis 1 and the creation of Eve in Genesis 2. Where these are clearly two different women, it had to be reconciled lest the creation myth go off the rails as it was just pulling out of the station.
3. *Tanakh* is an acronym for Torah (the law), Nevi'im (the prophets), and Ketuvim (the writings).
4. Levin also notes that there is no story of demonic possession in the Hebrew bible, although Jewish literature such as *The Dybbuk* and the *Kabbala* have such stories. "Using *The Dybbuk* as a point of reference," Rabbi Levin says, "a Jewish Regan could have been possessed by a spirit, but it would not have been the Devil."

## Chapter 16

1. There is no reference in Genesis that humans are evil from birth, thus no Original Sin. This was introduced in the interpretation of the Christian Bible.
2. David Hume, ed., *Dialogues Concerning Natural Religion*, with an introduction by Norman Kemp Smith (Indianapolis: Bobbs-Merrill, 1980), Part X, p. 198.

3. There is also the response to "Why doesn't God answer my prayers?" which is "He did, and the answer was No."

4. Per the plot, Kane is not really a psychiatrist, but let's ignore this. Blatty also noted that there are no Marine psychiatrists, that they were a contrivance for his book.

5. Referencing a famous E. B. White quote.

6. Saying "God is dead" implies that he must have once existed. Blatty, among others, cannot conceive of a universe that evolved without God's hand.

7. Correspondence with the author, July 16, 2021.

8. Travers and Reiff, *The Story Behind The Exorcist*.

9. Friedkin, "The Devil and Father Amorth."

## Appendix: Colloquy with William Peter Blatty

1. The missing scenes to which Blatty refers were restored in later editions of the film.

2. This and other inconsistences were addressed in various subsequent DVD and Blu-ray releases.

3. William Friedkin, in his memoir, *The Friedkin Connection*, reveals that Father Robert J. Henle of Georgetown University connected him with the aunt of the young boy in the actual case (this would have been Aunt Tillie or Harriet) and he assured her that he would protect her and her nephew's identities.

4. Blatty makes an intriguing observation in his "making of" book that "*The Exorcist* is about an atheist heroine who comes to believe that her daughter is possessed, in opposition to a Jesuit hero who does not."

# Extended Credits

# Index